Brooklands: Behind the Scenes

Charles Mortimer

ISBN 0 85429 262 4

© Charles Mortimer

First published November 1980

A FOULIS Motorcycling book

Printed in England by the publishers
Haynes Publishing Group
Sparkford, Yeovil, Somerset BA22 7JJ, England

Distributed in North America by
Haynes Publications Inc
861 Lawrence Drive, Newbury Park, California 91320, USA

Editor: **Jeff Clew**
Cover design: **Phill Jennings**
Layout design: **Joe Fitzgerald**

Contents

Part One – Brooklands in the twenties:

Part Two – The riders point of view

Foreword

Memories of Brooklands not only linger on among those who were there but are being revived by a new, young generation of enthusiasts who were not. Gratifying for the older people, but also inexplicable unless one contends, as I do, that Brooklands really did have an indefinable magic of its own.

Now that this is recognised by old and young alike, it seems to me that anything that can be done to perpetuate the memories of Brooklands and its 'regulars' should be encouraged. The track gave me fifteen wonderful years, the first five as a spectator and the last ten – to 1939 – as a competitor. I enjoyed them all but, to me, it has always seemed that, from every point of view, it was the 1920 to 1930 period at Brooklands that held the most fascination and glamour.

Few of the books so far written about racing at Brooklands tell you much about the people who raced there and, on the motorcycle side, the position is far worse, for almost nothing has been written about the history made there, at least until recently.

It was chance that brought this home to me when, early in 1974, I acquired some bound volumes of *The Motor Cycle* and *Motor Cycling* that covered almost the whole of the 1920 to 1930 period. Reading through the race reports made me wonder how many of these great men were still living and whether those who were had recollections that could be got together to form a story. I knew of Bert Denly, Victor Horsman, Woolly Worters and Bill Lacey, whose achievements alone would fill a book, and felt there could well be others. I needn't have worried. The Brooklands stars of that period were iron men and every time I met one I found that he, in turn, knew of another. 'He's getting on now, Charles. I don't know how you'll find him, but I know he's still going.' One by one I found them and what a wonderful time I had talking to them.

A pattern emerged. The first part of the book must be, not a full history of racing bikes at Brooklands in the 1920 to 1930 period, not even a report of every meeting, but a story of some great races and some smaller ones, in which these great men made history. The second part would be a record of the talks I had with each, which proved to be really absorbing because each still had secrets from the other which, at long last, could be revealed. Each, of course, was pleased to know I had seen or was going to see the others and, in one or two cases, I was able to arrange meetings between them – the first time they had seen each other in, perhaps, forty-five years.

To date it hasn't stopped. The faster I write, the faster fresh 'discoveries' become known. I have travelled from Surrey to Cornwall, to Wales, and to almost every county in England and my rather basic tape recorder has had to have its batteries replaced after nearly every visit.

What has struck me is that they were such very nice men, contented in their old age, because nearly all are in their seventies and several well into the eighties. All seemed delighted to see me and although they were genuinely astonished that there should be so much interest in Brooklands and what went on there, all had dug out whatever notes or relics they still had.

I feel fairly certain that anyone who knew Brooklands and went there will enjoy this book. It is mainly for the younger people that I have written it, whose enthusiasm for the dear old track I particularly admire when there is so little first hand information to keep it alive.

Acknowledgements

I doubt whether any author can ever have had so much help from just a few sources as I have had with this book, and I find it hard to express in words my gratitude, not only to those whose names crop up in this story but also to others whose enthusiastic help and guidance I have had in writing it.

I know of no book on the subject of Brooklands which contains so much original material and for this I have to thank those whose stories feature in it. They not only let me invade their homes but took enormous trouble to dig up memories and notes which, when collated, go to make up the story. I am grateful to them all and particularly to J. S. 'Woolly' Worters whose contribution is, on its own, almost a book in itself and is the finest bit of 'original Brooklands' I've ever come across.

'Woolly's manuscript was laced with delightful asides saying 'Charles, you'd better be careful about this next bit – see a lawyer before you include it'. I did. The lawyer loved it and tried hard to keep as much as he possibly could so that, in the end, very little had to be 'cut'. I feel that anyone interested in Brooklands must love it and I must express my grateful thanks, again, to him for although, from time to time, I've heard bits of it from him, to collate and get it into sequence and then get it on tape must have taken hours.

The questionnaire I sent him was the one that I took with me when I talked to all the others because, at the time, I felt that, after some forty-five years, it would be difficult for them to have vivid memories but although I did use it quite often in my talks, there were times when it was hardly needed at all. Reading back through it now I feel that it does sometimes appear as though I had a bias about certain things such as the comparative inefficiency of big twins and the status of Bert Le Vack, but really I hadn't. I loved all the big twins that ran at the track, and rode one myself, but I confess to being a bit shocked on re-reading their finishing records in the long races and I wanted to get the views of the others on things like this. I did want to get strong reactions on as many aspects of Brooklands as possible and I confess to having put some of my questions, from time to time, in a slightly 'loaded' way with this in mind.

Where it all flowed easily, I hardly used the questionnaire. I hardly used it at all, for instance, in the talk I had with Pat Driscoll because Pat had vivid memories of nearly every big race. He and I were only at variance once, I think because, having been 'top of the class' at winning 200 Mile Races, we came to one that he'd won, whereupon he was adamant that he hadn't even finished! Faced with the documentary evidence of both *The Motor Cycle* and *Motor Cycling* he appeared quite crestfallen, but conceding in the end, saying, 'Oh well, if they both say so, I suppose they must be right.' In a world where many people claim that they've done things which they haven't, I found that rather refreshing!

Even having witnessed many of these long races, it isn't easy to convey in print how great these achievements were because, sometimes, the speeds tend to belie them. One has to bear in mind the number of pit stops that were necessary and that all this was done on what was, at the time, the most wickedly punishing and bumpy track on the world, forty-five or more years ago, with machines that, by today's standards, were hardly sprung at all, and on tyres that were, even then, suspect from the half distance mark on. Add to that the fact that the science of metallurgy was still in its infancy and you begin to get some idea of the problem of even finishing.

Knowing both Bert Denly and 'Woolly' as well as I do, I can imagine how they must have enjoyed their shooting during the winter. Both are countrymen and to get right away from the tensions of racing must have been great. All these people had a clear conception of how life should be lived. Not all were particularly wealthy at the time and it always seemed to me that the shorter you are of money, the more important this becomes.

I have my Secretary, Mrs. Barbara Haine, to thank for putting me in touch with her friend and neighbour, Mrs. Sue Weekes, because it was Sue who battled to get the tapes into typescript. It was a battle, too, because there were many occasions when both I and my 'interviewee' were talking technicalities and jargon at the same time and to interpret it into something readable and sensible would be a problem to anyone, let alone someone who was too young to know anything about Brooklands or the people who raced there.

There are a number of people to whom I want to express thanks for putting me in touch with the Brooklands riders of the era and others, notably Dr. Joe Bayley, for great help and advice concerning photographs which always seem to me to be a vital part of a story of this sort.

Though I made great efforts to find everyone involved, I do know that there are some who should have been included, one a well known tuner and another, a 200 Mile Race winner. The problem here has been that the book has taken a long time to get together, nearly four years in fact, so that time has run out in the end.

As I write this, I don't know yet who the proof readers and 'fact checkers' are likely to be but I want to thank them and also my friend and neighbour Nick Channing, the first apart from myself to cast eyes on the book, for offering to read it and correct some of my awful typing mistakes and any others he finds.

The worst chore of an author is, I think, reading back through a story but, on the whole, I found it a bit less painful this time. It is difficult, when describing a series of races, to prevent it becoming a procession of cold facts but as I read it, it seemed to me that the race patterns were mostly quite different so that, in the end, the outcome wasn't too bad.

I hope this book will be enjoyed even if only to reward those who have helped me in getting it together. In its way it is history, and the thing about history is that, if you don't put it down on paper, it dies.

Ewhurst
October 1980   Charles Mortimer   **9**

Chapter 1

The First Four Years

Few people would disagree with the claim that, in the motorcycle sphere at least, the decade of the 1920's at Brooklands excelled any other in interest, technical advance and even in excitement and glamour.

The machines themselves were shedding the spindly, spidery appearance of those of the 1910's, were diverse in size and appearance, and were the products of many different firms, large and small. Some, such as Zenith, constructed ranges including virtually everything from a 175 cc two-stroke to a 1000 cc overhead valve twin, while other interesting variants included air-, oil- and water-cooled singles and twins.

What went on at Brooklands was regarded by the British motorcycle industry as important from the point of view of advertising. Not by all, perhaps, but a great part of the industry was anxious to jump on the band wagon and profit, with a view to boosting sales, from the interest centred in the track.

From all this a pattern emerged centering partly on racing but more, perhaps, on record breaking for it seemed that this was the sphere considered important by the advertising and publicity departments of the motorcycle industry. In other words, from their point of view, they liked the image of man and machine covering a given distance in a shorter time than ever before.

At the time, it was understandable and, from that starting point there grew a miniature industry at Brooklands and Montlhéry, dedicated to give the industry what it wanted – an ever changing picture of race wins and records broken. And from that small circle, certain figures emerged, towering above the others. The giants are easy to identify – what is difficult is to draw the dividing line between the obvious giants and the next category who were very good. Then you have to draw a line between the very good and the good and another between the good and the rest which is, perhaps, the most difficult line of all. For among the rest were men who were, perhaps, brilliant technically but who, for commercial or other reasons, became embroiled only occasionally so that one just cannot know how successful they would have been had they gone in as deeply as the others.

Even among the 'good' there were participants so colourful, intelligent and perceptive that to leave them out of a story of this sort would be sacrilege. Men who, realising that certain capacity classes were too competitive to enter, concentrated on record breaking in smaller and less orthodox classes so that, not infrequently, they broke more records in one day than their bigger brothers had broken in a month. They had to build weird contraptions in order to do it and, sometimes, they had to cover vast distances. But they did it and made a living at it, by ingenuity, intelligence and co-operation with each other.

There had to be co-operation between record breakers of that period. A rider would go out one day and made a successful attack on a rival's records and be paid a bonus by the manufacturer of the machine and by the maker of the carburettor, magneto, chains, tyres and many other parts – provided the newly established records stood for one clear month. Later the rule became one clear month and a clear mile per hour, because so practised did the contestants become that records were, in the end, being broken by fractions and this was too costly, even for big business. Since records had to stand for a month if the record breakers were to be paid, it became obvious that there had to be close co-operation between rivals – and there was. And, where margins were concerned, there is more than one authenticated instance of record breaker 'A' running record breaker 'B's pit during a long distance attempt on his own ('A's) records to ensure that they were broken by the smallest possible margin acceptable.

This sort of thing applied less, of course, in the larger capacity and more competitive classes although co-operation regarding the monthly time limit was almost absolute. There were often deadly scrambles to be 'The First' to do something and, here, competition could be cut-throat. The first hundred miles in the hour on a five hundred was a classic example – and there were others. But once the record was established it usually stood, by mutual agreement.

It was a hard life for the manufacturer and riders of a machine as reliable but less fast than its rivals. The short distance records were obviously out of their reach and since they were determined to be in on the thing they were faced with long rides which, at times, could last for six hours or more before any hope could be held of breaking a record. From then on, records would probably fall hourly but what a long long ride that first six hours or more seemed.

So if, in the end, a few emerged taller in stature that the others, nearly everyone competing at the track in the 1920's played some part to complete the overall picture.

Who, then, were the 'giants' of the period? Sooner or later, when compiling a story of this nature, one has to stick one's neck out, and I suggest they were Denly, O'Donovan, Horsman, Driscoll, Lacey, Le Vack, Marchant, Staniland, Worters and Wright. I don't think anyone would leave out one of those names although they might want to add others. But what is so fascinating is that, when you get down to looking at the achievements and activities of each of these ten riders, it is practically impossible to draw a comparison of one against another.

Joe Wright's lap record performances, all on big twins, were electrifying, always standing out as highlights during those ten years. But, except in short races, his appearances were infrequent, so that he must have covered by far the smallest number of laps, of the ten, during the period under discussion.

Victor Horsman's span of years was the longest, 1912 to 1930, and during it he took part in numerous record attempts on 500s and 600s, both solo and sidecar, as well as in countless races, long and short, so he must rank as a giant among giants. But, of course, his efforts were concentrated on those two capacity classes.

Bert Denly had a shorter span of years on bikes, 1923 to 1930. He was, perhaps,

Horsman's number one rival in many respects but Bert also rode 350s solo and sidecar.

Versatility seems to come into it at this stage. Horsman never rode anything except 500s and 600s. Denly rode everything except 250s and 1000s; Worters, Marchant and, to some extent, Staniland, nothing bigger than 350s; Judd and O'Donovan 500s only; Wright 1000s mainly; and Lacey and Le Vack solos only although the latter rode 250s, 350s, 500s, 750s and 1000s.

At this point, one other figure must come into the picture – R. M. N. Spring for, despite the fact that it was O'Donovan who brought Denly into racing and gave him his initial big successes, it was Nigel Spring who took over early in Bert's career and managed him, from then on, to the finish. Brooklands would still have been good without the Spring stable but not as it was – superb.

And, again, if one looks at all this from the point of view of versatility, how does one assess the stature of J. S. Worters? Woolly was probably more successful as a tuner/manager for all his great successes as a rider, and why not? You can only ride one bike successfully in a race but, as a manager, he often had two in the first three. This line of thought takes one down another road. How far, for instance, would Wright have gone without Claude Temple, Judd without O'Donovan or Denly without both O'Donovan and Spring? Had it not been for O'Donovan, Bert might never have come into the game at all.

There are others, of course, O. M. Baldwin, Temple, Riddoch and Baragwanath. Giants in their sphere but all big twin mounted so excluded as far as versatility is concerned. Perhaps, over all, Le Vack emerges as number one, riding in the greatest number of classes, tuning and managing and nearly always successful.

Its hard to tell but, as so many of these great men are still around, it seemed clearly worth while to talk to them and get their own views. What they told me can be read later in this book. But first, a resumé of the highlights of the decade.

That is what the story is about. Not a complete history of motorcycle racing at Brooklands in the nineteen twenties but a record of the highlights and what was behind them. And also, of course, about other supporting riders, some of whom were to all intents and purposes successful private owners who made up the fields, competing for the love of the game on level terms with the factory backed 'greats'. Without these chaps there might well have been no motorcycle racing at Brooklands for, at that time, the fields were small enough anyway.

Exciting as Brooklands must have been in the period between its opening car race meeting in July 1907 and its closure, from the racing point of view, in August 1914, it has always seemed to me that it only really came into its own from the motorcycle point of view, after World War One. I must admit that I do stand to be corrected on this and could be biased, only having, myself, seen and followed closely the racing that took place there between 1924 and 1939. It may well be that the 1907 to 1914 period lacked nothing in excitement and interest, for one has to bear in mind, of course, that at the time, nothing like Brooklands had ever been seen. In fact, so little was known about either car or motorcycle racing on closed circuits that, initially, horse racing practice was followed, the prize money being quoted in sovereigns and the competitors wearing coloured jackets as do jockeys.

There was a very clear distinction between entrants and drivers, the former taking the role of gentlemen owners and the latter of professional pilots, as it were. To some extent this characteristic remained I think, right up to the start of World War Two. It was comic, but the proprietors seemed to regard Brooklands this way and even in the mid-thirties still advertised the track as having 'The right crowd and no crowding'. There was certainly no crowding at the track during the time I knew it and, at times, the problem seemed to be to get a crowd at all, although the big meetings did draw them. And, where motorcycle racing was concerned, it definitely was the right crowd.

As always, following the aftermath of a major war, the wheels turned slowly at first. Many of the pre-war riders had gone, but a few, including Horsman and O'Donovan returned to the track. New names arose including O. M. Baldwin, Jack Emerson, Kaye Don, I. P. Riddoch and Vivian Prestwich, older son of J. A. Prestwich whose JAP engines powered racing machines of every capacity, and, of course, Herbert Le Vack whose performances with the big 1000 cc Indians constituted the major interest at Brooklands right at the start. Among the highlights of this first year of post war racing at the track were Le Vack's unsuccessful duel with D. H. Davidson's big Harley, to become the first to record over a hundred miles an hour on two wheels.

The 500 cc hour record, too, was under constant seige by both Emerson and Horsman, Emerson putting it up by nearly three miles an hour in September 1920, to 70.46. This was too much for Vic, who retaliated two days later with 71.68 mph, bettering this to 72.48 again with his Norton, a month later, so that it was not until ten months after that, in August 1921, that it was again in the Douglas pocket.

All these riders, Le Vack particularly, constituted the major interest at Brooklands throughout 1920, 1921 and 1922, being joined by the colourful Freddie Dixon and diminutive Bert Denly in 1923.

In October 1921, Horsman made his last Norton-mounted attack on the 500 cc 'Hour', capturing it this time at 73.38 mph only to have Emerson take it back a month later at 74.26. The fact that Halford's Triumph then entered the picture at 76.74 mph, coupled with Vic's realisation that, while Norton's had O'Donovan, they were unlikely to be really interested in anyone else, may well have influenced him in his decision to switch mounts. In May 1922 Emerson, with his Douglas, became holder of the record for the last time at nearly seventy nine miles an hour and the honour of being first man to cover over eighty miles in one hour on a 500 fell to Bert Denly in June 1923.

Bert's entry to the motorcycle racing scene must surely be unique. Living at the time in Byfleet, and employed by a local butcher, one of his tasks was to deliver the meat to the customers and it was while doing this, mounted on his 350 cc Douglas, that he was spotted by 'Wizard' O'Donovan. Never had the 'Wizard' seen a side-valve Douglas ridden quite like that and, for a moment, he stood dumbfounded. Then it dawned on him that, if a chap really could ride such a bike like that on the road, while living on the doorstep of the World's greatest race track, there was only one place for him. Striding round to the only butcher's shop in the village he met Bert and asked him to come and see him, since he had a proposition to make. At first Bert didn't take him seriously but a month later, the 'Wizard' paid another visit to the butchers, being more insistent this time and, as a result, Bert went for an interview, ending his job in the meat trade on the Saturday and starting a new one on the following Monday morning as works rider for Norton, never having ridden one before and never having previously been on a track. The fact that, within two months, he became holder of the World's 500 cc Hour Record at 82.66 mph underlines not only his ability but, also O'Donovan's perception and judgement. Bert's descriptions of his first work for O'Donovan and his first rides astride the Norton at Brooklands border on being hilarious but are better for him to tell in his own words later in the story.

At this stage, conscious of Horsman's success in stimulating interest in racing at Triumphs, the 'Wizard' obviously felt it wise to put up the 'Hour' up as high as possible, sending his new protégé out again twice in October 1923 so that, on the 15th of that month Denly and the Norton raised the record to 85.58 mph. But despite this, Vic broke it again less than a month later, riding a Triumph for the first time, at 86.52 mph and it was not until mid-1924 that the O'Donovan – Denly partnership regained it.

In the meantime, records were falling in many other classes and, by the beginning of 1924, Brooklands had entered its greatest phase, from the point of view of motorcycle racing, even if the span was only to last for six years.

But, at this stage problems arose at Brooklands. Local residents, never keen on having the track on their doorstep, rebelled at the alleged noise and this seemed to be levelled more at the racing motorcyclists than at the car people. Possibly the staccato exhausts of the single cylinders did penetrate the tranquility of St Georges Hill to a greater extent than scream of the four-, six- and eight-cylinder car engines. Whatever the position, the fat was in the fire and the whole thing came to a head during the week prior to the third motorcycle meeting due to be held early in May. The events of this week at Brooklands were chaotic, with trackside observers eliminating machine after machine on the grounds of excess noise and the whole culminated in a mass meeting of riders presided over by A. V. ('Ebby') Ebblewhite, the Brooklands Timekeeper and Handicapper and held in the Clubhouse in the Paddock.

The result of this was the riders strike, the first and only one ever staged by the motorcycle racing fraternity at the track and the issuing of a Resolution proposed by the British Motor Racing Club Secretary, George Reynolds and seconded by Herbert Le Vack:

'That this meeting of the Members and Entrants of the BMCRC, on the occasion of the third race meeting, view with grave concern the restrictions that are placed on practise, racing and attempts on records consequent on the attitude of certain Weybridge residents. In view of the adequate fees, rents and other revenues provided by the Members of the Club and paid to the Brooklands authorities for specific facilities, this meeting calls upon the Brooklands authorities to take such action as will restore to the Club those rights which they have hitherto enjoyed.'

Obviously, it was an issue that was not going to be resolved overnight. The riders struck, the meeting was cancelled and it was the death knell of open exhausts at Brooklands. The result of it all was the addition of a rule which laid down that every machine, car or motorcycle, should thenceforth be fitted with a silencer, the capacity of which should be six times the capacity of one cylinder, and the length of which should be not more than six times its diameter, having an exit pipe the same size or smaller than the pipe leading from the cylinder to the silencer itself.

That was the beginning of the Brooklands silencer, blinding the residents with science and technically acceptable to the experts. Whether or not it made one scrap of difference to the noise level is debatable and, in the years that followed a new generation of residents grew up in Weybridge more acclimatised to road and aircraft noise and more tolerant of progress. But, even in the thirties, the rules were rigidly adhered to, silencers were probed and examined minutely by the scrutineers equipped with a veritable armoury of special gadgets to ensure that no exhaust, whatever its appearance, ran straight through the expansion chamber, joining the tail pipe to make a straight through assembly. Despite this, few machines appeared noticeably quieter and some of the smaller capacity single-port engines took on a defiant and resonant crackle which they certainly never had before the rule was introduced. So at least one of the attractions of racing – noise – changed little and honour was satisfied, although the Brooklands 'can' did impair efficiency, to a greater extent on some machines than on others.

In retrospect, the strike took place not so much because the riders and entrants objected to fitting silencers but because they were given insufficient time to construct and fit proper silencing equipment for this particular meeting. This may well not have been the fault of the Brooklands authorities, who probably found themselves suddenly confronted with a panel of irate and influential residents, determined to bring the thing to a head even if it meant closure of the track.

In the end the matter was resolved and the meeting postponed from May 10th until June 7th. But before then, another meeting was held at the track, at which both cars and motorcycles competed, organised by the Ealing Club on May 24th. This was really the one at which the silencer regulation was first implemented and the winner of the first race was Spikins 350cc Zenith at an average of 74.78 mph. Third man was one of the participants in this 'first hand' story – J. S. Worters, 348 cc Toronda, who scored again later that afternoon, taking second place after fitting a sidecar, in the Five Lap Club Championship.

At both this meeting and the next, interest centred on the widely differing conceptions that designers and riders had of what an efficient silencer should look like and many were the weird and wonderful designs that turned out.

There were two highlights at the next meeting, five wins by Le Vack in a programme of thirteen races and a magnificent ride by Claude Temple on the big 1000 cc overhead camshaft Anzani, who averaged 105.52 mph over five laps from a standing start to win the 1000 cc Scratch Race from Allchin's big Zenith, Temple's best lap being 109.94. Since, at that time, records set up during races were officially recognised, this netted him the Standing Start Ten Miles at 104.37 mph and the Flying Five Miles at 109.62. Le Vack won one race with his 250 cc New Imperial, three on the same make of 350 and one, Brough Superior mounted, in a one lap sprint at 94.50 mph. Checking back on this was interesting to me because the two best standing laps I ever did at Brooklands were 93.90 in 1934 on an identical machine to Le-Vack's and roughly the same vintage, with three speeds and hand gear change identical – and in 1936, a standing lap at just under 94 mph on a new 500cc Manx Norton. Both these standling laps won me races, my Brough averaging just over 100 mph in a three lap race and the Norton 99.51 mph in a two lap. All three machines, of course, had rigid frames and were running on alcohol. I think it says something for the wonderful old Brough, which could well have been one of Le Vack's old machines, and for its fine old JAP engine that, ten years later, in the hands of a then amateur, it could still get so close to the figures of the Master! At the time I owned it, having acquired it for £25, it had just emerged from four years of industrial slump, during which time no one had much money to spend on maintaining aged Brooklands machinery. It was slightly temperamental by the time I got it but a great ride if you knew the line to take with it and unforgiving if you made a mistake. The best lap I ever had with it in practise was just under 109 and, officially, in a race, 105.74 mph. The best flying lap I had on the Norton was identical, but so much easier to do and, of course, temperament free.

Other placemen at this June 1924 meeting included Denly, with a win and a second place, Worters with a second and Chris Staniland, later the number one of the Worters stable, with a win and a third. Other winners were Joe Wright on a 350 cc Zenith, Allchin, Marchant, Baxter and H. Beart with his Morgan.

There were two motorcycle meetings held in July. The first, consisting mainly of 50 Mile races, solo and sidecar, took place in brilliant weather, Le Vack scoring again with the 250 cc New Imperial at 71.35 while Joe Wright came home first among the 350s at 76.58 mph. But it was Vic Horsman's day, really, for besides winning the 500 cc solo at 85.32, he continued with his 600 cc Triumph and sidecar, winning the 1000 cc Passenger 50 Mile race at 76.95, and this constituted a World Record for Class F, Beart's Morgan finishing second.

This meeting was followed by one organised by the Surbiton Club on behalf of the South Eastern Centre, the programme consisting of eleven races, six of which were for cars and the remaining five for motorcycles. When talking to Vic Horsman recently I suggested that these mixed meetings may have come about through shortages in entries because, unlike today, Brooklands meetings tended, sometimes, to be under subscribed. But he thought that the idea, really, was to stimulate interest by having variety and, at the time, it certainly seems to have worked.

This time all five races were handicaps, the 350 cc race being won by Walters' Zenith, with Lacey's Cotton second and Worters' Toronda third. In the 350 cc to 1000 cc race, the talking feature was the O'Donovan-designed banana-shaped silencer fitted to Denly's Norton, which finished second, just failing to catch Grimes' Martinsyde, with Michael McEvoy's 994 cc McEvoy Anzani third, the limit man in this race being A. F. Mann's on his aged Rudge Multi, belt driven. Even so, he wasn't the last to use belt drive at the track. I had that doubtful honour, seven years later.

The day proved to be a good one for 'Woolly' who brought the 350 cc Toronda into second place in the Surbiton Three Lap Lightning Handicap, behind Glover's big Douglas, completing it by winning the Three Lap Passenger Handicap at 66.76 from Riddoch's 998 cc Zenith. Third man home was O'Donovan who, despite having the services of Denly, still turned out, himself, to ride occasionally.

The August meeting was marked by rather lean entries and a highish percentage of non-starters so that this time, in certain races, the skill of the experts lay, not in winning as fast as possible but rather as fast as they needed. Dougal Marchant's winning speed of the 250 cc Scratch Race – 63.39 mph – was a case in point, as was Horsman's win in the next race at 78.79 mph in contrast to his win in the last race of the day, on the same machine, at 90.06 mph. Once again, 'Woolly' Worters brought the Toronda home first in the 350 cc race at 79.03 and the 500 cc event fell to R.M.N. Spring's Norton at 83.84. One feels that O'Donovan could hardly have been pushed in winning the last but one race of the day, on his 600 cc Norton, and sidecar at 71.87 mph.

At the 'Five Clubs' meeting, a fortnight later, he was out again, winning the One Lap Sidecar Scratch Race from Worters, Toronda, and coming second to Baragwanath in the 1000 cc Passenger Scratch Event, the Toronda notching up another second and a third at this meeting, while Denly, solo mounted, won the 500 cc Two Lap Scratch and was second in the Unlimited. The One Lap Solo Scratch for Private Owners was won by Mitchell's big Zenith, with Milton's Norton second and Gordon Cobbold's Sunbeam third.

Heavy rain rather spoiled the last **BMCRC** meeting in October 1924 – the Championships – becoming so bad that the meeting had to be abandoned half way through. Even so, it didn't deter Horsman who won the 600 cc Sidecar Event from Tucker. The race was marked by a potentially dangerous accident to Nigel Spring, whose outfit was struck a glancing blow by another competitor on lap two while laying second to Vic. Unknown to its rider, the bump removed a number of spokes from the sidecar wheel, the wheel finally collapsing at the fork – the worst possible place for such a failure since all the weight of the outfit was on it at that point. The rim and tyre parted company, disappearing completely, and it took all Spring's ingenuity and skill to bring the outfit to rest – and at a time when sidecar skids weren't compulsory and were seldom fitted.

The season ended with a healthy crop of record breaking led by Horsman and Judd, backed by Teddy Prestwich, Greening and Anstice and, as though inspired by all this, O'Donovan went out as late as mid-November to take the 2 Hours, 200 Kilometres, 200 Miles and 300 Kilos, 500 cc solo at speeds around 84 mph. So the 1924 season which had begun rather unauspiciously, finished strongly – silencers or no silencers.

Chapter 2

The 1925 Season

The Essex Motor Club staged a nice little meeting at the track early in May, with a programme of five races, three of which were for bikes. The first, a Three Lap Handicap for Machines to 500 cc, was won easily by Hicks' 350 AJS at 76.03 mph. Wainwright's Cotton and Wheeler's Douglas were second and third but two other 350s, Joe Wright's Zenith and C.W.G. (Bill) Lacey's Cotton were close behind.

The Three Lap Handicap for Solos 350 cc to 1000 cc was won by Wheeler, with Chris Staniland's 490 cc Norton second and Walter's 750 cc Zenith third. Guyler's big Indian frightened the spectators – and probably its pilot as well – with a fearsome wobble as it passed the Vickers sheds at the end of lap two.

The Three Lap Passenger Handicap provided the spectacle of the Scratch man being handicapped right out of the picture, Millar's 348 cc Chater Lea outfit receiving no less than two minutes start from Baragwanath's 976 cc Brough Superior. Allowing the fact that Millar obviously went well to average 68.90 mph for the race this would mean that, giving him forty seconds start per lap, Barry would have had to average nearly 96 mph to dead heat with him. J. S. (Woolly) Worters whose 350 cc Excelsior outfit was second to Millar, conceded him nineteen seconds start per lap and, here again, 'Woolly' would have had to average 79 mph to cross the line at the same moment.

To those who, so to speak, were 'in residence' at Brooklands, it was no more difficult to forecast the race pattern of these individual handicap short races than it was to forecast that of the scratch races. Time, and a certain amount of low cunning, was needed, whether scratch or handicap. With a scratch race it was sometimes harder, in fact, for whereas, in theory, all one had to do was to study practice form so carefully that, when practice ended, you knew the lap speed of every runner in the race, the likely winners were all top professionals well versed in concealing true form from the 'watch clicking' Brooklands fraternity.

But if, say, rider 'A' was lapping in practice at 95 mph. and slightly faster than he had done previously, one knew he was 'in the hunt'. But if rider 'B' was also lapping at 95 mph and had lapped at 97 mph at a previous meeting one took it that what had been done once would almost certainly be done again so, if no one else was going faster, rider 'B' would be the chap on which to put your money.

Let's use this Three Lap Passenger Handicap to illustrate the same thing. The results were:

1. Millar   348 cc Chater Lea. Handicap 2 mins.
2. Worters   348 cc Excelsior. Handicap 1 min. 3 secs.
3. Fitzgerald   592 cc Zenith. Handicap 1 min. 3 secs.
                        Winner's speed 68.90 mph

Forget, now, that we know the result. We are opening the programme prior to the race to assess the handicaps. Look for any one runner, a regular and consistent performer not likely to spring any surprises, whose form is known. Always a bit easier to work it out if he happens to be the scratch man and easier still if there are others in the race rather like him – chaps who, meeting after meeting, lap at always the same speed, give or take a mile an hour.

In this case, there are certainly two: Baragwanath on scratch and Worters who receives from him one minute, three seconds in three laps or 21 seconds start per lap. Barry can do 93 mph – he did it last meeting and the one before that. On the Outer Circuit speed table 93.09 mph is a lap time of 107 seconds (one minute forty-seven seconds). So, to dead heat with Barry, Worters, who gets 21 seconds per lap start from him, must turn in a lap time of 107 seconds plus 21 seconds, which equals 128 seconds. A lap time of 128 seconds works out, on the speed table at 77.81 mph, exactly the lap time he did when last running the outfit.

Millar gets two minutes start from Barry, or forty seconds a lap. To have averaged nearly 69 mph Millar must have put in flying laps between 72 and 73 mph and was, therefore, an almost certain winner, with an improvement on his handicap speed of between 5 and 6 mph.

Yes, the handicap race results were easier to forecast because, in the first place, the big names were, almost on principle, handicapped out of it and, secondly, because the lesser lights were less skilled in concealing their potential. And thirdly, of course, when betting came into it, Mr Average Punter so often seemed to find the working out of handicap speeds beyond him, preferring to lay his money down on scratch races which he felt he understood, to the satisfaction of the 'residents' who really did know form.

Two days after this Essex MC Meeting Worters, who must have been pleased with his standing lap time, was out again with the 350 cc Excelsior outfit, breaking the World's Standing Kilo and Standing Mile in Class B/S. One can picture him, at the end of the Essex Meeting, standing at the door of the timing box, lap times in hand, saying 'That first lap was alright. Think I'd better look at the Mile and Kilo times when I go back to the shed'.

There was nothing complicated about the organisation of short distance record attempts at Brooklands, provided you and your machine were of the quality to do it. You just went up to the office next day and agreed a day and time, phoned the timekeeper in London, confirmed it with him and that was it. If the timekeeper was A.V. (Ebby) Ebblewhite, you met him at Weybridge station on the day, for 'Ebby' wasn't a motorist and always took the train to Brooklands. If it was George Reynolds, he would arrive by car. There were few, if any, rail strikes in those days and George's car had never been known to fail. A long record run of twelve hour duration would

Brooklands veteran and Lap Record Holder, always **Brough Superior and sidecar mounted.**
E.C.E. ('Ted') Baragwanath.

mean six o'clock starts for whoever was timekeeper – and a good alarm clock. But I never knew either of them fail to be there at the start.

The Hutchinson '100' Meeting on 16th May 1925 must go down in history as 'good in all respects'. Weather, racing and Bemsee organisation were all first class and the big names, including Le Vack, were all there.

The first event, a Three Lap Scratch 350 cc, was won by the great Bert astride an overhead camshaft Coventry Eagle at 81.51 mph. He was followed by Worters' Excelsior and Lacy on his Cotton. Bert wasn't too pushed in this one and followed the other two for most of the race, pulling out a twenty yard lead during the third lap.

The race for 500s was a cracker and was fought wheel to wheel throughout by Horsman and Judd, the Triumph leading by a length most of the way. But **Rex** cleverly reversed the order as they left the Byfleet banking for the last time, bringing the Douglas in to win at 89.90 mph breaking the World's Flying 5 Kilos and 5 miles in the process – this at a time when world's records could be broken in a race, of course. Staniland's Norton was third. Denly on O'Donovan's Norton didn't start and neither did Barrow whose Royal Enfield had lost its fishtail in the previous race.

Out of seven entries for the 1000 cc race only Temple (998 cc McEvoy), Horsman (599 cc Triumph), H. J. Knight (996 cc Zenith) and R.E. Humphries (989 cc Harley Davidson – with direct drive), came to the line. Horsman won easily at 82.06 mph from Temple, who spent most of the time trying to get the big McEvoy to fire on two, with Humphries third.

Vic also won the next one, a Five Lap All Comers Handicap, with his 599 cc Triumph at 94.68 mph, from Humphries, with Loweth's Norton third. The 'pre-curtain raiser' short races ended with a Three Lap Handicap for Private Owners which Staniland won with his Norton at 87.68 mph with Knight's big twin Zenith second and Welch's little 248 cc Excelsior third.

The Hutchinson '100' of 1925 must surely have broken all records entrywise with fifty-four entries so that four, among them Pat Driscoll, ranked as reserves. They all got in, though, for there were seven non-starters among the fifty accepted. Even so, forty-seven starters in any race was good going in 1925.

Although the race was run on an individual handicap basis, the Club tried to make it more interesting by introducing the 'coloured jersey' idea, the fastest runners (Numbers 1 to 11) in White, 12 to 22 in Green, 23 to 33 Yellow, 34 to 45 Blue and the slower boys, 46 to 54 in Red. The Club wasn't too wealthy in those days and fifty jerseys must have ranked as quite a large item in the Balance Sheet unless, perhaps, a Committee member was also connected with League Football!

Sadly, Horsman, Denly and Le Vack were all among the non-starters. Significant too was that it was a huge field containing a number of fairly inexperienced people, all on individual handicaps. All three were back markers, Le Vack having had one win and Vic two that day. It's good policy, sometimes, not to push your luck!

Long individual handicap races are always hard to follow and harder to describe in print. In this one Temple, the scratch man, was waiting astride the big McEvoy Anzani for nearly half an hour before he was flagged away but, once on his way he was soon lapping at around 96 mph. The first caller at the pits was Maund's Zenith, for a plug change after three laps and, soon afterwards, Kershaw's new Hudson was in with part of its cylinder missing. Staniland retired with a broken rocker standard, a trouble not unknown with Nortons in 1925, and Baxter's 350 cc Rex Acme was in with a flat tyre.

The Race wasn't without incident by any means for, prior to retiring, J. H. Evans had crashed twice on his 348 cc OEC Blackburne. At any period it was quite an achievement to make personal contact with Brooklands Outer Circuit concrete and walk away unhurt. To do it twice in one race and then be in a position to 'retire' was masterly – and very sensible, too.

Temple, who had now completed 21 laps to the leader's 26, came in to refuel, retiring shortly afterwards, and this put the limelight on Longman, who was going well and whose handicap of 6 mins 10 secs. was, so the experts thought, generous for one so experienced astride a big twin Harley. And they were right for, at the stage when the race was being led by Pearson's 348 cc Zenith with 30 laps covered, Longman was only a lap behind. So, when the Zenith broke its primary chain when leaving the pit after refuelling, the race was in the bag for the big Harley-Davidson and Longman won at 89.66 mph followed by P. M. Walters' 344 cc Zenith with H.J. Knight's big twin of the same make third. Every devotee of Brooklands, including Dr Joe Bayley, knows that Zeniths like Brooklands and Brooklands like them. Even Pearson, who must have been the most disappointed man of the day, knew it for, replacing his broken chain, he still managed to fill fourth place. A very good effort indeed.

During 1924 there had been only two successful attacks on the 500 cc Hour Record, Denly taking it back from Horsman in June at 87.07 mph, and interest began to centre on who would be the first man to put 90 miles into the hour on a 500. Horsman clearly had this in mind and so had Triumphs but it was no easy task and the speed was creeping up more slowly, now, with each fresh attack. In November, Horsman managed to push it up a fraction further, to 88. 21 mph but that had to be it until the Spring. He came out again, just missing the magic 90 with an average of 89.13 mph in May 1925. But now, the racing programme began to take up his time and there were other records to be got so, for the time being, it remained there until the Fall.

This particular attempt was more rewarding perhaps than previous ones to Vic, for it took place on the Monday following the 200 Miles Sidecar Races on Saturday at Brooklands. For a great part of the race, things had looked promising for him with the 600 cc Triumph. Dixon on his big Douglas had led off the line, closely followed by the Triumph which, in turn, was shadowed by the Norton outfits of O'Donovan, Staniland and Tucker. A not unusual picture, this the lone Triumph being harried by its Norton rivals in full force. Fred, though, usually rode the same race pattern, solo, sidecar, wet or fine, wherever the venue, Isle of Man or Brooklands – flat out and let the others follow. This may not have suited Vic completely but he certainly expected it and was well able to cope. Accepting the blistering pace but feeling reasonably sure that the reliability factor of his Triumph was greater than that of Dixon's Douglas, he was content to play a waiting game, allowing Fred to pull ahead gradually from the 100 yard lead he had held at the end of the 3rd lap. At the end of 10 laps Fred had a 300 yard lead. Rex Judd came in to change plugs on his Douglas, retiring a lap later and, on lap 11, O'Donovan came in to see what could be done with his silencer, which had collapsed. On the 15th lap Dixon slowed and came into his pit and, at last Vic and the Triumph were in the lead, pursued by Chris Staniland and Fred, who had taken on oil at his stop.

For a time, the wily Vic was content to let Chris take the lead, Tucker now laying third and Dixon fourth but, on lap 23 the Douglas pulled in again, this time to retire. As they neared the 100 mile mark trouble struck Tucker, one of the sidecar chassis members breaking and allowing the safety skid to touch the ground and on the 39th lap he was flagged in so that the outfit could be inspected. A few laps later he retired and from then on only Victor and Chris were in it. Lap 40 saw the Triumph in the lead but four laps later it was the Norton again – and no sign of the Horsman Triumph, for a piston had gone. Victor's retirement left Chris in a strong position and he went on to finish an easy winner – and popular too for, like Horsman, Chris Staniland was an immensely liked Brooklands figure. Winner's speed 68.88 mph.

The 1000 cc Race provided drama, Le Vack and his Brough Superior leading Ashby's big Zenith outfit all the way until, with 57 laps covered, two laps separated them. Then the Brough's back tyre burst and while the rear wheel was being changed, Ashby was seen to be approaching his pit and on fire. But in those days, fires were not unknown at Brooklands and were more easily dealt with than rear wheel changes so that in the end it was the Zenith that won, with the Brough Superior second and Claude Temple's McEvoy Anzani outfit third. Winner's speed 72.71 mph.

The 350 cc Race was, perhaps, not the most exciting that Brooklands had ever seen. The meeting was wet and it seemed to affect this class to a greater extent than the bigger ones. V. Baxter led for a lot of the way and emerged the winner while Marchant (Chater Lea), Handley (Rex Acme) and Worters (Excelsior) combated a variety of troubles. In the end, it was Greening who took second place – eighteen minutes behind the winner and then there was an even greater wait for the third man home. Finally, and twenty-eight minutes behind the second man, J. S. Worters limped home after at least three stops, one of which was to adjust an exhaust tappet which he did while the engine was running. Subsequently he suffered a puncture which involved changing the tyre and tube but third he was and he deserved to be. Winner's speed 59.64 mph.

All this was very much in contrast to the Hutchinson 100 which had been run a week earlier and had resulted in a win for Longman's big Harley-Davidson at 89.66 mph, with the Zeniths of Walters, Knight and Pearson in second, third and fourth places respectively. Nearly all Brooklands machines were interesting and exciting but some of the Zeniths seemed to epitomise Brooklands itself, no matter what make of engine was installed, – usually a JAP although sometimes Blackburne. In this context it is almost easier to name the unexciting machines. But where would Brooklands, and to a lesser extent the TT, have been without those wonderful JAP engines. They were, to all intents and purposes, in every other machine, 250 cc, 350 cc, 500 cc, yes – and even 175 cc. Brooklands and the whole motor cycling fraternity certainly owed a lot to Mr Prestwich and his sons Vivian and Teddy.

The contrast between Longman's solo winning speed in the 'Hutch' and Ashby's in the 200 Miles Sidecar Race is interesting because the pattern was repeated more than once. The moral of it was that the Outer Circuit at Brooklands was punishing to any machine, car or motorcycle, and especially so to those poor old rigid framed bikes. And it was the second half of a 200 miles race that really took the toll. Today, the problem just cannot be envisaged by those who never knew the place and have never known anything except the superb present day standards of suspension and roadholding. Looking back, it seems to me that engine development in the 1920's and even in the early thirties, was way ahead of frame and suspension technique. This was the Achilles heel.

A hundred miles an hour has always been a magic figure. There were machines that would approach this figure on the road in the twenties and few that will not today. But, boy, what a difference there is in momentarily touching the magic figure on a long straight road, and then in keeping it up mile after mile, hour after hour for fifty, a hundred, two hundred miles.

The hammering and pounding broke every imaginable cycle part on a machine. Frames, engine mountings, saddle stays, tank mountings, fork springs and damper mountings – nothing could withstand it. In my talk with Bert Denly, he told me of no less than three separate occasions on which he had handlebars snap off, twice on solos and once with a sidecar outfit – and what part of a machine can be simpler to make than the handlebars. Obviously the problem was immense, for men who could make machines travel at these speeds – nearly fifty year ago – weren't fools. So one is forced to the conclusion that the science of metallurgy must have been way behind other aspects of motorcycle engineering at the time.

And what wonderful chaps the riders of the twenties were. Picture, for instance, the problem of losing a handlebar on a big sidecar outfit when taking it onto the Byfleet banking on full song. To save distance, the rider would only be using half the banking and would be exerting strong left lock to keep the outfit as low as possible. With his sidecar outfit, Bert would have been lucky for, although he would have no clutch, he would still have a throttle to close. His problem would have been threefold. First, to stay on the machine at all, with only the right-hand bar to hang on to. Second, to exert enough effort with his right arm to prevent the outfit going up and over the banking. And thirdly, the most difficult of all – to close the throttle while doing this, because track machines had throttle levers with no return springs and, on top of all this, the adjustment was drawn up tightly so that one didn't have to be continually pushing the lever open on account of the continuous pounding the outfit was taking. Some people even went to the extent of fitting a tough rubber band – often cut from an inner tube – from the top fork link to the lever, looping it round the lever so that, to all intents and purposes it was impossible to close it. My own Brough Superior had this fitting when I acquired it from Geoffrey Davis but I didn't like it and removed it – it seemed altogether too much like burning one's bridges. But many people stuck to it even until the mid-thirties.

What wonderful engines they were – nearly all of them. Triumph, JAP, Norton, Rudge, Blackburne, Sunbeam and the rest. In the battle one was having with the machine, one hardly gave them a thought. But, of course, the poor old engine was taking the same bodily pounding as was the rider and the machine itself, all the time at maximum revs for hour after hour and mile after mile. The only time I can recall thinking about the engine was in 1935 when I partnered the late Eric Fernihough on a 250 cc Cotton in a Twelve Hour Record run in October. And, even then, I only did it as therapy because of tiredness and boredom after nine hours of hammering and sliding. I recall wondering how it could possibly have done what it had and still have three more hours of work to do. It was a JAP and I gave it another thought about half an hour before the twelve hour run ended. It was dark then and one could no longer look down, along the railway straight, to see if anything was visibly wrong. We had no lights and were running in the headlights of a fast car. It was an eerie and unforgettable moment, unreal somehow for, by that time, one was deaf as a post and numb with cold. But, although you could neither see nor hear it, you could still feel that wonderful little motor hammering away beneath you, uncomplaining and still willing even after its long ordeal. As the long day wore on, it did seem tired and weary in accelerating after pit stops, finding it harder every time to get the big fuel load on the move again on the long pull up from the pits up to and round the Home Banking. It was slower then for on those standing lap one didn't need to use the Home Banking at all – you could stay right in close at the bottom. This was something I never recall when starting from the same place in a short race. But, once the Member's Bridge was reached it would regain its revs on the run down to the Railway Straight and, by the end of the straight it was singing just as happily as it had all day so that, fuel load or no fuel load, one was glad of a bit of banking as one heeled over left after passing the Vickers sheds.

I suppose that raises another point for the reader who never saw or went round Brooklands for it could be thought that since the track was banked and you went round it anti-clockwise, no steering effort was required. Let me try to give an idea of what had to be done in the course of a lap. First look at the time that one took for the lap and the distance that you covered. The track was a hundred feet wide for the whole of its length so that, on the 'fifty foot' line you were half way up the Home and Byfleet bankings. On that line, the lap distance was 2.767 miles. It was longer if you used more of the banking and went higher, shorter if you kept lower. The lower you went, the more the bike slid and the more you wore out the rear tyre. This didn't matter in short races but was a factor to be considered in long ones and even more so, of course, in very long distance records runs even with a 250.

The Byfleet banking had the longest radius lasting nearly a mile and with a well set up solo 500 which steered you had no need to use the banking at a lap speed of 105 to 108 mph, taking the machine in right at the bottom, within ten feet of the grass verge on your left where the Byfleet section began. You 'peeled off' as it were, heeling over hard to the left, concentrating only on keeping the front wheel roughly five feet from the inside grass verge – no banking at all – dead level ground. Immediately you did this, the rear wheel would 'step out' into a long and bumpy 105 mph plus slide which would last for a mile. With a good steering and carefully set up machine such as a Norton or a Grindlay Peerless or, no doubt, a Horsman Triumph, the slide would be reasonably stable. Now and again, the bike might find a strange uncharted bump which would make the rear end chop out slightly visciously but, as a rule, it would go the whole distance heeled right over to the left with the rear wheel 'hanging out' a foot or eighteen inches all the way round. Certain other makes, at the same speed, would 'chop' unpleasantly most of the way round, particularly it seemed, Sunbeams and the big Excelsiors and, to a lesser extent Rudges. If one found oneself following one of these, it looked an uncomfortable and, often, a dangerous business. But the riders of those bikes knew them and were always far less worried by the phenomenon than those who observed them from a few yards astern. Two riders particularly come to mind during my Outer Circuit rides, 'Laddy' Courtney with his Sunbeam '95' and P. A. Refoy who rode a B14 Excelsior. Both looked absolutely terrifying viewed from astern and, if you got alongside him, 'Laddy's' facial expression, round the Byfleet, was something never to be forgotten. I do recall him complaining after one race when we'd been in close company – anyone would have, that day.

As the bike left the Byfleet Banking one brought it up and immediately heeled it over to the right. For the line across the Fork was not straight, as it appeared to the spectator, but a full bore right hander. Even with a 350 cc sidecar outfit one used a lot of right lock here and with a fast 600 cc sidecar set up it was nearly full right lock as the outfit crabbed away to the left and you fought to keep well over to the right, close to the Vickers sheds so as to get a correct line onto the Home Bank. With his big supercharged Brough and sidecar set up, Baragwanath, and later Noel Pope, frequently used full right lock at the Fork and 'Barry' once told me that, if things didn't go right as he left the Byfleet Banking, he would have to keep on full right lock and 'roll back' momentarily in order to keep the correct line there. The problem was worse, with a big twin, solo or sidecar, because one had to use nearly all the Byfleet Banking so that, when one arrived at the Fork, the right hander was so sharp that you literally couldn't see the Home Banking onto which you were trying to line up.

The Home banking, having a much shorter radius and being, therefore, much steeper, had to be used at anything over over about eighty-five. Even with a quick 500 you needed nearly all of it and some people on slower machines tended to use far more than they needed so that, with a quick bike you had a passing problem which sometimes amounted to passing slower machines underneath because, even on a 110 mile an hour machine you had to be conscious of at least two who had started after you in a handicap race, the Broughs of Eric Fernihough and Noel Pope, both capable of 120 mile an hour lap speeds. The prospect of a Brough up the backside was always one to remember, one felt. And there were others – the 115 mile an hour brigade, Bickell on the copper plated Bickell JAP, Hewitt on 'Woolly's Excelsior, Dennis Minett's Rudge or one of the big Francis Beart Nortons. With all the problems you had ahead of you, it was essential to know what was likely to be happening behind you.

The dive off the Home Banking brought you into the Railway Straight and this really was straight for about half a mile or more. Here again, Baragwanath once told me that he used to practise relaxing completely here, in long races. I sometimes tried it on long rides and it did seem to work. His theory was that it was good for one's muscles to be relaxed instead of in tension all the time. But I was always very careful not to be still 'relaxed' when the Byfleet loomed up again!

So that was the lap. If you took two minutes to do it, you were averaging exactly eighty-three miles an hour. Ninety miles an hour laps took one minute fifty seconds, a hundred miles an hour one minute thirty-nine seconds, and a hundred and ten took one minute thirty. A hundred and twenty came out at one minute twenty-three. The late John Cobb's car lap record of 143 mph took him one minute nine seconds and it was after having done this that he, a very modest man and prone to understatement, told a friend that lapping Brooklands at that speed was like leaning as far out of a skyscraper window as you could, while making as sure as you could that you didn't actually fall! The Railton had a maximum of a hundred and sixty plus, of course.

The problems of passing and being passed existed only in races for, in record attempts one had the track to oneself and, other considerations apart, one really needed it during long distance record runs particularly as, by this time – mid 1925 – engine development was tending to progress faster than frame and suspension design.

Inch by inch or, at least, yard by yard, the 500 cc Hour record rose nearer and nearer the magic three figure mark. When, on the last day in October, Fred Dixon's Douglas took it from Vic Horsman's Triumph at 89.92 mph his satisfaction at breaking the record must have been mixed with disappointment at not being the first to take it to ninety. Vic, despite a busy season of racing, had had five months for further development. It was Motor Cycle Show time – a good time to make a successful attempt – and Brooklands was due to shut down for the winter at any moment. He either had to wait till 1926 or go at once. He chose to go, made a successful atttempt and became the first to put ninety miles into one hour on a five hundred – speed 90.79 mph – and that was it for 1925.

Rather surprisingly, no one rushed out to make another attempt the moment the 1926 season opened. In fact no one seemed interested in breaking the 500 cc 'Hour' until mid-season, when the whole thing took a unexpected turn. On 24th July, Wal Handley brought out his 348 cc Rex Acme Blackburne to make an attempt on the Class 'B' Hour and to the astonishment of everyone put it up to 91.20 mph, continuing the run to annexe the Two Hours as well at 88.31 mph. In his first hour, Walter covered 91 miles, 360 yards and, in the two hour run 176 miles, 1083 yards thus, in one attempt taking both these records, not only for Class 'B' but for the 500 cc Class 'C' as well. The excellence of this run is in no way dimmed by the fact that Horsman could, in fact, have broken the 500 cc hour at that time, had he wished to do so.

Handley's run was an absolute classic of its period and, in the 350 cc class the records stood until the latter part of 1928. But to allow them to stand in the bigger class as well was more than Vic could accept and, just two months later he brought the big Triumph out again and gave the 'Hour' a real knock, leaving it, this time, at 94.15 mph. There it stood for nearly nine months until a new challenger and make of machine, albeit both previous holders of the 'Hour' were to reappear, denting it, at first slightly and then very badly indeed.

Good weather favoured the Cup Day Meeting in July and the opening 350 cc Scratch Race was won by Le Vack on the Coventry Eagle from Worters' Excelsior, with H.M. Walters' Zenith third, the winner's speed being a rousing 90.39 mph.

Chris Staniland won the three Lap Private Owners Scratch from the Sunbeams of Williams and Cobbold. His winning speed was 87.99 mph and Cobbold won the Sealed Handicap.

The Five Lap Scratch up to 1000 cc looked a certainty for Le Vack's Brough Superior but he was out quickly with an oiled plug which left Walters' big twin Zenith the winner, followed home by Horsman's 607 cc Triumph and Baldwin's big twin Matchless. Winner's speed 97.27 mph. Big twins were tricky, plugwise, in those days. My own Brough Superior, in the 1930's, always left the line with a 50/50 chance of a plug oiling on the back cylinder, always hitting on two immediately and, if it was going to, losing the back cylinder on the change from second to top gear at between 85 and 90 mph just as it climbed up onto the Home Banking. Once that happened that was it – you never got it back again. It made betting tricky and, if I was putting money on it, I used to have a runner up in the control tower watching the bike as it came out from behind the Member's Hill on the standing lap. If it did lose a plug I used to pull it right down the banking and come out from behind the hill at the bottom and very slowly. If it was on two, I kept it very high on lap one and, on seeing it there, the runner would shin down the steps, sprint across to the bookies and place the bet.

The Ten Lap Scratch for the G. E. Tottey Cup was won by Horsman's Triumph, with the Nortons of Denly and Staniland following. Vic's winning speed was 91.22 mph but he wasn't pushed in this one, even being able to look over his shoulder each lap as he went under the Member's Bridge to watch the position astern.

A 350 cc Three Lap Handicap was won by Hopkins' Chater Lea at 85.87 mph, with Tottey's New Imperial and Wainwright's Cotton as placemen, but it was the next event, a Three Lap Handicap to 1000 cc, that was the highlight of the day. Wright was making his debut on a 'big un' in this one and a very good first outing it proved for, with a second lap speed of 108.98 mph he was able to ease to 103.76 on the third lap and still win easily from Knight and Horsman at an average of 103.76 mph, the same speed as his last lap. Joe's first outing on a big twin must have put the idea of smaller bikes right out of his mind from then on and a good thing too, for his wonderful rides on big bikes were to become a legend.

Nigel Spring's Norton and sidecar won the first heat of the Wakefield Cup and Worters' Excelsior Blackburne the second. Sidecar outfits were first, second and third in the final, crafty old 'Wizard' O'Donovan heading home the outfits of Spring and Horsman.

The Five Lap Scratch Race for the O'Donovan cup for two fifties produced a tremendous scrap between Le Vack's Coventry Eagle JAP and Worters' Cotton Blackburne when Woolly pushed the great man every inch of the way. But the pace was too hot for Woolly's Blackburne engine and it failed in the fifth lap, letting in Milton's Beardmore and Welch's Excelsior. Le Vack had, by that time, a huge lead over the others and was able to cruise home to win at 74.55 mph.

Welch won the last race, a Private Owner Three Lap Handicap, from Evans, whose OEC Blackburne didn't cast him off this time. Gordon Cobbold's Sunbeam was third.

At this point, the long wrangle that had been going on, concerning Brooklands vis-à-vis the local residents, was settled, the principal points agreed being that there would be no activities on Sundays, no motorcycles on Mondays and no events to last longer than three hours. Three hour events were limited to one in any one day and four hour events permitted on four days of each year. It was agreed that restrictions on motorcycles would be withdrawn if, and when, a silencing device could be found and enforced to make them no more noisy than the average of racing cars. The latter point, one would think, must have been quite difficult to define. It's strange, too, that the agreement seems to have taken only race days into account because, on every other day throughout the season, or at least on many days, there was an almost continuous roar of car and motorcycle exhausts in chorus. This was certainly the case when I was resident there in the thirties and couldn't possibly have been less in the much busier 1920s.

Perfect weather again marked the 200 Mile Solo Races and, although spectators were thin on the ground at the start, they rolled in well as the day wore on. This time, the 250 cc and 350 cc races were run off concurrently in the morning and the 500 cc and 1000 cc in the afternoon.

Le Vack and Worters immediately resumed their battle in the 250 cc race, Le Vack leading and lapping at first at around 71 mph, at which stage Woolly stayed only a few yards astern. Le Vack stepped it up to 73 mph, Woolly dropping back fifty yards, but when the leader stepped it up another mile an hour, Worters decided to let him go on a bit for both were now a long way ahead of the rest. The Cotton refuelled on the 38th lap, getting away again cleanly, but when Le Vack came in a few laps later the Coventry Eagle was reluctant to restart, leaving Woolly now leading by two laps. Shortly afterwards, it was all over, Le Vack going out with a broken valve spring, so that the Cotton was able to take a breather and continue to the end at around the 70 mph mark, finally averaging 69.24 mph for the race and being followed home by Briggs' OK Supreme and Colgan's Cotton.

An early scrap in the 350 cc race between Emerson's Zenith and Handley's **Rex Acme** ended when the Zenith dropped an exhaust valve. Marchant must have been wild, for he had to stop after four laps due to handling problems caused by the rear wheel being fitted the wrong way round. Dreadful for him but nice to know that such great experts were just as fallible as the rest of us and just as able to drop 'clangers'. A terrible 'gaffe' of this sort can be all that is required to produce fireworks and it did this time for, at the forty lap refuelling stage, it was Marchant who led, followed by Handley. After refuelling, Handley led again, followed by Hopkins, with Marchant third, a lap behind. Seven laps from the end, Handley led Marchant by one lap and Hopkins by two. At this point Worters, leading the 250 cc race, pulled in to say that an ambulance was needed on the Byfleet side of the track where it was found that, after hitting a bump and striking his chin on the handlebars, Marchant was semi-conscious and out of the race.

So Handley's Rex Acme emerged the winner at 78.37 mph, Hopkins Chater Lea was second and Kay Don's Zenith third. Winner's Speed 78.37 mph.

Twenty-one riders lined up for the start of the 500 cc Class at 3 pm and the first drama occurred when W. Van Horne slowed on the third lap and discarded what appeared to be his steering damper. Obviously not a wise move for, after proceeding in a series of wobbles for several more laps he then crashed and was out of the contest. At thirteen laps, Horsman led Judd and Denly and he was still in the lead at 32 laps. Shortly afterwards, Denly and Judd, who had been lapping at over 90 mph, came in to refuel, Bert going out almost immediately afterwards with a broken rocker standard. Never let it be said that racing doesn't improve the breed. How long would it have taken Nortons, I wonder, to discover this rocker standard weakness without the aid of long distance racing. It could well be that, at the time these troubles were befalling the Brooklands boys, very few or possibly no failures of rocker standards had been experienced in ordinary road running although the weakness would have been there all the time.

It is interesting, too, to note how many fine runs in these long races went superbly well until the time came to refuel. Reluctant starters were common after pit stops and one reason for this was the fitting of a brakeless front wheel because with no front brake and, usually a very poor back brake, one just had to rely on the engine for braking when running into the pit. This added up to shutting off with the engine on the over-run and the rear and only brake hard on for a quarter of a mile or more so that, once stopped at the pit, the cylinder was filled with cold vapour and oil. I never ran in a 200 Mile Race but, twigging this one after my first Hutchinson '100', with the Chater Lea in 1933, I never again started a long race at Brooklands involving a pit stop without either a front brake or no front brake and a rear one that one felt absolutely certain would do its job when the time came. In that way one could cut the engine when leaving the Byfleet banking and come in with it dead – and it always started cleanly.

It's strange too, how many of the major breakages causing retirements seemed to happen a few laps after the first pit stop. I don't know why. Possibly the run in and the thirty seconds stopped allowed the stinking hot engine to cool rapidly and then, as the heat came on again, that was all that was needed for the metals of those days to fracture.

With 41 laps of the 500 cc Race covered, Denly's Norton was second and Hough's AJS third but Pat Driscoll's Norton was coming up slowly and relentlessly and when Horsman failed to appear at the end of the 58th lap it was he who took the lead followed by Hough and E. W. Guyler (DOT). This was the order maintained to the finish, Pat's winning speed working out at 82.80 and Hough, who was just fifteen seconds behind him averaging 82.67 mph. Guyler was third, Grogan's Norton fourth and the only other runner was flagged off as being outside the time limit.

For some reason, Staniland stood in for Le Vack in the 1000 cc Race, riding the for-mer's Brough Superior. A really interesting development for it was almost unknown for anyone to take over one of the great master's mounts and it shows how highly Le Vack must have rated Chris. Later on, it may well have influenced J. S. Worters to include him in his team when he – Worters – retired from riding and became an even more successful tuner and manager. Even more disappointing, then, that at the end of the first lap the big machine should have been in at the pits for the first of a long series of stops to sort out a carburation trouble that, in the end, put it out of the race.

The ding-dong this time was between Wright's Zenith and Longman's Harley-Davidson and this lasted until the 46th lap, when Joe arrived at the pits, pushing the Zenith, to retire. Meanwhile, Staniland was having the ride of his life, working up to a secure third place, then, momentarily, second before retiring just before the end of the race so that, once again, it was Longman first and Wright second, the Harley averaging 69.56 mph for the race.

On to the Championship Meeting in October – and the end of the 1925 Season. The first event at this meeting was an innovation which produced a surprise. The innovation was a scratch race for 175 cc machines and the surprise was a chap called Dallison who won it on a 170 cc Elfson Norman and won it by a mile from Blackburne-engined Cottons of Worters and Johnston at 67.74 mph. This must have been a real surprise for both Woolly and Paddy, particularly as the former had only recently taken records in the class with his Cotton. Dallison duly annexed the Flying 5 Miles and 5 Kilos, together with the Standing 10 Miles and 10 Kilos – a really rousing effort acknowledged by all concerned.

The 250 cc Championship centered on Le Vack, Handley, Worters and Johnston and Bert played his usual watching and waiting game. Handley fell out when his silencing system came adrift and Bert took the lead towards the end, winning at 73.24 mph, followed home by Worters and Johnston, both Cotton mounted.

Dixon wasn't able to present Horsman with a real challenge in the 600 cc Sidecar Race, Vic winning at 80.98, Fred's Douglas coming home second with Tucker's Norton outfit third.

P.G. Dallison (170cc Elfson Norman). 175cc Championship Winner, 1925. Speed 67.74 mph.

There was a disappointment in the 350 cc scratch race for Emerson was disqualified at the start because his silencing system was held by the stewards not to conform to regulations. Once again Le Vack's Coventry Eagle won, Handley's Rex Acme was second and Lacey's Cotton third. At this point Bill was getting the Cotton going better at each appearance and must have been pleased to bring it in ahead of Worters' New Gerrard.

Records fell again in the 1000 cc Sidecar Class, Wright's Zenith taking the 5 Miles and 5 Kilos Flying Start and 10 Miles and 10 Kilos Standing at speeds between 86 and 90 mph, averaging 90.06 mph for the race and heading home Riddoch's Zenith Blackburne and Longman's Harley.

Right. **The great little man who 'tyred' them all. 'Dunlop Mac'.**

Below H.Le Vack (246cc Coventry Eagle JAP). 1925 250cc Championship winner at 73.24 mph.

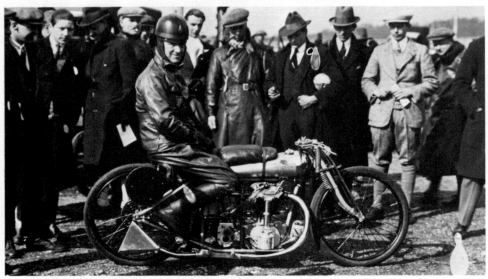

Four starters only in the 750 cc Solo Race! Among them was Dixon, who was riding his 596 cc Douglas in place of the 744 cc machine and who, even so, was pulling the wrong gear because the right engine sprocket wasn't available. So the race became a scrap between Horsman's Triumph and H. M. Walters' Zenith JAP and although Vic put in one lap at 103.11, it was the Zenith that got it, averaging 97.65 mph with Fred third.

Marchant won the 350 cc Sidecar Race at 76.73 mph from Worters and Baxter, annexing the same distance records as Wright and Dallison after Le Vack had had starting bothers, but Bert scored again in the 500 cc Solo Race, winning from Horsman and Denly at 97.08 mph and netting the World's 10 Mile Standing Start in the process.

The last race, run in failing light and slight fog, was won by Wright's 1000 cc Zenith at 102.90 mph after Le Vack and Temple non-started. It was a one-two-three for Zeniths for he headed Knight and Baldwin to victory. Only Joe, one would think, would be the man to average nearly 103 mph in conditions like these.

October 24th marked the end of the 1925 season, the meeting being made up principally, of short handicap races. Worters scored a third place in the Up to 350 cc Race and Rex Judd won the 500 cc from Longman and Wheeler at a creditable 95.59 mph.

Then in the 500 cc to 1000 cc Race came disaster, for at the start of the second lap Judd, who was in the process of passing a tightly bunched group, fouled Horsman's footrest. Both were doing over 100 mph and Judd came off, falling right in the middle of the bunch. Miraculously, he wasn't badly hurt and the ambulance was quickly on the scene. Baldwin, Knight and Staniland were the placemen, in that order, and the average for the big Zenith was 94.23 mph.

A Consolation Handicap was won by Teddy Prestwich's DOT sidecar outfit but quite why Teddy should have needed 'consolation' or ranked for it, is hard to understand. Dixon won the Passenger Handicap on his 596 cc Douglas from Riddoch and Fitzgerald at 83 mph and Cobbold brought his 493 cc Sunbeam into second place behind Webb's 1000 cc Indian and sidecar in the Private Owner's Handicap.

Horsman won the last race of the year, a scratch affair, from Dixon and H. M. Walters – 50 miles at 92.55 mph and obviously wasn't too pushed to pull off this one. The Walters brothers, H.M. and P.M., were regulars at Brooklands and both fast and consistent performers over long and short distances.

True to form, the daily papers, after hardly acknowledging the existence of Brooklands throughout the season, made headlines of the accident. Things still haven't changed a bit in this respect!

Throughout the season there had been successful record attempts galore by all the main protagonists right up to the end. Far too many to list and mainly over short distances solo and sidecar. Short distance records were still breakable at this stage and no one seemed to be faced with marathon rides, at this time, in order to procure the necessary advertising material.

A 'mixed bag' in close company. The high mounted André fork damper obscures the front number of 'big twin' rider No 2.

Chapter 3

The 1926 Season

Nineteen twenty six opened, as racing seasons have a habit, with, according to one report, 'A devastating wind which pierced one to the marrow' coupled with snow and sleet falling heavily. Nothing new about that for the diehards of Brooklands but far from ideal for the date was March 20th. Three scratch races and ten handicaps formed the programme and all were quite well supported, at least from the point of view of quality.

This meeting really marked the elevation of C.W.G. (Bill) Lacey to the 'peerage' for although Bill had made a very good start in motorcycle racing with his Cotton in 1925, he now made an entry as 'Number One' man for Grindlay Peerless. In the past there had been several whose preparation of machinery had stood out head and shoulders above the rest, notably Horsman and Worters, both of whom had obviously mastered the art of building machinery fast enough to win and strong enough to withstand the punishment of Brooklands concrete, but Bill now proceeded to do both these things and, at the same time add a third quality – showmanship. From now on, all his bikes were to appear not only fast and reliable but with the frame finished in superb nickel plating.

But it wasn't for showmanship that they appeared like this, it was pure common sense for, nickel plated, the bikes were easier to clean and it was also easier to inspect the running gear for cracks or other signs of wear. Whatever the reason, Bill's bikes added enormous interest to the Brooklands scene as from that moment. The sight of a 'Lacey' Grindlay Peerless or later, a Norton, out on the track in bright sunlight piloted by the minute, immaculately clad figure astride it, was something, literally, never to be forgotten. Even if the bikes had not been record breakers it would have been impressive. But they were record breakers and Bill's presence brought an entirely new 'dimension' to the scene as from this point.

Heaven only knows how many hours of painstaking work went into even one of Bill's track bikes. Everything was right – everything – and it was once said that if, when starting a bike, prior to warming up for a race, it coughed or spat back through the carburettor that was enough – he would put it away for the day and look at it again when the meeting was over. That was probably an exaggeration but it indicated the standard he set.

Be that as it may, he set the seal by winning the first motorcycle race at Brooklands in 1926, a Three Lap Scratch for machines to 350 cc. Winning speed 83.84 mph, Johnston's Cotton second and Tottey's New Imperial third. To some extent Bill may have been just the tiniest bit lucky with this one because Marchant was out quickly with a flat rear tyre, but it was a great start to a new era and a fine reward to what must have been a busy winter for C.W.G. Lacey and, probably, quite a big decision for the Grindlay Peerless set up.

The Three lap Scratch to 500 cc was won by Horsman at 90.22 mph, with Judd and Denly second and third, whilst Cobbold's Sunbeam won the Sealed Handicap. Wright's 976 cc Zenith won the 1000 cc from Vic's 595 cc Triumph at 98.82 mph – the only single in the race, with Patchett's big McEvoy third. McEvoy scored again in the Novice Handicap, Birkin's 350 finishing second this time, at 75.12. Strange that Birkin should rate as a novice and that there is no record of what must have been a thin line dividing 'novices' from 'private owners',

Lacey scored again in the three lapper 250cc to 350 cc, second to Colgan's Cotton and ahead of Tottey's New Imperial. He was second again in the next handicap, a Three Lap Experts to 350 cc, this time sandwiched between Greenfield's 250 Connaught and Greening's 250 Zenith. How delighted Grindlay's must have been that day. Always nice to know you've picked a winner.

The results of the Private Owner's Handicap were Gray (New Imperial), Marshall (Norton) and Knight (Zenith) at 69.08 mph and the 350 cc to 1000 cc Handicap results recorded Cobbold, Horsman and Driscoll, at the same speed.

E.W. Guyler, Brough Superior mounted this time, won the Experts 350 cc to 1000 cc at 96.62 mph, from Dixon and Horsman, and I have a sneaking feeling that this machine could have been the one that I raced at the track much later, in 1934. I never knew the full history of that bike but it had one feature that made it easy to identify and that was that the fuel tank was mounted on a flat baseplate with semi-circular metal straps running over the top of the tank to secure it.

For a long time it frightened me on every trip but, in the end, Ted Baragwanath sorted its handling problems for me and from then on it was a great ride. You had to take only one look at it to see that had been built for Brooklands at birth and was never a road bike converted for racing. I always thought of it, nostalgically, as a Le Vack legacy and still think it almost certainly was. I just wish I had it now.

The last race at this opening meeting of 1926 was a three lap passenger handicap. Chris Staniland won it, Wright was second and Milne third. Speed 77.81 mph. How happy everyone must have been to get back to the fireside that day. Even so, I bet that more than a few not only went up to the bar at the end of the day but made more than one stop at the pub on the way home. And for those unfortunates who brought their racers to Brooklands, not in vans, but on sidecar floats, the all-time low must have been roping them on at the end of the meeting with frozen fingers and in semi-darkness. Yes, it all comes back very vividly. It's great once you've made the grade a bit but hard going on the way up. But if you've won, or even been placed in a Private Owner's or a Novice handicap for the first time, nothing matters – nothing.

Weather conditions for the next meeting on April 10th had improved – in fact they were described as being 'congenial'. Another programme of Scratch and Handicap races to give everyone a chance with Handley, Johnston and Greening filling the places in the 250 cc Scratch. Handley's speed was 76.03 and next came the same sort of race for the next size up.

This time Marchant made no mistake, winning it at 89.90 mph, a long way ahead of Worters, who beat Lacey to the line by twenty yards. Bill's Grindlay was described as 'shining' and looking 'as if it would have been more in its element on a stand at the Olympia Show'. Obviously the reporters had not yet got their eye adjusted to the new look, a look that was to become more and more evident later when, in addition to Bill's bikes, Nigel Spring was to take Denly under his wing and put him astride the big AJS stable. But there was still a long wait ahead for that.

From now on Worters was contracted to one make. The Cottons, Torondas and New Gerrards had all gone and Excelsior was to be the banner for him and very well he did for Excelsior, who also did very well for Brooklands.

Horsman, P.M. Walters and Staniland were the highlights of the 500 cc Solos. Vic won at 92.57 mph and Dixon provided light relief by making pedalling motions as he passed the stands which surely proved that, even if it wasn't fast enough, the Douglas handled well – at that point anyway. I don't think, even in 1936, I would have felt it a chance worth taking on anything except a Manx Norton. For a wager, yes. But not for the amusement of spectators with nothing to come.

The 1000 cc Scratch Race was the highlight of the day, Wright winning from Patchett and Knight. But it was the speed and not the win that rang the bell – five laps at an average of 108.51 mph – the fastest race ever at Brooklands at the time. Standing Lap 95.05, second 112.42, third 113.45, fourth 112.42 and fifth 111.92 mph. Terrific! No other word for it.

A back-handed compliment for Lacey in the next one. Scratch man in the 350 cc Handicap, I think this must have been Bill's sixth meeting at Brooklands; four on the Cotton in 1924 and 1925, the opening (arctic) meeting in 1926 and now this one. I could be wrong about this but it's a point I want to check with him. Not surprisingly he didn't score this time and, since the race was for bikes up to 350 cc its second and third places were filled by 250s, Hill's Diamond and Godwin's Connaught, the winner being Packman's Cotton at 79.17 mph.

The Three Lap Handicap for the big boys was Patchett's, with the McEvoy at 102.69 mph. A.R. Quinn, Horsman's mechanic and sidecar passenger, making one of his first appearances astride one of Vic's Triumphs, was second and Gibson's Sunbeam third. But Dixon really did earn entertainment money this time for a lower link pin on his forks fractured at over a hundred and, after fighting it for nearly a quarter of a mile, Fred cast it away and was lucky to come out of it with nothing worse than cuts and bruises. Fred, the 'iron man' of all periods, didn't cut or bruise easily and, no doubt made light of the thing, but it was almost as nasty a tumble as ever happened at Brooklands so it must have made him think. Apart from reflecting about how lucky he'd been, things like this didn't happen to Fred without him getting down to root causes. Not so much was known about metal fatigue at that time but I'd wager that, within a very short time, Fred W. Dixon knew as much about the subject as most. That would be the best aspect of it and, with Fred still around, not too high a price to pay.

Baldwin must have been pleased to equal Wright's 113.45 mph in the next one but disappointed to be robbed of a win when the plot faded on the last lap, letting in Quinn who got it at 71.56 mph from a fairly generous handicap of 2 mins. 12 secs., with McEvoy on one of his own productions second and Staniland third.

Another win for Worters came in the 250 cc Handicap, at 77.81 mph and for

The ohv Douglas circa 1926. Always exciting, but performance sometimes outmatched braking.
— Even so, performance was paramount!

Marchant in the 90 Mile and Hour All Comers, his winning speed – 90.72 mph matching the title of the race. Guyler's Brough was on the scratch mark in this one and was reported as 'missing throughout the race.'

The last race, a Passenger Handicap, was won by Milne's 350 cc Rex Acme at 64.84 mph and it was noticed that Marchant's chin was bleeding again despite the fact that this time the tank top and other wounding sections of the bike were Sorbo covered. Such a shame that Dougal is not still around. I never knew him at the time he was racing but saw a lot of him later because he settled in to become a neighbour of ours at Weybridge. I used to meet him almost daily, with his shopping basket, in Weybridge High Street and he always had something amusing to say.

Few long races at Brooklands were noteworthy for their high percentage of finishers, particularly in the larger engine capacity classes, but of them all, the 200 Mile Sidecar Races held in July 1926 must surely rank lower than any. Out of seventeen starters in the 350 cc class, only five finished.

If that was bad, worse was to follow for, the 600 cc race produced one finisher and the 1000 cc class none!

Even in the 350 cc event Teddy Prestwich, the winner, was the only one to complete the course without trouble and one is left wondering what those enthusiasts who paid their hard earned money to see the races must have thought about it. Were such a situation to arise today one feels that, enthusiasts or not, a paying public would certainly feel inclined to ask for their money back but, even in the mid-twenties, mechanical reliability was hailed as something remarkable rather than being taken for granted as it has come to be now. Even so, one is left wondering whether, perhaps, debacles of this nature may have led to the smaller gates that Brooklands was to enjoy in later years.

On this occasion tyre trouble, caused by the hot weather, was partly to blame, but only partly, because throughout the day almost every other hazard imaginable, including fire, was instrumental in eliminating one machine or another. Looking back over the record of this race it is hard to pinpoint, exactly, the reasons for such a huge mortality rate.

Entrywise, long races at Brooklands tended to be under, rather than over subscribed and there is no doubt that, from time to time, entries that were well below the standard required were accepted for long races. Great enthusiasts as these chaps were, they were sometimes competing in a long distance race for the first time, with the experience of only a few short races behind them, so that they had really only a vague idea of the problems they would have to face. If their retirement came within the first twenty or thirty miles, they still hadn't learned much about long distance racing at Brooklands but, if it came within thirty miles of the end, they'd learned a lot – and had done very well to get that far regardless of their position in the race itself.

A hundred mile race on the Outer Circuit at Brooklands was a very long way in 1926. In terms of things that were likely to break, fall off, or otherwise go wrong, two hundred miles was more than twice as long and this can be seen time and time again if you study the comparatively high percentage of finishers in the Hutchinson 100 as compared with the percentage in races of two hundred mile distance.

Even so, the programme for the 350 cc 200 Mile Sidecar Race in 1926 included names like Worters, Handley, Marchant, Hopkins and Johnston, all of whom were names with which to conjure. Yet only two of them – Worters and Johnston – were to figure in the results, and neither as outright winners.

Prior to the race, it would probably have been true to say that, good as he was, among such a list of names, Prestwich would have been rated as a likely placeman but hardly as a winner of the race by a margin of well over twelve minutes. So the moral there was that it was speed plus reliability rather than speed alone that counted. The determining of this combination was probably the key to outright success – in every class.

Seventeen 350 cc outfits came to the start line at one o'clock and a gay bunch they looked for, in each class, the riders were identified by different coloured jerseys, the colour chosen for the Class 'B' boys being blue. There was some technical interest in the machinery for, while Prestwich's JAP engine had a 'seven spring' arrangement for closing its valves, Gordon Cobbold's Sunbeam had those of the hairpin type. The latter is certainly interesting because, in the first place, Cobbold usually competed as a private owner – not as a works rider – and secondly because one would think that this could well have been the first time that a Sunbeam used 'hairpin' type springs in a long race at Brooklands.

One would expect Teddy Prestwich to have had all the latest 'mods' fitted to an engine carrying his own name but, with the Isle of Man TT having been run off only a month previously, one is led to think that, for all his 'private' status, Gordon probably did have quite a close link with Wolverhampton and John Marston.

Unfortunately, when writing this part of the story, it was sometimes necessary for me to talk to participants before setting out the chronicle of their activities and, to some extent one was 'flying blind' except for the very high highlights. The big names of the nineteen twenties were perfectionists in the truest sense and the evening of life hasn't changed them. One preferred not to be interviewed 'on tape' but generously offered to tell the story in his own time, in his own way and using his own tape recorder. Another did a 'stint' on tape with me, listened to it and then preferred to do likewise.

But, in the case of G.C. Cobbold (Sunbeam) I am writing the story before I had talked to him, although I had enjoyed one very pleasant lunch with him where no 'work' ensued. So, when the time comes for me to talk to him again, I shall switch on my tape recorder and ask awkward questions without prior notice.

There was some 'personality' interest on the line at the start of this race for two of the sidecar passengers were very small boys, both of whom were recorded as experiencing 'a goodly share of pushing when trouble befell their drivers'.

Lucky chaps. Their light weight would certainly have helped the hard working 350 cc motors but, while wondering whether they had had previous experience of sidecar passengering at Brooklands, one hopes that this particular 'ride' didn't swing them away from motorcycle racing for ever. One wonders, too, how small they were vis-a-vis the minimum weight limit called for regarding sidecar passengers – or ballast – at the time.

Rather strangely, bearing in mind the disasterous nature of the race – not one outfit failed to get off the line cleanly and, at the end of lap one A.P. Hamilton (Velocette) led the first 'wave', consisting of W.L. Handley (Rex Acme), J.S. Worters (Excelsior) C.W. (Paddy) Johnston (Zenith) H. Glover (Douglas) and E.S. Prestwich (Coventry Eagle). Cobbold's Sunbeam lay tenth ahead, surprisingly, of Dougal Marchant's and Ron Hopkin's Chater Leas. The race must have been a disappointment for Dougal for, after running up fairly quickly through the field, he faded from the picture while lying fifth and within yards of the tightly bunched leading group. Cobbold was also in at the pits at this stage and Glover's Douglas was out of the hunt after eight laps, with a sheared magneto armature.

Meanwhile, both Worters and Johnson had overtaken Hamilton. All three had been riding, as it were, on a pocket handkerchief and both 'Woolly' and 'Paddy' may well have been happy to let someone else set the pace in the early stages.

At 20 laps Johnston came in to replace a rear tyre, which was treadless. This is quite interesting because, here again, one comes up against the compromise as one did in the 'speed vis-a-vis reliability' arguement. But here it becomes 'to use the banking, save the rear tyre and take a longer way round' or 'grass cut' all the way round the Byfleet, saving distance at its expense. Even in 1926, twenty laps was a very short life for the rear tyre on a 350 cc 'chair' outfit and one can't help feeling that Paddy may have been taking a calculated risk which, in the event, didn't pay off. It is certainly doubtful whether, in only twenty laps, he could have gained in distance more than he lost in time in having to stop for a tyre change.

Handley now moved into third place behind Worters and Hamilton, displacing them both at the twenty five lap mark – a third of the race distance covered. At this point Prestwich, the ultimate winner, lay fourth. Handley was lapping around the seventy-four mile an hour mark at this stage, thirty seconds ahead of Worters who, in turn, led Hamilton's Velocette outfit by thirty-five seconds.

Retirements now included Marchant, Glover, Hopkins (magneto trouble), Hutchings (McEvoy) with piston trouble and Greenaway whose Matchless had been suffering from clutch slip. To make things more exciting, the red jerseyed runners – the 600 cc Class – had now joined the fray and had, themselves, completed ten laps.

But in the 350 cc class the order now remained unchanged from laps 25 to 33 when the whole race pattern underwent a dramatic change, Handley's Rex Acme coasting into the pits with a broken rocker.

At half distance – 36 laps – the order was Worters, Hamilton, Milne (Rex Acme) and Prestwich but a lap later, Hamilton's Velocette was out with a broken primary chain, just at the moment when the three leading outfits, Excelsior, Rex Acme and Coventry Eagle were all in at the pits simultaneously for refuelling.

They did not leave in the same order, Worters being delayed at his pit for tappet adjustment. Handley, meanwhile, was back in the race having replaced his broken rocker. Young's OK Supreme came in with a flat tyre and Harrington, whose Zenith outfit had been lying fifth, was out with fifty laps covered. With fifteen to go for the leaders, there were now only eight runners, the order being Milne, Prestwich, Handley and Johnston. But, ten laps later, both Milne and Handley were in trouble with tyres. Prestwich now led for the first time, with Johnston second and Worters fourth after a long pit stop.

Harman, whose OK Supreme occupied third spot at this stage, now dropped out, Worters passed Johnston and, in the end, Prestwich crossed the line a comfortable winner followed by Worters, Johnston, Milne and Young, the machine order being Coventry Eagle, Excelsior, Zenith, Rex Acme and OK Supreme. Winner's speed 63.52 mph and time 3 hours, 10 minutes and 51 seconds.

No less promising a field lined up for the 600 cc Race, among them being Horsman (Triumph), Anstice and Dixon (Douglases), Emerson (HRD), Denly, Staniland, Spring, Driscoll and Tucker (Nortons) and Kaye Don, D.E. Calder and P. Brewster (Zeniths).

E.S. (Teddy) Prestwich (344cc Coventry Eagle JAP). Winner of the 200 Mile Sidecar Race 1926. Speed 63.52 mph.

One man among them stood out right from the start and it was V.E. Horsman once again. Lapping consistently as fast as he needed but not one fraction of a mile an hour faster, Vic underlined every racing maxim and came out on top.

The sad tale of mechanical failure repeated itself again. Emerson's big HRD outfit led off the line but Dixon's Douglas was leading the field at the end of lap one, followed by Horsman, with Spring's Norton in third place and Emerson fourth. And at the end of lap two, the four had already begun to draw away from the rest of the field, with Spring now ahead of Horsman. But on lap four, Dixon's engine locked up so solidly and with such suddenness that the rear tyre was torn from its rim – and that was the end of Fred.

Almost at the same moment, the Nortons of Spring and Staniland went out with a missing sump drain plug and a broken rocker standard respectively and Emerson now came up to take over the lead from Vic and his Triumph, followed by Denly on O'Donovan's Norton.

The suspension of Driscoll's outfit appeared to be collapsing slowly and, on lap nine, the Triumph led for three laps, only to be passed by the HRD on lap twelve, the stragglers already having been lapped twice. Anstice and Tucker were enjoying a 'no holds barred' scrap and, by now, Parker (Douglas) was in at the pits with a burst rear tyre. At eighteen laps Emerson still led, followed relentlessly by Horsman, twenty yards astern. At this point only Anstice's Douglas and Brewster's Zenith outfits were unlapped by the leaders, despite the relatively low lap speeds of the first two placemen, so low in fact, that for a time Handley's 350 cc **Rex Acme** was holding Emerson.

At 24 laps the order was Horsman, Tucker, Emerson and Anstice, with Brewster now a lap astern. The Zeniths of Kaye Don and Calder had completed 21 laps and Braidwood's AJS and Cowley's Norton 18, Parker's Douglas having retired a lap earlier while Denly's Norton had faded after 14 laps.

Half distance saw the race order as —

1	Horsman	(Triumph)	36 laps
2	Emerson	(HRD)	35 "
3	Anstice	(Douglas)	34 "
4	Tucker	(Norton)	34 "
5	Brewster	(Zenith)	34 "
6	Driscoll	(Norton)	33 "
7	Don	(Zenith)	29 "
8	Bagshawe	(Norton)	27 "
9	Cowley	(Norton)	25 "
10	Matthews	(Norton)	23 "

The field was now made up of six 600 cc outfits, those of Anstice, Don, Bagshawe and Cowley having 500 cc engines, the moral of this seeming to add up the fact that reliability and good preparation were probably of greater importance than sheer engine capacity.

Emerson's fine run ended at exactly half distance, with a broken fork spring. This, in itself, seems a strange end to an outfit so obviously well prepared and ridden for, at that time, a fork spring must have been an obvious thing to have at the pit and among the easiest and quickest of components to replace.

So the sad story drew to its close, one competitor after another dropping by the wayside till it was Vic Horsman and the big Triumph alone crossing the line, the sole finisher within the time limit although Bagshawe was still running just one lap astern and 'Pa' Cowley was circulating with 67 laps to his credit.

In retrospect, it almost seems as though Vic had planned the run in advance as a long distance record attempt for not only did he go through the three hour run non stop without even taking on fuel but he also broke the 600 cc Sidecar Class records for 100 Miles, 200 Miles, 2 Hours and 3 Hours at speeds between 77 and 73 mph; the fact that it was concurrent with a 200 Mile Race win seeming almost co-incidental.

What were the Golden Rules needed to notch up such a victory? They added up to impeccable preparation, knowledge of the outfit and the problems to be faced, foresight, restraint in both the early and late stages of the race, a good information service on the developing race pattern, and ability to be influenced in only what concerned the rider and stamina. It should be remembered that in Vic Horsman's case he was no longer in the first flush of youth and had, by now, been competing at Brooklands prior to World War One. Even today, 200 miles is no mean run on an independently sprung machine. Picture then, the problem of fighting a rigid 600 cc outfit for nearly two and three-quarter hours on bumpy old Brooklands.

How then, were all these qualities amounting, really, to years of experience, deployed by Vic? Preparation, knowledge of the outfit and its problems spoke for themselves – nothing broke, nothing fell off and nothing went wrong.

Foresight? He seemed almost to have had access to a crystal ball in his pre-judgement of the race pattern. Restraint? It must have been tempting to push the trusty Triumph too hard in the close fought early stages of the race and even towards the end when comfortably in the lead. Yet when almost coasting to victory he was content to be passed by the still scrapping leaders of the 350 cc class. But his superb information service decided he was not to be influenced by events that didn't concern him and he exercised the necessary restraint and continued to cruise steadily on to win.

If the 350 cc Race was poor and the 600 cc Race dull – barring Horsman's wonderful run – the 1000 cc event – one can hardly call it a race – was deplorable. So bad in fact that it is better to pass by it quickly to happier and more thrilling races later in the reason.

But it must be chronicled, however briefly, and the sad fact is that, out of ten entries, only nine came to the line, G.L. Parkes' big twin Zenith being the absentee.

The only interest, at this stage consisted in the weird and wonderful arrangements that some entrants had made to offset the fuel thirsts of their big twins, the most comic of all being B.S. Allen's Brough Superior which had a huge cylindrical auxiliary fuel tank strapped – literally – on top of the sidecar nose. Nearly all the eight others had vast and, in some cases, hideously ugly main tanks, but for all the good it did their unfortunate pilots, they might almost as well have allowed ingenuity to go to less length.

At first, it was Wright's big Zenith that led the dismal procession, the Zenith carrying no less than ten and a half gallons of fuel and two and a half gallons of oil in three vast tanks mounted, one in the normal position, one on the saddle tube and one in the sidecar. Temple on the big OEC was almost immediately in trouble and Humphries Brough Superior arrived at the pits minus its sidecar tyre. By lap three, Wright had stopped and Ashby's Zenith led so that, with 18 laps covered, the order was –

1	C. T. Ashby	(980 Zenith)
2	C. F. Temple	(996 OEC Temple)
3	H. J. Knight	(980 Zenith)
4	B. S. Allen	(980 Brough Superior)
5	E. C. E. Baragwanath	(980 Brough Superior)
6	R. E. Humphries	(980 Brough Superior)
7	F. A. Longman	(989 Harley-Davidson)
8	M. A. McEvoy	(980 McEvoy)

Allen's Brough Superior broke a petrol pipe and Baragwanath's oil tank split, emptying its contents over the exterior of the engine instead of the interior and, at 25 laps, Ashby stopped for fuel putting Temple in the lead on a machine that was running on one cylinder only. Longman retired, McEvoy was suffering from steering troubles and Allen seemed to be having bothers in getting the fuel from his various tanks to the carburettor which needed it.

At half distance, Ashby still led from Knight, Temple, Allen and Humphries and, by now, had more than a lap's lead over the others. But another pit stop revealed that there was a split in his silencer and, until a repair could be effected, he was pit-bound.

Temple came in to change a rear tyre and, he too, was held for the same reason. Humphries ran out of oil and pushed in with a rear tyre down to the canvas and so it went on, silencers being repaired and falling apart again until, in the end, everyone in the class who had survived found himself running outside the time limit. As nobody got back within it, the race ended with only Temple, Knight and McEvoy still running so that, as one reporter put it 'The flagman walked out and the tale of the ten little nigger boys ended abruptly'.

It's hard to say quite what moral can be drawn from all this but the picture does seem to indicate that the higher the engine capacity class, the lower the general efficiency and the reliability factor, too. Obviously, the main problems were, firstly, the problem of keeping two cylinders firing as opposed to one and, secondly the life of the rear tyre vis-a-vis the fuel load carried. The greater the fuel load, the lesser the number of fuel stops needed but, on the other hand, the greater the fuel load, the faster the wear on the tyre. No-one seemed to have been able to strike the happy medium.

But, if the 200 Mile Sidecar Races had proved to be rather a debacle, July wasn't a completely barren month for the Cup Day Meeting also fell within it and this was a lot better.

The 350 cc Solo Scratch Race was the first event of the day and proved to a really well contested race so that throughout the whole five laps no-one really knew who the winner would be until right at the end. Worters proved to be the man, coming home with an average of 91.89 mph, his best lap being 94.50 mph. At the time, this was the fastest average ever for a 350 cc race at Brooklands and Woolly deservedly won the Sealed Handicap as well.

The Sealed Handicap was really a ruse to encourage slower riders to enter for scratch races in which they knew they had no chance so that scratch races became, as it were, a race within a race. No-one knew what his handicap was until the announcement after the race had been run.

Handley on his Rex Acme-Blackburne was a close second and Bill Lacey, his Grindlay Peerless 'literally steeped in nickel plate' as one report said, was third, followed by Gordon Cobbold's Sunbeam.

A Three Lap Scratch Race for private owners followed and was won by R. V. Packman's Cotton Blackburne, with Jeffrey's OK Blackburne second – both three fifties, while J. A. Welch's 250 cc Excelsior Blackburne was third and was winner of the Sealed Handicap.

Joe Wright was the hero of the next race, the 1000 cc Five Lap Scratch, winning it with his big Zenith from O. M. Baldwin's sister machine, his average for the race working out at 107.34 mph. But this was by no means all the story for Joe was having handling problems of the nastiest kind. The report in *the Motor Cycle* of this race said 'Each time he approached the Lap Scoring Box from the Byfleet Banking he took off at the same bump in the track and was in the air for a few sickening thousandth's of a second. Then he thudded back and the tussle began. The whole machine appeared to the spectators at the Fork to bend in the middle and, at 115 mph was snaking for twenty yards before the rider had control again. The worst wobble occurred during the second lap and Wright seemed to be almost done as he thundered past the scoring box shaking his head as if to convey to anxious Freddy Barnes that many more struggles like that would drain the very dregs of his strength.

That could well have been true because, more than all others, a big twin did require strength as well as judgement at Brooklands and this one was really fast for its day, Joe's laps working out at 102.27 mph (Standing) and 112.68 for his best 'Flying' (lap two). Once established in the lead, he was able to ease to 111, 109 and finally 101 mph. Deservedly, he, too, was winner of the Sealed Handicap and the ride also netted him records for the Standing Start 10 Kilos and 10 Miles. Baldwin also averaged over 100 mph for the race, Walter's 750 cc Zenith was third and Horsman fourth on a 607 cc Triumph. Vic's Triumph must have had the edge of Joe's big Zenith for steering since, according to the record, his steering damper consisted of a narrow strip of rubber cut from an inner tube and twined round the 'T' piece at the fork crown and the front down tube. The machine had obviously done stints with a sidecar for the forks were laterally braced.

As a race, the 500 cc 10 Lap Solo Scratch was unexciting. But the entry was interesting for it included Le Vack who was turning out for the first time under the New Hudson banner and who, according to rumour, had lapped in practice at over a hundred. And while Handley had the first of the vee twin Rex Acmes, Dixon's Douglas had a long stroke engine that had been prepared for the Belgian Grand Prix. But, after leading at the end of lap three, Le Vack retired, followed by Handley, who had lost a push rod, and it was Chris Staniland's Norton that emerged as winner at 93mph, followed by Dixon. Here again, it was the outright winner who netted the Sealed Handicap award also.

A 350 cc Three Lap Handicap followed. It proved to be another dull race, with 31 entries and nine non-starters, and was won by Greenfield's 250 cc Connaught Blackburne at 73.24 mph.

Fourteen starters came to the line for the 351 cc to 1000 cc Handicap, including Staniland, Dixon and Cobbold. Clearly, this was one of Chris's many good days for he won it, averaging 94.50 mph with a best lap of 99 mph, which must have been a slight disappointment for, at the time, he still hadn't notched up a Gold Star lap. Walters' and Cobbold's Sunbeams were second and third respectively.

Even way back in 1926, the Wakefield Cup Races attracted strong entries, for the trophies outshone most of the others and there was prestige value as well. This time the entry was so big that, as in later years, the race was run in two heats and since an almost equal number of solos and sidecars had entered, there was a heat for each.

The solo heat produced the rather sad sight of the hares being unable to catch a tortoise and was won by W. A. Jacobs' 250 cc Rex Acme from the 3 mins 30 secs mark, with Walters' 500 cc Sunbeam second (5 secs) and R. V. Packman's 350 cc Cotton from the 1 min 30 secs mark, third. Winner's speed 67.85 mph.

The sidecar heat included Wright, Baragwanath, Marchant, Riddoch, Horsman, Spring, Worters and McEvoy and was won by the first – still in trouble with steering – at 85.13 mph, with Spring second and Marchant third. Horsman and Worters were fifth and sixth respectively. It was a handicap race, of course. The final was run in the rain and the results were –

1	W. D. Marchant	348 cc	Chater Lea sidecar	2 mins 10 secs
2	W. A. Jacobs	249 cc	Rex Acme-Blackburne	3 mins 30 secs
3	V. Horsman	599 cc	Triumph sidecar	1 min 30 secs

Dixon's Douglas refused to leave the line but started first push afterwards when back in the Paddock, McEvoy's throttle wire pulled out and Walters hurriedly wheeled his Sunbeam off the line finding a crack in the forks.

Worters notched up his second win of the day in the 5 Lap 250 cc Scratch Race, followed by Paddy Johnston's Cotton Blackburne and Goodwin's Connaught and the programme was brought to a close with a win by A. G. Walker's Chater Lea Blackburne in the Three Lap Private Owner's Handicap.

Later in that week both Worters and Wright turned out to make successful attempts on World's records, both riding solo, in the 250 cc and 1000 cc classes respectively. For them, at least, July must have been a busy month, because, within a week from then, the 200 Mile Solo races were due to be held.

In contrast to the sidecar races, the 200 Mile Solo races were full of interest and contained quite a high percentage of excitement, perhaps the most noteworthy thing being that all four classes were won by machines powered by JAP engines. Again, there was a high rate of retirement, bringing forth the remark from one disappointed competitor that 'all machines are bad but some are less bad than others'!

Among the 'less bad' must certainly have ranked Worters' Excelsiors because, not content with winning the 250 cc Race outright, Woolly then went on to notch up second place in the 500 cc event riding, if you please, a 350 cc Excelsior at a finishing speed that would have earned him third place among the 'thousands'.

Brooklands had a habit of producing its own particular problems and the one it trotted out this time was a shortage of PMS 2 racing fuel. PMS 2 and RD 1 were the principal alcohol fuels fashionable at the track for as far back as I can remember, the latter for extremely high compression ratio engines and the former for ratios used for longer races. A third variant – RD 2 – appears to have been trotted out for this meeting and it was presumably octane rated somewhere between the two. RD in this context refers to 'Racing Discol' for it was Discol who produced it and I think PMS stood for Pratts Motor Spirit although I certainly was supplied with both via 'Jazz' of the Discol company who manned their store at Brooklands in the 1930's.

Whatever the facts, shortage of the required fuel was blamed for the high retirement rate this time and there must have been something in it because Handley withdrew the Rex Acme twin on finding that the fuel he wanted wasn't available.

Content to let others make the running, Woolly sensibly sat back and watched the race pattern emerge, coming through slowly and taking the lead from Johnston's Cotton and Greening's Zenith around the ten lap mark. For a time he allowed Millar's Zenith to go into the lead, staying himself in company with Greening and Prestwich (Coventry Eagle) and this was still the race order at 18 laps. Millar continued to lead until lap 25 when he called to refuel and it was at this point that Greening and Prestwich must have slowed at the same time as Woolly speeded up. By now, there were nearly two laps separating them so that, when he stopped for fuel at half distance, he was able to change a plug without losing his lead.

But the plug change didn't cure the slight misfire that was bothering him and another pit stop for the same reason now put Millar back into the lead. By now he was having to press on to maintain his position but on lap 49 Millar went out with a bent exhaust valve so that this brought Johnston up into third place, behind Prestwich. In his turn, Prestwich went out on lap 53 with a broken exhaust valve spring, Johnston disappearing shortly afterwards so the Hungarian rider Balazs now became second man on another 250 cc Zenith – on his first visit to Brooklands! And it stayed that way to the finish, Woolly and his faithful little Excelsior winning at 69.56 mph. Seventeen minutes behind him came Balazs and seven minutes further back still came W. M. (Mike) Couper, later to become famous as a driver of ultra-fast Talbot cars at the track.

The results were :-

			hrs	mins	secs	mph
1	J. S. Worters	246 cc Excelsior	2	54	34	69.56
2	L. Balazs	246 cc Zenith	3	11	21	63.22
3	W. M. Couper	246 cc P & P	3	19	25.5	60.76
4	C. S. Barrow	246 cc Royal Enfield	3	23	35.5	59.53

Dixon, Judd and, nearly, Handley were among the non-starters in the 350 cc class of the 1926 200 Mile Solo Race. Handley, in fact, wheeled his Rex Acme off the line on discovering that it had a bad gash in the wall of the front tyre. But, effecting a quick repair, Walter was still able to rank among the starters although entering the contest when the leaders had already covered no less than seven laps. Lacey's Grindlay Peerless led at the end of the first lap, Marchant's Chater Lea at the end of the second pulling out quite a long lead from the immaculate Grindlay by the time Handley was leaving the start line, and at the 18 lap mark the order was Longman (AJS), Hicks (Velocette) and Marchant, whose clutch had decided that it didn't like the treatment.

This was the cause of Dougal's retirement and, shortly afterwards, Hicks came too quickly into the pits in order to change a plug, crashed in the process and lost time straightening things that had been bent. Pit stops at Brooklands were always rather difficult in long Outer Circuit races, for sustained high speed makes very low speeds hard to judge at any time and the problem in these races was always made worse by the fact that Outer Circuit front wheels had no brakes. Coupled with this, one sometimes found, at the very last moment, that oil which had made its way on to the rear tyre, or even on to the brake itself, had rendered one virtually brakeless so that, intending to be down to thirty or forty miles an hour by the time one reached the pit area, one was sometimes still in the seventy to eighty mile an hour bracket.

At half distance – 36 laps – the order was –

1   Lacey, (Grindlay Peerless)
2   A. P. Hamilton (Velocette)
3   H. M. Walters (Zenith)

Interest now began to be centred on Handley, who was burning up the track as only he could when the situation demanded it for, at the forty lap mark, it suddenly began to dawn on all concerned that Handley was only three laps behind Bill's Grindlay Peerless, which was in the lead.

Hamilton still lay second but he had suffered a not uncommon but very unpleasant Brooklands experience in hitting two Brooklands bumps in quick succession, the second one throwing him face forward onto the steering damper which cut his mouth badly and removed a tooth. This was a nasty experience which could sometimes happen and it might surprise people to know how many quite youthful Brooklands riders were around at one time sporting one or more false front teeth.

The only big change at the three quarter distance mark was that, amazingly, Handley was now in second place behind Lacey, with Walters and Hamilton third and fourth respectively.

With 62 laps covered, Walter was three minutes behind Bill and two laps later the gap was down to 2 minutes 38 seconds but Bill, of course, was well aware of the situation and would have been watching it develop lap by lap so that he could take things as fast as he had to and no faster than that. He finished more than a lap ahead of Walter whose ride, nevertheless, must rank as one of the greatest ever in a long distance Brooklands race.

The results were :-

			hrs	mins	secs	mph
1	C.W.G. Lacey	344 cc Grindlay Peerless	2	29	14	81.20
2	W.L. Handley	348 cc Rex Acme	2	31	16	80.26
3	A.P. Hamilton	348 cc Velocette	2	37	48	76.79
4	H.M. Walters	344 cc Zenith	2	38	34	76.42
5	L.P. Driscoll	348 cc Zenith Chater Lea	2	39	44	75.86
6	J.A. Porter	348 cc New Gerrard	2	45	52	73.07
7	F.G. Hicks	348 cc Velocette	2	49	20	71.59
8	R.V. Crawford	348 cc OK Bradshaw	2	56	31	68.64
9	G.L. Wallis	344 cc Wallis	2	59	29	67.51
10	H. Glover	348 cc Douglas	2	24	51	59.16

Not a bad race at all, despite the fact that the winner was, perhaps, clearly the winner fairly early on. Handley's ride was absolutely outstanding – such a pity that it had to be done with so great a handicap and amazing that the engine stood up to such punishment for over two and half hours. It is interesting to speculate what might have happened had he and Bill started on level terms, lapwise. And, bearing in mind that his overall time counts from the drop of the flag, it is interesting to guess at his actual average speed from the time he left the start line until he finished. As usual, Bill's superb preparation paid dividends – one report said 'at the end of the race there was hardly a spot of oil anywhere on the machine, and the plated exhaust pipes were not even blued'. Bill could never accept that oil should come from an engine anywhere other than where there was a hole, that is to say from the exhaust or, possibly, a crankcase breather. Every joint in that engine must have had hours spent on it. In my own day, ten years later, many machines, including some of my own, used to finish even the Hutchinson 100 oil filmed and sometimes to the next stage – oil bathed.

Hamilton must have felt that a lost front tooth was well worth losing for a third place as a private owner in a Brooklands 200 Mile Race and Wallis must have been pleased to get his strange looking, centre steered brainchild to the finish at an acceptable, if not world shattering speed.

On, then, to the 500 cc Race. The bright lights of this were Emerson, whose HRD won after leading all the way, and Worters who brought a 350 cc Excelsior into second place. Emerson's tactics were to pull out a big initial lead straight away, and in this case it worked. This was always quite a difficult decision for a race favourite to make because you could work it out two ways. You could go for a big lead straight away, pushing the machine fairly hard and chancing a greater risk of engine failure. Or you could sit behind the next fastest man, secure in the knowledge that you could pass him at any time. But doing it that way did involve the possibility that some cycle part might fracture so that, having got to the pit and repaired it, one was then faced with a hard, engine punishing stage of the race later on, at a point when the engine would probably be a bit on the tired side anyway.

This time both Dixon and Rex Judd brought their Douglases in to the pits for plug changes at the end of the first lap and, for a time, Horsman and Denly lay second, both of them well astern. But Horsman was dropping back and, at ten laps, Emerson had a full lap's lead from Denly (Norton), Calder (Zenith), Worters (Excelsior), Walters (Sunbeam JAP) Staniland (Norton) Horsman (Triumph) and Anstice (Douglas), Le Vack's New Hudson having faded from the picture after only four laps.

The position had changed quite a lot at the 20 lap stage for Emerson now held a lap's lead from Horsman and Anstice. There were some who felt that Vic had felt happy to sit back, banking on the likelihood of Emerson falling out, but they were wrong. At this stage he pulled out, returning via the Finishing Straight to the Paddock, the machine having showed symptoms of partial seizure during the later stages of its run.

Very unusual for him, and his departure must have been a great relief for the leader, whose progress continued unchecked. Judd had a very bad moment opposite the pits when the rear tyre of his Douglas burst, Staniland melted a piston and Denly was involved in exploring the innards of his magneto. Calder retired with a broken magneto chain.

Chains of all sorts were Achilles heels in the 1920's and this can be seen in so many photographs of machines of winners in long races. Often the primary chain can be seen hanging in a loop so big that one would think it must have stretched almost to the stage of starting to jump the engine sprocket.

At half distance, the order was Emerson, Dixon, Worters and Walters but, at this point Emerson had a bad wobble opposite the pits and came in to make adjustments. Driscoll, whose magneto hadn't been tightened to its platform, retired when it fell off and, when Worters came in he adjusted the engine shaft shock absorber so that at three quarter distance the order was still the same. Emerson was now lapping around 87 mph to Worters' 83 mph and with 60 of the 73 laps completed Dixon was towed in by the travelling marshal, still in a hurry since he announced that he wanted to catch the 5.15 pm train back to Middlesborough. So it ended, resulting in —

			hrs	mins	secs	mph
1	Emerson	490 cc HRD – JAP	2	23	54	84.22
2	Worters	344 cc Excelsior JAP	2	32	48	78.66
3	Walters	490 cc Sunbeam JAP	2	37	30	76.94
4	Braidwood	498 cc AJS	2	41	40	74.97

For once, the 1000s fared better. There were twelve entries, mainly big twins, and twelve starters was a more than a usually good beginning. And thirty-three per cent of the entry finished, which was even better. Wright, still harbouring the memories of his last, terrifying ride, had fitted leaf spring trailing link forks to his Zenith, Longman had foregone a gearbox in favour of just a clutch and a countershaft and Baldwin's Zenith, by way of innovation, carried its oil tank on the front down tube, ahead of the engine.

Patchett (980 McEvoy) pulled out a huge lead from Humphries' Brough Superior, followed by Wright (Zenith), Parkes (Brough Superior) and Ashby (Zenith), all of whom were in close company. Humphries was the first to call in – to remove oil from his goggles, which seems strange since the oil couldn't possibly have come from another machine and could only have been thrown around by his own engine which, even by 1926 standards, must have been leaky to achieve this. Wright was still unhappy with handling problems but since Patchett had stopped with fuel feed problems, he now lay second to Baldwin, who was having a trouble free run with 18 laps covered. Ashby, Longman and Humphries followed, with the rest further behind.

Baldwin broke a rear chain but a quick stop kept him in the hunt so that, at half distance – 36 laps – he now lay second to Longman, with Wright third. Patchett was now out for good with a broken front down tube, Humphries suffered a flat rear tyre and at 54 laps – three quarter distance – it was Baldwin, Ashby, Longman, Wright and Knight who were there in that order, all Zeniths except for Longman's lone Harley.

Just before the end, Baldwin's fine run finished spectacularly with a burst rear tyre and poor Joe Wright went out with only one lap to go.

So the final results were –

			hrs	mins	secs	mph
1	C. T. Ashby	980 cc Zenith	2	22	28	85.06
2	F. A. Longman	989 cc Harley-Davidson	2	24	38	83.17
3	R. E. Humphries	980 cc Brough Superior	2	41	28	75.06
4	R. Charman	980 cc Zenith	2	41	53	74.85

Great as the big twins were to see and to hear in action, their performance figures were pretty lamentable in long races. Judging by his scintillating performances in short races, one would have had the feeling that, had Wright not been a starter in these long distance marathons, he would have shown them all the way home. But he was there and he didn't show them the way home so, hard as their problems are to define, they must have been real problems.

At first, as one looks back at some of these really very poor long distance events, one cannot help feeling that, with a few notable exceptions, the standard of machine preparation was, in many cases, poor and, in some cases appallingly bad, particularly among the 'also rans'. This stands out a mile when one looks at the comparatively trouble free long distance race runs and record runs put up by the top professionals, particularly Horsman and Worters for, to them, even a three hour run was not all that long when looked at in the light of some of their much longer and just as successful record runs.

But there is no doubt that very long sustained high speed runs on fairly short banked tracks do produce problems not encountered in ordinary road or circuit racing.

In 1963 I took to Montlhéry a current and very successful 250 cc two stroke production racer to explore the possibility of making a World Record attempt in that class on records between 500 Kilometres and 12 Hours which, at that time, stood at speeds only slightly higher than they did in 1935 when I broke them, partnering Eric Fernihough on a Cotton. The 1963 machine was ridden by the then works number one rider, had been prepared by the works and had works engineers looking after it. Literally numerous bothers arose, none of which had shown up in road races and the longest trouble-free run we had in nearly three days of testing was just under two hours. Not only that, but the highest recorded lap speed, after many changes of set up and gear ratio, was more than ten miles an hour slower than the maximum believed speed of the machine.

So, from this experience alone, one is led to believe that long, sustained high speed runs do tend to produce their own special species of headache and that there may be some excuse for the less successful long distance runners of the mid-nineteen twenties. The bumpiness of Brooklands and the rigid frames of 1926 certainly didn't help and, even with the sprung frames of 1963, Montlhéry had some bumps which produced similar problems thirty six years later.

So perhaps it isn't altogether surprising that, nearly thirty years earlier, the retirement rates were as high as they were. In 1935, I watched, day by day, Eric Fernihough's preparation of the 250 cc Cotton which we were going to share for the twelve hour record attempt. Some of his preparation I thought way out and even ridiculous but when the day came we were glad of it after six hours, needed it after nine and couldn't possibly have done without it for the last two hours of the run. Even today, I think, not many people have had a go at a twelve hour record run. Looking back on ours, I feel that there were really no problems in the first three hours but quite a few between three and six hours. There were a great many in the period from six to nine hours and I really think that in the last three hours of that run only Eric or 'Woolly' Worters could

A Brooklands Outer Circuit Handicap 'Line up', 1926.

have foreseen what would be required.

So perhaps it isn't surprising that way back in the mid-twenties the retirement rates were as high as they were. I must confess, though, that as a dedicated and dyed-in-the-wool devotee of Brooklands, I have been rather staggered by some of the dull race patterns of the mid-twenties when one now looks back on them – and surprised that what is now revealed as rather poor and, in some cases, amateurish motor cycle racing can, at the time, had seemed so thrilling and exciting.

Beauty, I feel, really is in the eye of the beholder and, to some extent, the beholder sees what he wants to see. My own recollections of motorcycle racing at Brooklands in the mid and late 1920's have always been that it was glamorous, exciting and closely fought stuff. Reading back now, through cold reporting at the time, reveals it to be anything but glamorous, completely unexciting and anything but closely fought, over long distances at least. But, as in my own time, there in the 1930's, the good chaps really were good. They stood out as the real professionals they were but, at the time, I suppose, a young and over enthusiastic spectator just didn't bother to analyse the thing and was content to let the others bask in the glory of the few. However it was, the memory of the place and the people remains and I don't like the idea of it changing just because stark print denies that it ever was as I saw it.

Certainly, at that time, tastes were far simpler and less sophisticated and since it was an era of great progress and experiment a fairly high percentage of mechanical failures were easily accepted or even expected. For all that, it was a great era if only because of the camaraderie between riders and the wonderful lack of officialdom.

In 1926, July was certainly the busiest month at Brooklands for the motorcycle people and, from then on, things slowed down quite a bit until October and November, when there were the usual spate of record attempts concurrent with the Motor Cycle Show.

The next motorcycle event after the 200 Mile Solo Race Meeting amounted, literally, from the sublime to the ridiculous, for this was the beginning of the era of mixed meetings.

At that time, probably more than any other, there was a closer mutual interest in each others affairs between car and motorcycle people, and particularly light car owners. At motorcycle meetings the car parks would be full of cars of all sorts and it was probably this fact that decided the Brooklands authorities to include some motorcycle races at some of the smaller car meetings.

So, in August, the Essex Motor Club included at their Brooklands Meeting a 25 mile Handicap for bikes and also a Match Race between two cars and two bikes. The results for the former were –

1	W. A. Jacobs	249 cc Rex Acme	7	mins.	30	secs.	start
2	F. G. Hicks	349 cc Velocette	3	"	45	"	"
3	C. W. G. Lacey	349 cc Grindlay	2	"	42	"	"

Won by 150 Yards. Winner's Speed 69.85 m.p.h.

The Match Race between Parry Thomas' 7 litre Leyland Thomas, Malcolm Campbell's 2 litre Bugatti, Knight's 980 cc Zenith and Bill Lacey's 344 cc Grindlay

Peerless resulted in a close finish and a win for Campbell from the 33 seconds mark, with Knight second (47 secs.), Thomas third (scratch) and Bill a very very close fourth.

Nothing else, then, till the end of August when that great favourite, the Hutchinson 100, together with a small programme of short races was run off, the first of which was a Three Lap Handicap for which eighteen starters out of twenty nine entries turned out. It was won by R. L. Briggs' 348 cc AJS at 75.57 mph with two 250s, Colgan's Cotton and Greening's Zenith second and third respectively.

The Three Lap Handicap 350 cc to 1000 cc Race was won by J. W. Marshall's 490 cc Norton, with Lance Loweth's similar machine second and Wright's big Zenith third. It is sometimes rather difficult to get at true facts when looking back so far and, reporting this race, one source of information said that Wright's Zenith was 'steering as well as ever'. Quite hard to understand when one looks back only one meeting earlier and found the machine described as almost unhandleable.

The Handicap Race for Passenger Machines up to 1000 cc was won comfortably by Worters' 344 cc Excelsior sidecar outfit followed home by Preston's 588 cc Norton and Webb's 998 cc Indian at 75.34 mph. Fernihough's 490 cc Fernihough Morgan wasn't allowed to start and was classified as 'unsafe', which must have maddened Eric to whom safety was a fetish, particularly as the machine had not long before successfully attacked records in its class. Without any doubt at all, this must have been the only occasion ever when he was refused a start for this reason and I would think that when the Morgan did start again, Eric would have argued the thing out successfully with the organisers and would have brought it to the line again in exactly the same form. That would have been his way of avenging such a slight.

Contemporary reports sometimes pinpoint their own absurdities. Describing the start of the 'Hutch', *The Motor Cycle,* doyen of all motorcyling periodicals, refers to Wright's big Zenith as 'the limit man', going on to say – in the same paragraph – that when Wright left the line, C. S. Barrow's 246 cc Royal Enfield had already completed twelve laps so, presumably Barrow must have been limit. But Joe, of course, as out-right Outer Circuit lap record holder, never in his life started from the limit mark on a 'thousand' or, I think, on a machine of any other capacity.

But both Joe and Patchett's big McEvoy were out after 9 laps, the former with a tight engine – after lapping at 102 mph and the latter with a rear tyre that had shed its tread. This particular 'Hutch' seems to have had the Handicapper smiling on the limit men and frowning on the owners of the faster machinery, for when Joe Wright's big Zenith left the start line from the scratch mark, C. S. Barrow's 250 cc Royal Enfield had already covered 12 laps, four other 250s had covered 11, three 350s, including Hick's Velocette had covered 6, Worters' 250 cc Excelsior 7 and even Chris Staniland's fast 500 cc Norton was 3 laps ahead. Barrow won at 74.39 mph followed by Packman's 250 cc Zenith, Hick's Velocette, Miller, Greening and Jacobs on 250s, and Staniland's Norton.

The highlight of the BMCRC Championship Brooklands Meeting in mid-September was, without doubt, the weather, for the sun shone throughout. As one report said 'The Championship Meeting is apparently made to consist entirely of 5 lap scratch races on the assumption that a dozen super cracks, who have been beating one another by split seconds throughout the season, will enter each race and proceed – meta-phorically speaking – to cut one another's throats with the utmost savagery, to the vast entertainment of everybody concerned'. The report went on to say that due to small entries, non-starters and high machine mortality, scratch races didn't work out like that and they certainly didn't this time.

Sticking my neck right out, I would go a stage further and say that, on occasions, closely contested scratch races were really not closely contested at all. At one meeting, and I really can't recall now which it was, when closeted in the gentleman's loo, I was privileged to hear the most enlightening conversation I ever did hear at Brooklands. Unaware of my presence, the loo was visited by three very famous riders who, in the belief that they were alone there, proceeded to carve up the programme so effectively that the winners of five out of the seven or eight races were decided then and there. It was a friendly, even jocular conversation and it has been a source of great sorrow to me ever since that, on that particular day, there was not one bookmaker in the Paddock because the plan was adhered to and carried out so superbly that the crowd left the circuit that evening convinced that they had witnessed the finest day's racing they had seen at Brooklands for many a month. Even the motorcycle papers appeared to have fallen for it for the reporters went into raptures concerning the thrillingly close finishes that day.

And, after all, why not. The winning speeds were all acceptably high, the race leaders changed place from time to time and yet no one was forced to thrash his engine to bursting point or to do anything mean to his mate in riding. Had each of those races been contested outright it isn't impossible that someone might have been hurt and quite likely that at least one expensive engine might have finished the day with its innards hanging out. There was no one else in the running in any of those five races anyway. How often this happened it is hard to say. It certainly happened that day and may have done on other similar occasions. But days like that sent the spectators home happy and even to someone 'in the know' it was quite fascinating to see the plan carried out so beautifully and with just enough, but not too much, window dressing.

Clearly, the 1926 Brooklands Championship Meeting didn't fall into this category for engine failures ruined the chances of many riders, including some top names.

The 250 cc Class 'A' 5 lapper opened the proceedings. Le Vack was not there and Worters and Handley were the likely ones but, after taking an initial lead, Handley faded temporarily and Worters took over a lead he was to keep to the end. Handley dropped further back behind Millar's Zenith and Colgan's Cotton but rallied towards the end, repassing Colgan and finishing third to Worters and Millar, the winning speed being a highly creditable 81.77 mph and the win by a big margin.

Class 'F', 600 cc Sidecars followed, with the Douglases of both Dixon and Judd figuring among the non starters. But, despite that, the entry was good, including as it did such names as Horsman, Staniland, Denly and Brewster. Good as it was, it didn't produce a race, for Denly went out almost immediately, closely followed by Chris's Norton, leaving only two main protagonists to fight it out, Horsman who already had a big lead over them all, and Brewster's 599 cc Zenith. The Zenith fizzled on the last lap and – believe it or not – even Vic's super reliable Triumph engine did likewise as he came off the Byfleet banking, leaving him to coast over the line – winner of the race but with a dead engine. Average speed 81.24 mph. No other finishers.

The 350 cc Solo Race probably came just in time to prevent the spectators leaving in disgust, although even here, six did not start out of an entry of fifteen. But the quality of the starters was good and, right from the beginning there was a great battle between Marchant's Chater Lea and Worters' Excelsior, with Handley not far behind and Lacey scrapping with Archie Birkin – brother of Sir Henry (Tim) Birkin of Bentley fame. But the first three had quite a long and increasing lead from these two and the real fight was between Marchant and Worters. It was only really decided towards the end, when Marchant managed to place a slower rider, who had been lapped, between himself and Woolly, thereby turning a knife edge lead to one that could still be described only as slender. But slender was enough and he won at 93.97 mph.

Living well up to their reputations, the thousands again produced the now familiar ration of temperament, coupled with 'way out' features of design and improvisation. Patchett's supercharged 1000 cc McEvoy provided a disappointment by failing to make its initial bow and Riddoch's Zenith Blackburne had an elaborate system of hot air jackets for its induction pipe. Wright took the lead, followed by Riddoch, who dropped out after three laps leaving Baragwanath's Brough Superior lying a poor second. Joe then faded and 'Barry' took over to win. 2nd and 3rd placemen? J. S. Wright (Zenith) – on one cylinder and I. P. Riddoch (Zenith) – after clearing a choked fuel pipe. Really!

The programme seems to have lurched from imminent disaster back to good racing in turns and the fifth race, the 750 cc Championship, was by far the best of the afternoon although its pattern was weird.

The new 745 cc Rex Acme Blackburne twin, ridden by Handley, led for three laps, during which time Horsman passed the reigning championship holder Walters and Staniland's Norton trailed along astern. Then Chris miraculously found speed up his sleeve and proceeded to pass Worters and, on the last lap, Horsman and Handley as well, so that he won at 98.82 mph. Chris, of course, was a highly intelligent and

A 'mixed field' handicap. Solos and sidecars.

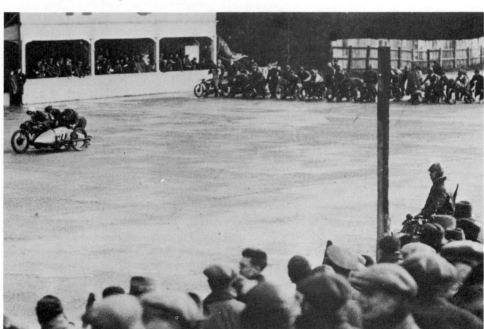

perceptive rider, a test pilot and later a star driver of cars who succeeded in lapping Brooklands faster on four wheels than anyone else, with the sole exception of John Cobb.

Back to the sidecars and, again, an unexciting race of 350s. It was, in reality, the 350 cc Solo Race again, with sidecars attached, and it provided the same result – Marchant, Worters and then Milne's OEC-JAP a long way behind. There were five starters, Birkin retiring on lap one and Emerson on lap two. Only three finished. The winner's speed was 77.93 mph. A two horse race really.

Another lurch towards better racing came with the 500 cc Championship. This time Judd's Douglas did start and although the carburettor of Denly's Norton was shrouded in a tin structure which made it invisible – the rider alleging that it contained white mice – the mice must have been fierce ones for it won at 95.59 mph closely followed by Staniland, with Judd third and R. Gibson's Sunbeam fourth.

The 1000 cc Championship was a repeat 'thousand' performance of past patterns, made slightly more interesting by the reliability of Staniland's 588 cc Norton although, obviously, it could not match the speed of Wright's big Zenith, which won at 102.06 mph. Chris had a very bad moment indeed in this race when following Baldwin's 996 cc Zenith, which stopped very suddenly. Patchett, who must either have had enormous initial power or very poor tyres retired again with no tread on the rear.

I sincerely hope that the reader hasn't found all this past history too repetitive. Not, at least, to the extent that the Brooklands habitués were finding it 'in the flesh' as it were, for spectator attendance had been dropping off steadily for some time and the powers that be now came to a rather belated conclusion that repetition was one of the reasons and decided that something must be done about it.

So far, in the story, I have covered it all rather fully so as not to miss anything but, from now on we will get over the ground a bit faster. Remember, won't you, that when we have covered the exploits of these chaps, we shall be getting their recollections of it verbatim in the second half of the book. Remember too, the ones who will be talking to us. They are Archer (who hasn't yet come on the scene), Cobbold, Denly, Driscoll, Horsman, Lacey, Tottey and Worters. There are others who I know to be around. The problem is finding them.

Having reached the decision that bike racing at Brooklands now needed a face lift, the Club sat down and had a good think, coming to the conclusion that, in addition to full bore racing on the outer circuit, the fans ought to be treated to some 'round the corners' stuff for a change.

So, enter the first 'Brooklands Grand Prix' with solo classes for 250, 350 and 500 cc solos, and 350 cc, 500 cc and 1000 cc sidecars. The course consisted of 43 laps of what later came to be known as the Mountain Circuit, in other words up the Finishing Straight the correct way turn right on to the Home Banking – the reverse way outer circuitwise, down to the timing box and right again – almost a hairpin – into the straight again. This gave a circuit of rather over a mile and a total distance of roughly fifty miles, with sandbags set up along the straight to form chicanes. Later, the chicaned Straight still came into it, but the turn at the end went left onto the Outer Circuit, to include the Railway Straight and the Byfleet Banking. This gave a much longer circuit, the race distance in the thirties being a hundred miles – and for solos only.

This time, not knowing how many entries they would get, the administration decided that the 250 cc and 350 cc races would be held concurrently. This proved to be right because, although they got enough entries to run off the programme, there were some – among them Horsman and Lacey – to whom this sort of thing didn't appeal. Although they probably turned up to spectate, they didn't enter.

But there were others who came in to fill the gaps, among them Eric Fernihough, who won the 250 cc race on a Zenith with Colgan second on his Cotton, the winning speed working out at 51.50 mph, which doesn't sound earth shattering but was respectable in view of the course layout. There were six starters in this one and ten in the 350 cc race from a total of twenty-four entries for both togehter.

This sort of thing was Handley's handwriting and he led the 350's first time round but both Barrow and Hicks liked it too and were close behind, followed by the inimitable Dixon who would have a go at most things, Brooklands particularly. By lap three Fred was in second place and reported as 'cornering luridly, wobbling slightly but always master of his mount'. Those poor Douglases. They really must have been much better bikes than most people realised. Barrow's ride ended abruptly with a 'head on' collision with a sandbag on lap 19. A nasty ending to a good ride because sandbags are much much harder than they look. Not only judgement but brakes and brake fade must have come into this because on this circuit the run down from the Home Banking to the hairpin at Chronograph Villa was punishing to brakes.

The usual crop of retirements came up, Handley with clutch trouble, Longman with a flat tyre and Dixon with a single cylinder Douglas. The result of all this was that Freddie Hicks's Velocette romped home to win, seven minutes ahead of Birkin's McEvoy.

There were twelve starters out of sixteen entries in the 500 cc race and Dixon took the lead at the end of lap 1. Staniland, whose entry had been a late one and who may not have had too much practise on the circuit, lay well back at first and began to come up strongly but in the seventeen to twenty lap period both he and Dixon went out, Fred with engine trouble and Chris – very unusually for him – 'on the floor'. This let in Tommy Bullus's New Hudson, which won at 59.07 mph., Hicks was second this time and Cobbold's reliable Sunbeam third.

The sidecar classes could hardly be said to have been well supported, having seventeen entries in three classes out of whom only ten came to the line, two 350's, four 600's and four 1000's.

One of the 350's fell out after seven laps, leaving the other, J.S. Holdroyd's OEC to complete the course and win at 45.28 mph. Patchetts' big McEvoy and Dixon's 600 cc Douglas outfits began to pull away from the rest and these two emerged the winners of their classes at speeds of 50.30 and 50.38 mph respectively. Patchett had a stop out on the course, which enabled Fred to get on ahead a bit.

The 1926 season ended gracefully with the nice little MCC meeting in mid-October. It was nothing to get excited about except that it marked the first appearance of another one of those who was to become a 'regular' – L. J. (Les) Archer of New Imperial and Velocette fame. Les won a 'Gold' on this, his first Brooklands outing, and others who enjoyed the day were George Brough and Gordon Cobbold.

Chapter 4

The 1927 Season

The first tremor of Brooklands re-awakening came towards the end of January, with the announcement that Norton's racing interests would, as from then, be in the hands of Nigel Spring. This amounted virtually to the end of O'Donovan's long reign and the end also of R.M.N. Spring's career as a rider. Bert Denly was the only rider nominated although from time to time, others were designated to partner him in long distance record attempts.

The R.M.N. Spring – A. Denly partnership was to last a long time. It was in fact such a firm one that when the time did arrive for a change, they both stuck together and went from Norton to perform the same tasks, possibly on a greater scale, for AJS.

The opening BMCRC Meeting that year took place in the usual and seasonal weather conditions. As one report put it 'Gusts of wind made the holding of a fast machine on full throttle a task for he men but in spite of this, of the wet state of the track and of the blinding stinging rain which fell during several of the races, some extremely high speeds were attained'.

Gordon Cobbold's Sunbeam was first to get away in the first race of the season, the Three Lap 350 cc Scratch but it was Worters, Handley, Lacey and Hicks who were ahead at the end of the lap. The central electrode of Handley's plug blew out and Woolly was able to pull out a big lead from the others, winning at 86.77 mph with Lacey heading Hicks.

On the start line for the 500 cc Scratch an official was getting riders opinions on the weather conditions. 'What do you think of it Vic?' he asked Horsman. 'Wet' was the answer. If you ask a silly question you must expect a silly answer.

Cobbold's Sunbeam had a crafty air intake, enclosed in tinware, with an adjustable opening facing forwards and two balance pipes – one from the box to the float chamber and the other leading to the filler cap of the tank. Le Vack's New Hudson led at the end of the first lap followed by Judd's Douglas, Cobbold, Horsman, P. M. Walters and Denly, the last riding for the first time under the Spring banner. At the end of the second lap Le Vack had half a mile lead over all the rest and the order was now Denly, Judd and Cobbold. It stayed that way until the end, Bert's speed working out at 94.68 mph. So many riders reported nearly losing it in this race that it was decided to postpone the 1000 cc race and substitute the Novice Handicap. A good idea. It must have been pretty awful for the really fast boys and, of course, good experience for the Novices. Their speeds would be much lower anyway. Kirby's Sunbeam won this one, at 76.39 mph.

Eric Fernihough wheeled out his 'brainchild' for the Up To 350 cc Handicap – the machine which was later to become my first Brooklands mount, for I bought it from him much later – in 1931. On this occasion it was entered as a Montgomery JAP which, in the main, it was, although before I did the deal with Eric, it had become known as the EF – JAP. *The Motor Cycle* described it saying 'The engine has two vertical overhead valves operated by push rods, a single exhaust port, and, except for the crankcase, is stated to be half a pre-war twin cylinder ohv 350 cc JAP. The rest of the machine is standard Montgomery ultra-lightweight with chain-cum-belt transmission and front forks with horizontal springing'. I don't think I can add much to that really, except to say that the crankcase, so Eric told me, was originally the lower half of a 250 cc side valve single. I've the very fondest feelings for that bike, which was my first racing bike ever, my first Brooklands mount, the first on which I ever got a place in a race and the last belt driven bike ever to compete at Brooklands – when I had it in 1933. It certainly could have been quicker but couldn't possibly have been more loved.

Sadly, as was its wont, it chose to misbehave this time and Eric, its creator, was towed ignominiously back to his shed so that the 350 cc three Lap Handicap was run without them, being won by Lacey's Grindlay Peerless, with the Cottons of Colgan and Johnston second and third.

There were three big twins in the 1000 cc Race, two of them McEvoys, with Patchett and A. P. Hamilton aboard, while Wright had temporarily forsaken Zenith to ride a Brough Superior. He won at 96.33 mph from Horsman and Staniland but was slow off the mark so that Vic led the race for quite a distance in the early and mid-stages.

Torrents of rain now fell so that the programme had to be suspended and several races were scrubbed altogether but one more, a Three Lap Handicap for Sidecars up to 1000 cc was won by Calder's Calder Special, powered by a 350 cc JAP, at 65.10 mph, followed home by the 600 cc outfits of Denly and Horsman. The Spring – Denly alliance will have been happy with two second places at their first meeting and pleased by the comment in one paper that, during the winter, good use seemed to have been made of enamel and metal polish, going on to say that never had the Norton race bikes looked so smart and workmanlike. If one were to make a guess, it would be that Nigel Spring would really have liked to go in for nickel plating the frames and running gear right from the start. Time or possibly the expense of it, at least until his potential as a manager was known, may have been what prevented it. Within the week, the outfit was attacking 600 cc sidecar records successfully, at standing and flying speeds between 83 and 88 mph respectively.

Later in April details were announced of special Brooklands machines being produced by Excelsior – for Worters – and by Grindlay Peerless for Lacey. Both looked extremely workmanlike, the Grindlay being nickel plated, extremely compact and generally giving an appearance of increased strength and robustness compared with what were probably only modified production machines on which Bill had raced till that time.

Denly was out again only a few days later, this time with a five hundred, on which he took the standing start 50 kilos, 50 miles and 100 kilos. Could it be that R.M.N.S. had his eye on the 500 cc 'Hour'? It looked like it for the speed for the 100 kilos was 96.30

Solos 'scrapping it out' low down on the Home Banking. Square front numbers and big tanks denote a long race.

'Two pushers per machine – and the bigger, the better'.

J.S. Wright (996cc Brough Superior JAP). Winner Race 3 Opening Meeting 1927 at 96.33 mph.

mph and it would be logical to try this one and then take the plot apart and see what it looked like after covering this distance.

Just as, at this stage, O'Donovan had faded from the picture and whilst others like Emerson were beginning to fade, new names like Denly and Lacey were now starting to come into it strongly. Two , Le Vack and Horsman, went on and on, but things were becoming more evenly matched and I think, really, that the two golden years were 1927 and 1928 from this point of view.

The opening 350 cc Scratch Race took on an unusual pattern for not only Worters but Lacey also struck trouble and both were very, very unusual troubles. Bill discovered his first, on the line in fact, and it was that the immaculate Grindlay Peerless – the new one – had disgraced itself on its very first appearance by shedding a steering damper bolt. This must, surely, mark the only occasion when one of Bill's bikes started in a race with any part of it fixed up with wire. Woolly's trouble was even worse and could have been serious had he got going. On leaving the line he found that he couldn't get any gears and, looking down, he found to his horror that the two frame tubes which formed the gearbox mounting had sheared and that the gearbox was now held in place only by the drive chains. In Bill's case it could well be that the Grindlay had been built at the works and not by him and possibly against time, too. In the case of Woolly's Excelsior it was not the new bike but his old one and, surmising, it would seem possible that, after spending time on getting the new one right and then not being entirely satisfied with it, he had fallen back on an old friend which had, at last, let him down.

Whatever the facts, Bill disappeared from the scene early on in the race and so did Handley, letting in Freddy Hicks's Velocette to win at 86.02 mph, followed home by Colgan and Birkin. These two must have held the record, at the time, for second and third places with only an occasional first to keep the spark alight!

The 500 cc Scratch Race really did produce a sensation for, with Le Vack trailing Denly at the end of the first lap; everyone felt that the old master was playing his usual 'cat and mouse' act. But to the astonishment of all, he wasn't, and this wasn't surprising because Denly's standing lap had been done at 92.47 and his second at a rousing 104.19 mph. With a race average of 100.82 mph there was nothing Le Vack could do about it. Judd was third and Nortons must have been not only rubbing their hands with delight but also looking into the archives to see what remuneration they had agreed with Nigel Spring!

The 1000 cc Scratch Race provided the rarest of sights – a changing race pattern, high speeds and some good scraps for the lead. There were only five starters and, at the end of the first lap it was Baldwin, Wright, Staniland, Patchett and Horsman or – put another way – Zenith, Brough, Norton, McEvoy and Triumph. This wasn't Vic's sort of race. He would take on all comers in the 500 cc and 600 cc classes and beat them on level terms. When it came to the thousands he had to rely on the capriciousness of the big twins – and this time they weren't being capricious. Chris, with his 588 cc Norton, may possibly have been willing to take just a few more changes – to bring the plot round the Byfleet to within a foot of the grass instead of ten feet and to being it down so far on the Home Banking that the rear tyre really did take a pasting – but Vic was at the time, a little bit older, a little bit wiser and a little bit wilier. These qualities would have paid off in any other race, but they didn't in this one. Chris ought to have scrubbed the rear tyre till the tread departed, but it didn't. The big twins ought to have given more trouble but, for once, they didn't – except for Wright's Brough Superior.

This must surely have been the only motorcycle race ever to have been run at Brooklands in which Vic Horsman started and finished last. Wright edged into the lead on the second lap and then the order was Baldwin, Patchett, Staniland and Horsman but at the end of the third lap, Patchett had taken Joe, whose engine then began to emit clouds of smoke and was obviously on the point of seizing. This enabled George to ease the big McEvoy and cruise home to win at a mere 100.82 mph, with Baldwin second and Chris's 588 cc Norton third. Such a change.

Next was a Private Owner's Handicap Race won by H. O. Matthew's 588 cc Norton and Sidecar at 76.03 mph. It was followed by a Three Lap Expert's Race in which Woolly scored with his 250 at 84.84 mph, a success which he followed by promptly winning the next one with the same bike, this time at 86.62 mph.

Denly, Horsman and Cobbold were the placemen in the 1000 cc Handicap, Denly winning at 97.65 mph and, after another Private Owner's Handicap had been won this time by Haverson's HLH Blackburne, the boys then lined up for the 90 mph Three Lap Handicap.

This one, too, was a bit unusual. False starts were rare at Brooklands but this was one such occasion the handicapper getting his lines crossed so that the rest were held after Lacey and Judd had left. Back to the start and a change of plugs for the two fleet ones after which Bill annexed first place with the 500 cc bike, with Staniland's 600 and

G.W. Patchett (996cc McEvoy JAP). Winner Race 3 at the April 1927 Meeting. Speed 100.82 mph. Standing (in light jacket) A.P. Hamilton, Velocette and McEvoy rider, later to drive Alfa Romeo cars at Brooklands.

Horsman's 500 taking the places. Speed 97.08 mph.

The last race of the day was a Three Lap Passenger Handicap in which Chater Lea annexed first place followed by Staniland's big Norton. Nice to see a manufacturer riding one of his own productions. Speed 72.28 mph.

Once again, the 200 Mile Sidecar Races produced, in equal measure, anticipation, ecstasy, innovation, humour, disappointment and frustration in that order, to which one must add some thrills and a certain amount of real racing.

The 350 cc Race was notable for the appearance, for the first time, of the new overhead camshaft Blackburne engine installed in Paddy Johnston's Zenith outfit, with two coil springs for each valve – just becoming in fashion – and duralumin rockers with steel tips. Worters had his new track Excelsior with a 350 cc engine. In the earlier photographs of this bike there could been seen a vast and empty looking space behind the saddle tube, for the gearbox was mounted high up. Now Woolly had craftily filled the space with a big oil tank, or rather two of them. The prize for the biggest fuel tank in relation to engine capacity went to Broadbent's Chater Lea, which carried seven and a half gallons and, for the most thoughtful and kind rider, to Hopkins who had fixed a broomstick to the body of the Chater Lea so that the end protruded rearwards. As one report put it 'the passenger, when lying full length on his stomach, could hold on to the end of the stick and so save himself from making a nose dive onto the track in the event of the machine hitting one of the worst bumps'. Not too much to ask, one would think but, although I never met him, everyone I have talked to when compiling this story makes a point of saying what a very nice man Hopkins was. From what his contempories have told me, I would imagine that Ron Hopkins was possibly the nicest and most helpful of them all.

Brooklands sidecar passengers took an awful pasting and no one who acted in this capacity will disagree with that. In this race, six outfits carried ballast and, on the face of it, this would seem to be better. But to take any part in a long race at the track was the coveted ambition of hundreds of young men over the years so that there was always a queue of would-be sidecar passengers waiting. And sometimes, of course, it was good to have a passenger. If the outfit suffered a minor breakdown on the far side of the track it was easier with two. One could take turns at pushing while the other rode in the chair. Two miles are a long way on a hot day and, in circumstances like these, a ballast loaded sidecar becomes heavier to push at every yard. Only the passenger of the winning outfit in each class got an award – a small silver cup, and a description of the passengers standing on the line at the start of this race describes them as being 'swathed in bandages' and having 'pieces of rubber tied to various portions of their anatomies'. It doesn't go on to state which parts. A pity, really – every portion could be involved if the circumstances arose. The passenger of F. J. Young's OK Blackburne was a case in point for history records that 'the tail of the sidecar body dropped clean off, leaving the poor fellow clinging for dear life to the remnants; just as the officials realised his plight and were thinking of flagging the machine off, the engine gave up the ghost owing to a rocker standard giving way.' Note, carefully, that the officials, wise old men all of them, were only thinking about it when blessed relief came. No one, surely, can ever have viewed a broken rocker standard with more delight than this chap.

Almost invariably Brooklands passengers lay feet first, facing backwards, but I do recall a few who managed to get their sidecar bodies mounted low enough for the passenger to sit up and face forwards. One particularly, a 'thousand' outfit, the comfort of the 'chair' was a pre-race matter of pride to both its pilot and passenger. For many laps this chap did look very very comfortable indeed. But soon the sidecar body seemed to be slightly nose down – or was it imagination? The phenomenon began just as the Stewards were beginning to enjoy their beer and sandwiches. They seemed not to have noticed it and nor did the driver. Down and down it went, lap after lap and, as it did so, the poor passenger, who certainly had noticed it, leaned further and further back. Then, as this obviously wasn't going to be enough, he began to slide further rearwards, still laying on his back facing the sky. Further back he slid and still further, till he must have been hanging almost by his toes alone. One wondered why. Every spectator knew he was fighting a losing battle and, ere long, he was so far back that he was completely out of contact with the rider. Still the nose of the chair became closer to the track and it was only when it began to scrape it that alarm among the spectators overcame curiosity. Only just in time, too for when it was at last flagged in, there was quite a big hole in the front of the floor through which the poor hero was in danger of sliding.

Johnston's new engine didn't take him far in this race, just four laps. Driscoll's Zenith Chater Lea went out with mag trouble, Hopkins had, as he put it, a spot of trouble with the dear engine and, for all his vast fuel load, Broadbent stopped with a choked fuel system.

At quarter distance it was Handley, Worters and Millar, and at the halfway point, Worters, Handley and Hicks. Then Handley's rear tyre picked up a nail so that, with three quarters of the race run, it was Worters, Millar and Handley. One lap later, Woolly was out with a broken exhaust valve rocker spindle and this let Millar into the lead. But, bit by bit, Handley caught up and finally won, Millar coming in behind him and ahead of Hicks. Unfortunately, though, Millar was excluded from the award list since he finished minus one of his silencers, even though this was something that could happen to anyone and frequently did. Winner's speed 69.00 mph exactly. The record shows that, in this race, Eric Fernihough finished seventh on a Zenith outfit. It represented one of Eric's few efforts with a chair and when, ten years later, I was getting into the sidecar of his Brough Superior at its first outing at Brooklands, it suddenly occurred to me that I'd never seen him ride one. I felt I ought to check the position having been brought up sharply with a momentary twinge of alarm because chair or no chair, I'd never seen him ride anything bigger than 350s on the Outer Circuit, except for standing miles and kilos on his sprint 500 cc Excelsior during the time I knew him. With the thought of ninety odd brake horse beneath us I said

'By the way Eric, can you ride a chair'?

'Of course I can'.

'I've never seen you do it'.

'Well, you're going to now.' And I had to be satisfied with that.

We did a few slow laps, came in to check the thing over and then went out again and did a standing start kilo and mile. The big outfit was really marching at the end of the Railway Straight and I was sure he would take a high line onto the Byfleet Banking. But he didn't, going on instead about half way up and, instantly, I was sure we were in for big trouble. Suddenly the outfit lurched and the sidecar wheel jolted up and stayed a foot off the ground so that my instant reaction was to calculate at what point we would be going over the top. I looked right and saw that we were still alongside the sewage farm and was glad about that for I knew, then, that we wouldn't necessarily both be killed instantly by being dashed to pieces on the parapet of the Byfleet Bridge. It was to be a heavy landing in the gorse, on the other side of the banking, I decided, and instantly wondered whether Eric was going to take Ted Baragwanath's advice because Barry always said that once you knew you were going over the top it was better to slide off the back of the bike and let it go on its own rather than hang on and take a full trip. That way, Barry maintained, you'd have a long trip down the concrete but better that than a long trip through the trees. Quickly I looked left and was astonished to see the pilot not only still in situ but apparently still in control. It's strange how things like that stick with you. I even recall a fleeting moment of irritation mixed with pleasure. Irritation that Eric should have been so cocky about being able to ride sidecars and pleasure that, for once, he'd been proved wrong for Eric was practically never wrong, which was so trying for those of us who were almost never right.

Instantly, the pleasure died and the irritation turned to anger for I realised that I was being given a demonstration of just how well he could ride a 'chair' as we returned the whole way to the Paddock, more than a mile and a half, on the two offside wheels and with the third wheel airborne. What was worse was that he took us the whole way back, left turn into the Paddock, a left circle and stop – still with the wheel off the ground. I think if he'd had a lighter passenger, he might have circled right. My weight put paid to that.

The 600 cc Race lost two of its thirteen starters, Bullus (New Hudson) and Parker (Douglas) within six laps – both out with magneto trouble. Bert Denly, Staniland and Le Vack set the pace for the first quarter of the race but Chris went out shortly afterwards when his fuel tank fell to pieces and, to half distance his place was taken by Tucker's Norton. The engine of Matthew's Norton burst in a big way, in view of the pits, so spectacularly that, by the time it came to rest, the accessory people were still arguing about whether the cause of the drama was a burst tyre or a broken chain and all were relieved to see it arrive with the con rod hanging out. Tucker was delayed for ten minutes with a broken fuel pipe and, later, with tyre trouble but still managed to hold third place behind Denly and Le Vack at three quarter distance.

In racing, nothing is certain. At the three quarter distance point of this one, Denly was more than sixteen minutes ahead of Le Vack. Put another way, when he set out to cover the final fifty miles of the race, Le Vack still had more than sixty five miles ahead of him – it was just a matter of cruising to win. I bet Bert had thoughts of only tyres or chains giving trouble. Possibly, I suppose, the dreaded broken rocker standard too although with Spring's guidance they had probably left this one behind them. Anyway, it was none of these things. The bit that broke was the extension spindle from the exhaust cam pinion – driving the magneto – and who could possibly have foreseen that. At the three quarter distance point, Denly had averaged 79.87 mph, even with the huge lead he had over the other Bert. Le Vack's winning speed was a mere 68.90 and he was followed by Tucker at 65.27 mph and C.M. Harley's Zenith at 58.27 mph. Yes, long distance racing at the track did have its full quota of heartaches.

In the 1000 cc race Ashby's Zenith was in at the pits at the end of the first lap, pushed by his passenger and with its overheated driver trotting along astern. His trouble was a magneto chain adrift and, fourteen laps later Patchett was in and had changed the gearbox of the big McEvoy in ten minutes. Temple was in with a broken fuel pipe and Wright's Brough Superior was leading Baldwin and Longman at an average of 83 mph. Temple got going again and promptly ran into tyre trouble, finally running out of rear wheels and gratefully accepting the offer of a rival tyre representative to fit another make. Good publicity for the rep and his firm at good odds, for he was now no longer a menace. By half distance Baragwanath had replaced Longman and six laps later Wright was out with a broken exhaust rocker so that, with three quarters of the race run, Baldwin, in the lead, had a four minute lead over the second man H. M. Walters, also Zenith mounted. This was the order to the end, Baldwin averaging 73.97 mph ahead of Walters, Baragwanath and R.E. Humphries, also Brough Superior mounted. At least there were four finishers within the time limit in this one.

Immediately after this, the Spring/Denly combination was out breaking the World's Flying Mile and Kilo with the 588 cc Norton sidecar outfit. As if to underline to Le Vack that they really did mean it, they put the Kilo up from 88.94 to 91.30 mph and the Mile from 88.28 to 92.02 mph – slightly faster over the greater distance – very unusual. Another one out on the same day was J. J. Hall, establishing, not breaking records in Class 'H', which was for 350 cc three wheeled cyclecars. To my great sorrow, I never met Jim Hall and I think it really was the greatest regret I ever had regarding Brooklands for, of all the characters there, he surely was the king.

He raced very little, concentrating solely on establishing and breaking records, in many cases in absurd classes like this one, and others such as the 75 cc solo and inter-mediate. It was purely business and he was the grand master at drawing bonus from anyone he could possibly interest in the record breaking scene. In this case he was establishing records with a vehicle called an HP – JAP over distances ranging from 5 Kilos (at 52.18 mph) to One Hour, which he took at the rousing speed of 46.73 mph. For this he used a JAP engine, ML Magneto, B and B Carburettor, KLG plug, Sternol oil, ROP Spirit, Palmer Tyres, Brampton chain and Don brake linings. Nine lots of bonus there alone and brake linings wouldn't have come into it at all except for pulling in at the end of the 'Hour'. And note, also, that it just wasn't on to lose even one bonus by using the same make of spirit and oil. Just great!

And that was only the tip of the iceberg for you would see him featuring in advertise-ments for numerous other things like hair cream and soap, well knowing that none of these manufacturers knew anything about Brooklands or records and had probably never been there. Ebby once told me that he heard Jimmy Hall chatting up a likely Director and the conversation went like this –;

'Would your firm be interested in advertising record breaking?'

'We could be.'

'What would you be prepared to pay for a record?'

'What do most people pay?'

'Oh around ten pounds.'

'Yes, we would certainly pay ten pounds.'

'And for two records?'

'Twenty I suppose.'

'And for three?' But at this point the advertiser became just a little suspicious and put forward the 'sliding scale' idea. This was agreed to by 'J.J.' with a fine show of disappointment but with the certain knowledge that a few more hundreds were in the bag. It was great business. There was absolutely nothing wrong with it and anyone could have done it. But although Jimmy Hall really would have liked one or two more to join and break some of his numerous records just so that he could go out and break them again, very few people did. Hall went on for years breaking records at first at absurdly low speeds and later at very creditable speeds indeed. But he went fast only when he had to and he must have been one of the most prolific record breakers of them all. And the people whose products he advertised were delighted, because, for them, it proved to be very cheap advertising. If any of them had, for instance, looked into the question of what it would cost to be able to advertise their product allied to the 500 cc 'Hour', they would have been even more sure of the splendid bargain they'd made. Many people told me that J.J. Hall was a genius but they all added that he was a very nice man. I wish I'd known him.

Some nice little Paddock items made the fourth Member's Meeting more interest-ing. Although it was a programme of short races, Baldwin's big Zenith had long distance tanks, for it had been prepared for a record attack on the World's 1000 cc 12 Hour. Rain had prevented this so, as one report put it 'he sportingly decided to have a shot at some of Saturday's races'. Yes, things like this did happen. Neither Le Vack or Handley were there but W.H. Phillips had Bill Lacey's old Cotton and went very well indeed with it. 'Wal', of course, was a nephew of Le Vack. At this stage Le Vack who, until then, had been having things more or less his own way, was coming up against the rising stars of Denly and Lacey and it could have been that he decided, this time, to stay at home and search for more horsepower. He had done magnificently for every manufacturer whose products he had ridden and he was certainly not one ever to take a back seat if it could possibly be avoided. There may have been other reasons for his non-appearance at this meeting but this one is a possibility.

Hopkins and Hicks appeared to be having a good scrap in the opening race, a 350 cc Scratch, followed by Cobbold's Sunbeam but, towards the end, Hicks pulled out quite a long lead and it was obvious that he was the man.

The next race, the 500 cc 5 Lap Scratch, was a queer one, partly because Bill Lacey made one of his very rare mistakes and partly because it wasn't altogether surprising. At nearly every previous meeting when the Club had held programmes consisting of short Scratch and Handicap races, the former had been run, class for class, over the same race distance. At this meeting, for some quite unaccountable reason, the 350 cc scratch race had been run over three laps and the 500 cc was to be run over five.

It must have been a very strange race for Bill for, coasting over the finishing line at the end of three laps, ahead of the Sunbeams of Gibson and Cobbold, he spotted a group of officials waving at him madly. Slowing down, he was then passed by Gibson, still flat out and, twigging that something was wrong, he got once more into his stride. He repassed the Sunbeam only to find, minutes later, that he was all alone again and not surprising either, for the Sunbeam had, by now, lost a silencer. He cruised for a bit and was then caught up by Cobbold so, resigning himself to the fact that he just didn't know how long the race distance was, he kept going. In the end, after winning at 84.56 mph from Cobbold, Bill had to be brought in by Reuben Harveyson armed with a red flag. But he did win!

The 1000 cc 5 Lap Scratch Race was good fun too, because it was between the big twins of Wright and Baldwin and Staniland's 588 cc Norton. Chris, clad in grey flannel trousers and gym shoes and an open neck shirt with the sleeves rolled up, beat both the 'big 'uns' off the line, although he couldn't hold Wright's Brough Superior for long. Joe got a useful lead and Baldwin pressed the Norton hard, eventually to gain a lead of about fifteen yards. But this was on the Railway Straight and, taking the Norton round the Byfleet within a foot of the inside edge, Chris got it all back from the Zenith, which had to be taken right round the top. Great, and with no leathers, either!

The first of the 3 Lap Handicaps, this one for Experts, was good too, although it provided a runaway win for Cobbold's Sunbeam. Baldwin didn't start, so Staniland was scratch man, but Chris still hadn't left the line when the limit man, Les Archer (250 cc New Imperial) came through at the end of his first lap. Not surprising since Les had done a 'standing' at just under 70 mph. At that rate, Chris would have had to average 104 to beat him! And Cobbold, Worters and Hicks weren't far behind anyway whilst Judd's Douglas was cleaving through the field. Gordon's winning speed worked out at 80.59 and Archer and Judd were the placemen.

A good day for Les who came second to Welch's HRD in the next Handicap. The next one, another Handicap, was won by Loweth's Norton from the Douglases of Judd and G.D. Brown. Brown was another one who had a long spell of riding, at Brooklands, always on Douglas, for whom he was an agent. A very long spell for he was still going there in the thirties, when I was competing.

Wal Phillips pulled off the Private Owner's Handicap on Lacey's old Cotton at a very respectable 80.85 mph and the Ninety Mile an Hour Handicap fell to Gibson, whose Sunbeam went well to average 87.88 mph. The Sunbeams of the period were

Rex Judd (494cc Douglas). Winner of Races 2 and 3 at the August 1927 Meeting at 98.62 and 99.61 mph. Gold Star Winner at 103.54 mph.

handsome, beautifully finished, reliable and fast, but nothing more. Gordon Cobbold told me, when I had lunch with him recently 'They were all right lapping around ninety but put another five miles an hour on to that and you had troubles'. He should know. He must have done more laps round Brooklands on Sunbeams than anyone else except, possibly, Gibson.

Horsman's 600 Triumph was second in the Ninety Miles an Hour Handicap and Bill Lacey's 500 Grindlay Peerless third, both from the scratch mark.

A rather uninspiring Passenger Handicap concluded the meeting and was won by L.J. Pellat's 344 cc McEvoy at 68.03 mph. McEvoy's had mixed fortunes at Brooklands but they were interesting and certainly contributed something to the scene. In fact, any small manufacturer who supported Brooklands had a soft place in the heart of the enthusiast, particularly one that tended to specialise in husky big twins!

Mid-July heralded the 200 Mile Solo races of 1927, the 250 cc and 350 cc even being held concurrently in the morning and the 500 cc and 1000 cc events in the afternoon.

From the start, the 250 cc showed the, by now, usual picture of 'Worters in the lead', the little Excelsior being tailed closely by Colgan's Zenith Blackburne for the first 33 laps. The Cotton stopped at this point, on the far side of the track, having still been on Woolly's tail at the time, both of them now being a lap ahead of the third man Hall, on a New Imperial. Finding no fuel in the float chamber, Colgan opened the filler cap and found, as he thought, none in the tank either, which must have mystified him since, on that basis, the consumption had halved since the day before when they did their final tests. He pushed back to the start where, at his pit, it was found that since the big tank was in two separate halves with a balance pipe connecting the two, and latter had become blocked. Not only had he been drawing fuel from one side of the tank but that all the distance had been covered with only one of the two carburettor float chambers being fed. By the time that had been discovered, Woolly, despite the appalling weather conditions, was in an unassailable position, provided nothing unexpected cropped up – and nothing did, so that he went on to win his third consecutive 200 Mile race. Throughout the race he steadily increased his lead over the rest, averaging 71.18 mph compared to the second man Edmunds. (OK Supreme JAP) whose average was a full 4 1/2 miles an hour slower. Hall's New Imperial was third and, after a great ride, the unlucky Colgan managed fourth.

In the same dreadful conditions, Handley took the lead in the 350 cc race, at first followed by Lacey, Hicks, Hamilton and Staniland. Since Hamilton was a private owner among full works supported riders, it would be logical to assume that he was probably the only one of the five flat out from the fall of the flag. When the rain recommenced after a short let up, soaking Handley's engine, it was the privately owned Velocette that went into the lead, followed at quarter distance by Staniland riding a beautifully judged race, with Lacey just astern. At half distance, the order was still the same, the leader's average having gone up from 83.70 to 84.70 mph but then came the changes. Two laps later, the studs holding the Velocette tank broke, fracturing one fuel pipe and letting Chris, who was a minute behind, into the lead. Lacey moved up to second place and, after a new flexible pipe had been fitted to the Velocette, Hamilton rejoined the race holding the tank between his knees. At three quarter distance the order was still Staniland, Lacey and Hamilton but, after pressing on hard and lapping at just under ninety to make an impression on Chris, Lacey's oil pump packed it in so that the final order was Staniland, Hamilton and Himing, on a Zenith. A very fine ride indeed and no wonder that Hamilton's average of 71.63 was nearly twelve miles an hour slower than that of the winner. A great day for the Worter-Staniland equipe, too.

Conditions were better for the big 'uns in the afternoon. Horsman and Wright had passed Judd, Denly came up alongside and they stayed together, dead heating for first place at quarter distance, the Triumph and the Zenith having faded along with Le Vack, Driscoll, Cobbold and Bullus. Shortly afterwards, Judd went out with a broken valve collar, followed by Lacey with a broken valve spring. There were only ten from the original seventeen starters still running at half distance, and at the half way mark it was Denly leading, with Staniland's Norton second, followed by Quinn's Triumph. Quinn, Victor Horsman's sidecar passenger and chief mechanic, was astride one of Vic's Triumphs, and by three-quarter distance nearly everyone was in serious trouble of some sort. Staniland had gone out with a broken valve collar, accompanied by Quinn, and Bert, although still in the lead and not really threatened by Gibson's Sunbeam in second place, now found he had a broken rocker standard. Hoping against hope that it might last if nursed, he began cruising, but the 61st of the 74th lap race saw him stop to try and fix it with wire so that it was the Sunbeam that crossed the line first at 79.98 mph, Walter's JAP-engined Sunbeam following, closely pursued by Eric Fernihough's HRD.

The 1000 cc race was no thriller, Vic Horsman's Triumph leading at quarter distance and averaging 93.79 mph but going out with a broken cam follower shortly afterwards so that at half distance Grogan led, his Norton followed by Longman's veteran Harley-Davidson and Baldwin's big Zenith, the Norton averaging 93.88 mph. At three quarter distance it was Longman and Baldwin, trailed by Patchett's McEvoy and the average had dropped to 86 odd. In the end Longman finished on his own at 86.89 mph. Not too inspiring but it tended to be the usual pattern in that class.

In retrospect it seems strange to have held the popular BMCRC Cup Day Meeting only a fortnight after such a marathon and this could well have been the reason for a rather poor turn out of professionals and a glut of wins by private owners, many of whom lacked the cash or the facilities to tackle a race of even a hundred miles, let alone two hundred.

But for all that, it seemed to be an enjoyable day and was at least graced by brilliant weather, Denly's Norton winning the 500 cc Scratch Race at 99.81 mph, Wright the 1000 cc at 101.43 and Rex Judd getting his 'Gold Star' at 101.43, a good speed at the time for a Douglas, but too much for it because it faded almost immediately afterwards. Handicap race winners were Phillips, Lacey and Edmunds and 'Pa' Brewster, on his big Zenith, romped away with the last race, a fifty miler at an average of 88.47, despite Le Vack's efforts on the New Hudson which finished unplaced, although it averaged 99.41 mph for the distance.

In September came the 'Hutchinson 100', Judd winning one of the 'curtain raisers' on his Douglas which held together to average creditable 98.62 mph over three laps. He followed it up by winning the next race, a five lap this time, at 99.61 mph, some consolation for his previous bad luck.

Dixon had a beautiful new Brough Superior for the 'Hutch' and was on the Scratch mark with Wright's big twin Zenith, but both had to give the limit man, Anderson on his Dunelt, so much start that they had cold engines by the time the flag fell and both were reluctant starters. Despite its newness and beauty, Fred's Brough cast him off on the first lap and he was a bit more than lucky to be thrown by a big twin and get away with nothing worse than a damaged elbow – but Fred was often lucky – and very brave too. Wright followed him into retirement five laps later.

Just as difficult to follow as usual, the pattern of the race began to emerge soon after half distance, at which point the plodding little Dunelt still held its lead. As usual, it was a question of the tortoises being chased by the hare, Ventura's Cotton being the other tortoise and Harold Willis's fleet Velocette the hare. But a few laps later it was seen than an even fleeter hare, Hicks's Velocette, was moving up on Willis and on lap 31 he passed him and went on to chase the 'tiddlers'. A lap later, though, he was out with a broken inlet valve spring. The Cotton overtook the Dunelt and Willis did the same on the 34th of the 37 laps, going into the lead on the 36th and holding it to win the 'Hutch' at an average of 88.39 mph, Ventura finishing second at 73.78. Longman's wonderful old Harley was third at 90.63 mph and Anderson fourth at 66.30 – who said that two strokes were unreliable!

When talking to Les Archer recently – his Brooklands recollections are in the latter part of the story – he told me he thought that 'valves and springs being in the open, in those days, had a simply wretched time'. They certainly did; one has only to look at the record of the 200 Mile Solo Races and, in this case Hicks's Velocette. Let it never be said that racing didn't improve the breed or that Brooklands didn't serve a very good purpose, at that time anyway.

Chapter 5

The 1928 Season

All through this part of the story I've been hoping to describe an opening meeting with the words 'nineteen so and so dawned fine and clear' but poor old Brooklands really did take the prize for bad weather on opening motorcycle meets. One of the reasons, I think, was that the Club had a lot of meetings to run off each season, coupled with the fact that they had to be fitted in with the car side of it and the result of this was that the first bike meeting had to take place early in the season and the last one very late.

Nineteen Twenty Eight broke all records and the opening meeting scheduled for March 31st was washed out and had to be re-run on Wednesday, April 11th. This was quite a blow, particularly from the spectator point of view because, in the nineteen twenties and early thirties, it wasn't at all easy to get time to spectate at race meetings or even, in some cases, to compete in them. But this time it was alright for the entry was good and the crowd not bad at all so, presumably, a lot of mothers-in-law must have died and had funerals that day!

Paddock gossip? Le Vack was there and was said to have spent the winter profitably, Colgan's Zenith had the new TT Blackburne engine with adjustable push rod return springs and Pellat's OK Supreme JAP sidecar outfit must surely have been one of the lightest ever to compete for it weighed only 310 pounds complete.

Lacey had the opening 350 cc Scratch Race well in hand when a mammoth leak sprung from his fuel filler cap, which brought Staniland wheel to wheel with him so that Chris won by a whisker, both of them heading Freddie Hicks's Velocette. Chris averaged 93.27 mph but there seems to have been slight disagreement about the distance between them for one report gives it as one inch whereas, in the classified results, it is described as the thickness of a tyre tread. I don't think, somehow, that even in 1928 tyres had treads one inch thick.

Le Vack made no mistake about the 500 cc Scratch race, three laps again, this time winning it from Lacey by fifty yards at 101.43 mph. He oiled a plug in the next one, the 1000 cc Scratch race so that Baldwin won from Denly at almost the same average – 101.23 mph, this time. Bacon's Norton won the Private Owner's Novice Handicap at 87.84 mph from E.M. Thomas's Rex Acme. Crowther Smith's similar machine won the up to 350 cc Handicap from Driscoll's Zenith Chater Lea, and Cobbold and Pat scored again in the next one – up to 1000 cc, on a Norton, this time behind Tucker's Norton

H.J. Bacon (490cc Norton). Winner Race 4 at the April 1928 Brooklands Meeting at 88.08 mph. Continued to ride through the 1930's with Velocette and Sunbeams.

and only two yards ahead of Potts's HRD. Thomas won the next Private Owner's at 82.28 mph and then came the Three Lap Solo 'experts'.

Le Vack really drove the point home in this one, winning it by ten yards from Lacey and Hicks at 103.97 mph, a fine average for so short a race, his best lap being turned at 108.98 to Bill's 105 mph. Yes, speeds were now beginning to creep up.

Tucker concluded the meeting by winning the Passenger Handicap Race from Worters and Hicks at 80.33 mph.

The Clerk of the Weather still hadn't finished with Brooklands and sent another day of torrential rain for the second meeting. Rather depressing for everyone, especially for Staniland and Worters, because this meeting, I think, must have marked the tailing off of Woolly's riding era and his transition from rider to tuner-manager.

I think this must be so because, after riding Nortons for so long and so successfully and well, Chris won the opening 350 cc scratch race from Hicks and Lacey at 91.22 mph and on an Excelsior JAP.

But Bill turned the tables on Le Vack decisively in the five hundred scratch race, winning it from him at 102.27 mph with a best lap of 107.34 mph – and on a streaming wet track, too.

Wright turned out on a new monster for the 1000 cc race, an AJW Summit, but he was headed home by Baldwin and Denly. The winning speed was 102.90 mph. Le Vack didn't run in this for he had bent a valve trying to keep up with Lacey in the previous race. Wet weather did tend to cause bent valves at Brooklands for the rear wheel would be losing grip before it hit each bump and the revs would go even higher after hitting one than they did when the track was dry.

But he made up for it by beating Denly and Tucker at exactly 83 mph – in the Passenger Race, by only five yards, so he was still under pressure from the 'youngsters'.

The next two, and last, races of the day were watched by the spectators from the comparative comfort of the tea room. Both were run in torrential rain and the first was won by Gus Grose's Excelsior at 83.99 mph.

Price's win on his Douglas at 92.23 mph, ahead of C.J. Williams' Raleigh, was overshadowed by a monumental accident to Colgan, whose Zenith broke away in the wet round the Byfleet Banking heading for the top in a big way. But at the last moment Colgan remembered Barry's 'golden rule' and abandoned ship, getting away with nothing more than a cut elbow and abrasions. In doing so he laid the machine on its side so that it, too, lost momentum and slid back down the banking, remaining – what was left of it – on the track. The second placeman in this race was, Jack, father of Peter Williams and more of Jack will be heard later on. Who made that Raleigh go so fast? None other than 'Wizard' O'Donovan who, having left Nortons, was now entrusted with Raleigh development.

The 200 Mile Sidecar Race patterns were slightly different from previous ones, the main thing being that both the 350 cc and 600 cc races centred on scraps between two fast men. As previously, the 350s proved to be the most reliable, the 600s not as good as in the past and the 1000s a bit better. Staniland, on Worter's Excelsior, took the lead, followed by Longman and Hicks, with Wal Phillips and Cobbold not far away. After only eight laps, Longman had to stop to replace – guess what? – his sidecar passenger, a very early stop indeed for this one and it couldn't have pleased Frank a bit.

Staniland stopped for fuel just before half distance and took up station behind Hicks, with Ashton's Chater Lea and Longman's New Hudson behind him but, at 44 laps Chris came in again with a broken engine bolt and this gave Hicks a four lap lead. Before the race ended, poor Chris was in again so that, at the finish, it was Hicks at 70.84 mph, Ashton, Longman and the Excelsior.

With ten laps covered, Le Vack led the 600s with Tucker, Denly, Horsman, Price and Driscoll next in line but Vic dropped out on lap twenty and, at half time, it was Denly and Le Vack dead heating with Tucker and Pat Driscoll next. They had run the race like Siamese twins and now came in to refuel together, Denly taking 55 seconds and Le Vack 59. Their lap speeds now went up a mile an hour to eighty-three but, just before three quarter distance, Le Vack disappeared on the far side of the track where, as one report put it 'questions could not be asked'.

This put 'the other Bert' into an undisputed lead and he was able to ease off, for the lap prior to Le Vack's retirement had been their fastest – 85.4 mph. Tucker and Driscoll were lying quite a bit further back and Pat now had the carburettor stub break off. But making his way back to the Paddock, along the Finishing Straight, he found a Norton there, removed the carburettor stub, fitted it to his racer and still made third place at the finish, albeit nearly 27 minutes behind the winner and at an average of 67.30 mph compared to Denly's 78.73 mph. But it was worth it. A.J. Dussek, a private owner, was fourth, thirty-two minutes after that.

The 1000 cc race proved to be a good one for Brough Superior, at the expense of the Zenith boys. Wright's change of mount to the AJW Summit did nothing for him and Kempster's big McEvoy broke its frame under the steering head, scaring the wits out of the VIP's when, at 24 laps, it charged them with its engine and sidecar chassis scraping the ground. Then Baldwin, whose Zenith had been leading at the half way mark, nearly went 'over the top' when the saddle tube connection to the sidecar snapped when he was high up on the Byfleet banking at the 44 lap point. This left Baragwanath's Brough Superior with a four lap lead over P.M. Walter's Zenith and this was how they stayed, followed home by C.F. Edwards' Brough outfit, the winning speed being 73.95 mph.

From the bike point of view Brooklands tended to slow down in late May and early June, the Isle of Man TT being the reason. True, very few Outer Circuit riders ran in the Island although there were some that did and others, of course, were 'all rounders' anyway. But the TT took from Brooklands the engineering brains and the backroom boys and, to some extent, the lessons that had been learned at Brooklands went into the building of the works bikes for the TT. Many of the TT machines were brought down to Brooklands in late April and in May and, suddenly, both the machinery and the 'boffins' would all disappear almost overnight and not be seen again till the races were over. And it worked the other way, too. They could come back with lessons learned in the Island that could be, and were, applied to racing at Brooklands. The 'inter Brooklands – TT' gossip was something everyone looked forward to and enjoyed.

The 200 Mile Solo Races were run off at Brooklands on 23rd June, 1928 in perfect weather. The quality of the entry list was good and so was the quality spectatorwise, for those watching included Alec Bennett, Walter Handley and Jimmy Simpson.

The start line arrangements for the 250 cc and 350 cc races would hardly have met with the approval of today's ACU for the fourteen 250s and twenty-one 350s were lined up in two lots across the track, thirty-five machines in all. That was alright but remember that at Brooklands, each bike had two pushers. So with seventy pushers in all, and with twenty-eight of them in the front line, this meant that on starting, the 350s had to thread their way through and in between the 'pushers off' of the smaller class in the front line and, having done that, they had to thread themselves through the accelerating 250s on the run up to the Home Banking. Great fun. Every precaution was taken, of course. The 'pushers off' of the 250 were lectured prior to the start and told to 'stand their ground' once their job was done. That was the sort of thing that was so nice about Brooklands. It could never happen today and was one of the reasons why one went to Brooklands.

Nothing dreadful happened, though, and all got under way, the two fifty class being led by Staniland's Excelsior, chased by Fernihough's similar machine. At first, both were lapping around the same speed, approximately 77 mph, but at half distance Chris put it up a mile an hour and this decided Eric to ease a bit to around 74 mph so as to be sure of second place. This was it, then, till the finish, Staniland winning at 74.34, followed by Eric with three others, Taylor, Bilney and Couper behind them.

In the 350 cc class, Hicks quickly built up a twenty-four second lead over Le Vack and no one else seemed to be in the picture. E.M. Thomas's Rex Acme faded on the Byfleet side of the track and while its pilot was investigating the trouble, the Rex was hit head on by the Chater Lea of A.G. Walker who was really close in. This was always a risk when 'grass cutting' The grass wasn't always cut back as low as it might be and a bike that was 'clipping' it was heeled over so far resulting in the eye level of the driver being so low that visibility was reduced more than one realised. Both bikes were very badly damaged indeed this time, although Walker somehow managed to get around to the pits where it was found that he had a broken arm. A good effort to ride a mile and a half with a broken arm and a good thing he didn't stop – he probably couldn't have anyway for when he did arrive at the pits he coasted into the arms of a knot of officials.

Hicks still led at half way mark followed by Le Vack and Wal Phillips, and had averaged just over ninety at this stage. Le Vack went out, having been lapped and everything looked set for another Velocette win. It wasn't though. The oil tank burst and Phillips's Grindlay Peerless took the lead and held it to the end, winning at 86.69 mph from the Chater Leas of Hopkins and Bickell.

The 600 cc race was, with a few notable exceptions, an almost continuous procession of riders and machinery into and out of the pits.. Nothing is to be gained from listing all the troubles, which seemed to cover every possible part of a racing motor cycle. Only Denly, Le Vack, Ernie Nott (Rudge) and Tommy Bullus (Raleigh) were immune and the Raleigh wasn't fast enough to be in the picture. But Denly was out after 23 laps after setting a blistering pace and this left the race open to Le Vack, who won it followed by Lacey, Nott and Gordon Cobbold. Le Vack's winning speed was 94.85 mph and both he and Gordon must have been pleased with the day's work.

The 1000 cc race? There were five starters and three finishers. Pat Driscoll's 588 cc Norton won it at 87.07 mph after Baldwin's Zenith had made numerous stops for plugs. But it did brighten up a bit towards the end for, at last, Baldwin got the Zenith going and really motored in an effort to pull the fat out of the fire. But it was to no avail and Pat deserved his win.

The 'Mountain' Circuit, with two lots of chicanes, was chosen for the Brooklands Grand Prix in August 1928, the first artificial turn being in the Finishing Straight and the second on the rise up to the banking, after the Paddock. This type of racing was proving popular among both riders and spectators so the entry was good and varied. Staniland won the 250 cc class from Taylor's OK Supreme and Ventura's Cotton, with Fernihough's DOT – JAP in fourth place. It would'nt be true to say that this was Staniland's sort of racing. Chris enjoyed everything provided it was exciting and fast

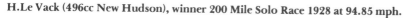

H.Le Vack (496cc New Hudson), winner 200 Mile Solo Race 1928 at 94.85 mph.

and if anything in life came under those headings it was for him. Motorcycles, cars and aircraft – he rose to the top in each – he just couldn't help it. He was certainly the best all rounder I can recall, utterly uncommercial, quietly enthusiastic, a unique man among unusual men. Chris talked in clipped phrases, always with a twinkle in his eye. Never a phrase without humour and often with a double meaning so that it was minutes later that you got round to it. Often with sarcasm too, but it was never unkind sarcasm, always mild and always humerous. It was a great thing to count Chris as a friend and I rated my friendship with him more highly, almost, than anyone I came to know at Brooklands. I never could understand how the Worters – Staniland association worked so well because Woolly and he were so very very different. Both had a keen sense of humour, Woolly's being dry and Chris's willow-the-wisp.

The secret was, of course, that both knew the worth of the other and realised what a splended team they were together, so, to some extent, they must have accepted each other's characteristics although one just couldn't imagine either accepting compromise in any form.

I remember an incident once when, later, both had passed from the bike scene and were after Jim Cobb's Brooklands Outer Circuit lap record, which then stood at 143 mph. The car was the Multi Union, Alfa Romeo based – a brilliant piece of development carried out by Woolly with finanace arranged by Chris.

It had then lapped at over 140 mph and was the second fastest car ever to have gone round Brooklands. After doing this lap, Chris had told Woolly of changes in the set up which he felt should be made. They were big changes and involved hours and hours of detail work and, on the day I was there, everyone, Woolly particularly, was anxious to see what Chris thought of the results. He took the car out and it lapped at just over 141 mph. It returned to the Paddock, swung through the gate with the engine dead and stopped opposite the waiting group. Chris raised his goggles and Woolly took a step forward. Chris shook his head and said 'Hopeless, Woolly'. We all strolled off. It was awful but it was only what he felt at that moment. It took no account at all of the work that had been done and it could have been put so differently, one felt. It was, I suppose, put in the manner he would have adopted after testing a Fairey Battle bomber for, at the time, he was their Test Pilot. But it wasn't the result of the work of a team. It was the hard, grinding work of one man that had gone into the Multi Union that day. But that was Chris.

His death when flying during the war was a tragedy. But I really can't recall anyone who enjoyed life as much as he did or anyone who accepted the possibility of death more readily.

Having won the 250 cc Brooklands Grand Prix, Chris was in the picture again in the 350 cc race. Alec Bennett, Velocette mounted, was the odds-on favourite for this one and, whatever the odds, Alec carried a lot of money that day. But he was out of it at the end of lap one and it was Chris in the lead being chased by Hicks, Taylor, Cobbold and Willis. Velocettes were seriously interested in racing at this time and were spending money on it. Fast as the Worters Excelsior was, it was really under pressure this time. Hicks stopped and this was the spur that Harold Willis needed for, slowly and relentlessly, he cut down Chris' lead and, despite hitting one of the sandbags on lap 18, he got the lead and kept it till the end, the Excelsior being second and Cobbold third.

Not a very exciting 500 cc race. Bennett's Norton made the running for the first half of the race but then began to misfire and was passed by Bernard Hieatt's Cotton Blackburne which won, with Hicks second and H.M. Walters third.

The 350 cc Sidecar Race was better, a wheel to wheel scrap between Hicks and Staniland keeping the crowd on its toes. That was the finishing order and Les Archer's New Imperial outfit was third.

Nine starters for the last one, 600 cc the Sidecar which Tucker led all the way. But Hicks, giving away 250 cc kept him at it throughout. Try as he would, Pat Driscoll could do no better than third. And that was it.

Then, only a fortnight later, it was the Hutchinson '100' again. This time the Worters equipe produced a novelty for the first short handicap, Chris being astride a 173 cc Excelsior. And they nearly pulled it off, too, for the little bike led to within yards of the finish, lapping at nearly eighty – a great speed for a 'baby' at that time. Hicks won again, by half a length at 96.15 mph.

Dicker's Rudge won the next one and then it was Hicks again – at 97.65 mph, but over five laps this time as against the three lap distance of the opening race. Baragwanath's Brough Superior won the Passenger Handicap at 84.84 mph and then they lined up for the 100 mile 'blind'.

There were the usual crop of retirements in this one but no real incident, and in the end, the winner proved to be P. Brewster (495 cc Matchless) and Hicks second and Fernihough's 250 cc Excelsior third, Brewster's winning speed being 93.52 mph.

Brewster was another great Brooklands character, who I never met, although he was popular with everyone. He was a good and consistent rider but I always regarded him more as a tuner and a technical expert. He certainly had the reputation of being a very kind and helpful man and I must tell the only story I can recall about him although I cannot vouch for its truth. He lived, so I was told, in the little village of Peaslake, in Surrey, where he was much liked and respected by his neighbours. One year, in November, there was a rending explosion which did no good at all to the 'Chateau Brewster'. As the horrified villagers rushed to the scene, the great man appeared at the door, blackened and with torn clothes, but still master of the situation 'Back to your cottages, all of you' he shouted. 'Nothing to worry about – just making a few fireworks for the kiddies'. I hope it was true. It seemed to fit the character perfectly.

It was difficult to get the right combination of circumstances for a successful meeting at Brooklands. The weather could be bad, the entry list good, and you could have a good gate. The pre-race publicity wasn't too bad and nothing could be done about the weather anyway. The 1928 Championship Meeting on September 8th was really good entrywise and so was the weather. But the gate was small, which was a pity, because the racing really was good. Maybe the summer holiday period had something to do with it but, whatever the reason, a lot of potential spectators missed some interesting racing.

If Hicks scored a good day at the Grand Prix Meeting, it was nothing to the day he had this time, for he pulled off almost every race entered.

The Worters – Staniland stable set the ball rolling by winning the 250 cc Championship with a lead of 300 yards over the second man and at an average of 78.31 mph. Then Hicks 'got into gear' and began by winning the 350 cc Championship at 96.90 mph from Birch's Chater Lea and Staniland. To set the record straight it should be said that Lacey, the title holder, was unable to defend his crown but even Bill would have had to go some to bear this average which was nearly two and a half miles an hour faster than the winning 1927 speed. Bill's absence was caused by the fact that he'd parted company from the model at over 108 mph when record breaking at Montlhéry and this had come about by his hitting an unlucky Montlhéry bump just at the moment when he had one hand off the bars and was adjusting the steering damper.

The 500 cc Championship and the 350 cc Sidecar Championship both proceeded to fall to the Hicks challenge, the first at 100.41 mph and the second at 78.31 mph, after which he proceeded to win the 3 Lap All Comers Passenger Handicap at 81.37 mph and to come second to Gibson's Sunbeam in the 3 Lap Senior Solo Handicap, ahead of Weslake's Sunbeam, ridden by Cobbold.

In the 600 cc Sidecar Championship Race, Spring's entry was ridden by Driscoll, winning by half a mile at 82.59 mph. Pat then went on to finish second, on the same outfit, to Baragwanath's Brough, winner of the 1000 cc Championship, at 84.56 mph and the only other race, a 3 Lap Junior Solo Handicap was won by Les Archer's 350 cc New Imperial at 87.07 mph.

As if to avenge his enforced absence from the Championship Meeting, Lacey came out strongly at the next one, the Cup Day Meet, but although he won two of the seven races, Staniland won three and was second in another.

Chris set the ball rolling by winning the 350 cc Solo Scratch Race at 88.62 mph and Bill countered by pulling off the 500 cc Scratch at 101.43 mph and the next Handicap at 107.10 mph – a great effort. A Private Owner's Handicap was won by E.M. Thomas's Rex Acme at 90.06 mph.

This was altogether too much for Worters and Staniland who proceeded to annexe the 3 Lap Scratch Race for the Harry Jay Cup and the 5 Lap All Comers Passenger Handicap in quick succession, after which they could really have afforded to rest on their laurels.

They could have but didn't, preferring instead to bring their impudent little 175 cc Excelsior to the line for the Fifty Mile Solo and Sidecar Handicap for the George Newman Cup.

Knowing both Woolly and Chris, one can picture them trying to decide which was the right bike to run in this race. Chris always liked to go as fast as possible and would probably have preferred something larger. But Woolly, whose decision it would have to be, probably chose the 'little 'un' because, in the first place, there would be no problems of passing and because, secondly, the other strings would all have done quite a lot of work that day.

The result of the Fifty Mile Race was that Hopkins won it on his 350 cc Chater Lea and Sidecar at 76.85 mph, Chris was second and Les Archer's 250 cc New Imperial third. But if Woolly and Chris had harboured any illusions that they would be limit men in this one for a change, they were wrong, for Hopkins got 14 mins 15 secs start from the Scratch man, the tiny Excelsior 11 mins 5 secs and Les's New Imperial 9 mins 30 secs.

October 20th marked the last meeting of the 1928 season and, to make his presence known, the Weather Man made sure that heavy rain was the order of the day so that the whole programme had to be delayed, the first race being run off at 2.30 pm. It was a poorly supported meeting – all handicaps, which didn't attract the faster boys, but Pat Driscoll did turn out to win the Three Lap Passenger Handicap at 80.07 mph and scored another first at 79.17 mph while George Tottey also got a win at 78.79 mph, the other winners being W.M. Couper, Gus Grose, F.C. Kirby and Reg Barber. Not a very exciting ending, really, to what had been rather a good season's racing.

Chapter 6

The
1929 Season

In many ways, the opening meeting of each season was often the best, mainly because there was so much that had changed during the winter. For those in 'residence', the usual pattern was that, immediately the track was usable, testing began, usually in early March, the machinery being ready 'for use' a fortnight or three weeks later.

Then the 'home counties' riders would start to arrive for what was, to them, some early testing and this would normally be in mid-March. A few Northerners would turn up prior to the first official practice but most of them waited for the first meeting, for there were no motorways in those days and the run down was long and slow so that one day's practice really amounted to the loss of nearly a week's work when travelling had been taken into account. It was a good time for all – new riders, old riders with re-hashed machinery, old riders with fresh machinery and sometimes old riders who had changed allegiance to another make.

It didn't always work out that way, though, and it certainly didn't in 1929 for, only two days prior to the opening meeting on March 24th, the track was nowhere near ready and poor George Reynolds, then Secretary of the BMCRC was almost tearing his hair out with worry. But feverish work was put in and, in the end, everything was alright, although only just.

The principal interest at this meeting centred round the Spring-Denly stable for, during the winter the equipe had left Nortons and had contracted themselves to AJS, the result being a really superb stable of beautifully turned out race machinery. It consisted of four 'units', 346 cc, 495 cc and 743 cc solos and a 598 cc sidecar outfit – all single overhead camshaft models, all the frames and running gear being chrome plated – a superb turnout and a real shot in the arm for the Brooklands motorcycle racing scene. Interest centred particularly round the giant 743 cc single and this was, on the face of it, a well thought out choice aimed at the 1000 cc class races in which the retirement proportion had been so big and the finishing speeds appallingly low.

Unfortunately, the 350 was a non-starter at the opening meeting, the trouble being that, since the front fork spring was too strong for Denly's light weight, the handling had suffered, so, once again, Hicks's Velocette won the 350 cc Scratch Race, ahead of Bickell and Archer.

C.J. Williams's Raleigh won the 500 cc Scratch Race from Hicks at 98.43 mph, as compared with Hicks's winning speed of 90.39 in the previous race. Hicks must have picked up more places running in races out of his class than anyone else one would think. Velocettes were rather good at this – the pattern came to be repeated, years later, by Les Archer when, after Hicks's tragic death in the Isle of Man, he took over from him the Velocette mantle.

Frewin's Raleigh won the Private Owner's Handicap at 88.15 mph – a good speed for a 350 cc Raleigh – and it was good to see two first places scored by Raleighs. Cliff Lewis, later to become Secretary of the BMCRC, won the next one on his little 172 cc Baker Villiers, at 63.68 mph and then came the 1000 cc Three Lap Handicap, in which Wright was to ride the big Zenith. It was good to see Joe back on his old love and results proved that he had been right to go back to it for he not only won it convincingly but also broke the lap record at a speed of 113.71 mph to average 106.88 mph for the race. Denly won his first ride on the big 743 cc single cylinder AJS in this race, receiving nine seconds start from Joe in three laps and finishing third behind Loweth's Norton.

Two more handicaps followed and finally, the meeting was brought to a close with the 1100 cc 3 Lap Passenger Handicap which had three starters only and was won by Horsman at 84.84 mph, with Baragwanath second and Denly third.

A modest beginning for the new AJS stable, it must be admitted. But an awful lot had been learned and by the time the April meeting came along, they had done much

J.S. Wright (996cc Zenith JAP). Winner Race 3 at the April 1929 Meeting at 111.52 with a Record Lap at 117.19. Second in Race 4 averaging 112.33 with a new Lap Record of 118.96 mph.

homework and were ready to put it into practice. The irrepressible Hicks certainly won the 350 cc Scratch Race easily, from the AJS but, for a 350, the three lap average from a standing start – 99.14 mph – was fantastic and if Hicks was going to be able to put up this sort of performance it would be a long time before anyone would beat him.

But even this great performance was overshadowed in the next Handicap, which Wright won at an average of 115.52 mph, lapping at no less than 117.19 mph on his second time round.

Fernihough and Archer, both from the 1 min 30 sec mark finished first and second in the next Handicap, followed by Denly's 350 cc AJS from the eighteen second mark, with Cobbold fourth.

Baragwanath won the Five Lap Passenger Handicap from the scratch mark at 92.06 mph, Bert being second this time with the 600 cc sidecar outfit and Horsman third, but Bert then proceeded to pull off the next one with his giant single – a 90 mph Handicap – at 94.86 mph, after which Eggleton's 250 cc OK Supreme won the other Private Owners' Handicap at 74.11 mph.

The meeting ended with a Fifty Mile Race for the J.A. Prestwich Cup – another Scratch Race in which Denly, Lacey, Hicks and Williams all started but Lacey was soon out of it with handling bothers attributed, in one report, to incorrect wheel alignment. Something very wrong about this because Bill never lined up wheels wrongly – I must take it up with him when we next talk.

The scrap in this race was between Williams and Denly, the latter shadowing the Raleigh throughout till, when two laps from the finish, its primary chain broke so that the immaculate Spring AJS won at 99.40 mph.

May 4th and it was the 200 miles Sidecar Races again, poorly supported in terms of members although there was nothing lacking in quality.

At first the 350 cc Race was led by Handley on one of Spring's AJSs, followed by Cobbold, who had forsaken his faithful Sunbeam for an OK Supreme, with Staniland third on a Worters-entered Excelsior. Worters other entry, ridden by M.V. McCudden, retired with engine trouble on lap nine and Johnston's Rex outfit went out with a broken sidecar connection. At quarter distance Handley still led, followed by Cobbold and Staniland, with Freddie Hicks watching it all from behind. Poor Les Archer, who had been going well, now ran into trouble after trouble – carburettor, plug, magneto – you name them, Les had them all that day.

Cobbold's fine run ended with a broken magneto platform and, halfway, it was Hicks at 71.15 mph, Handley at 71.14 mph and Chris, in his first long distance ride for Worters, at 70.49 mph – all close stuff. The finish was closer, for Handley went out with a broken inlet valve spring which let the valve drop so that it was the Velocette which led the Excelsior home, their respective speeds being 70.70 and 70.69 mph respectively – and with fifteen yards between them. One would suspect that Hicks could have pulled quite a bit out if necessary and that Chris probably could have as well. Both were loaded with trackcraft and both will have known what was the sensible thing to do.

At quarter distance, Horsman, Denly and Tucker – all very close together – led the 600s but, with half the race gone, Denly led at just under 80 mph, while Vic was now third. But only a few minutes later Denly's gearbox mainshaft sheared coming off the Home Banking and, a lap or two later, the sidecar wheel spindle of the Triumph broke, which must have given Vic a nasty end to the race and let Tucker cruise home to

G.H. Tucker (588cc Norton). Winner 200 Mile, 600cc Sidecar Race 1929 at 70.95 mph.

win at 70.95 mph followed by A.J. Dussek's Norton.

One little story here, concerning a tuner who, it was said, at one time, prepared engines for Driscoll. Again, I can't vouch for its truth although I did check it with Chris after it was told to me. The rumour – I'd rather call it that – was that, for some reason, Driscoll felt unhappy with the performance of an engine and changed allegiance to a rival tuner, the first boffin then taking on work for Chris. The three then met on the start line and, just before the start, the first tuner turned to Chris with the words 'Well, good luck Staniland' and, thinking that wasn't pointed enough, swung round to Driscoll with 'As for you Driscoll, I hopes you breaks your bloody neck', whereupon Chris quipped 'Well said, Jim, a fine sporting phrase'.

In the 1000 cc Race Driscoll's 588 cc Norton lined up with an assortment of JAP-engined twins, the engine capacities of which were variously quoted at 976, 980, 986 and 996 cc. Whatever the capacity, it did them no good, for the single ran steadily throughout to win at 77.78 mph from Baldwin's Zenith, Longman's Brough Superior being still a runner at the end but outside the time limit. On the face of it, the big single AJS could have done well in this one but troubles were being experienced with engine balance at the time, and this produced vibration. And vibration of any sort was the kiss of death in a race of this length, of course.

Good weather, a fair crowd but not very exciting racing at the next meeting held on

June 1st, although there were some highlights – and some light relief.

Staniland won the 350 cc Scratch Race by 300 yards at 92.74 mph and Lacey lapped at nearly 108 mph to head the 500s home. On the line, at the start, Denly discovered that he had only top gear but, having two very strong pushers, he decided to have a go. Start it they did, so that he ran home second to Bill. Rather brave of him, really, for it isn't a good thing to know that, somewhere in the box, two spare gears are floating around and that, even if they can't engage, there could always be a bit of broken selector to lock the whole thing up.

Wright shone again, breaking the lap record twice at 118.86 mph but the race was won by Gus Grose at 93.97 mph by three yards. Dreadful for Joe, after taking all those risks and demonstrating so much skill. Why anyone ever bothered to ride fast bikes in handicaps at Brooklands is a mystery still unexplained.

Cobbold won the Five Lap Passenger Handicap with his OK Supreme at 72.71 mph followed home by Archer's New Imperial and then came the last race – a 50 Mile Handicap.

The programme was running a bit late at this stage for the light relief at this meeting had been provided by a swan which, after being startled by an aircraft, had become airborne and, in circling, had hit the telephone wires where it hung precariously before falling, wounded, onto the track. Races couldn't be started with such a hazard pending and it was some time before the problem swan was caught and taken to the first aid post.

Lacey's 500 cc Grindlay Peerless was on scratch in the fifty mile event but Bill came through the lot to win at 103.76 mph, ahead of Fernihough and Horsman, and this pleased everyone and particularly 'Ebby' who had set him to average exactly this speed.

The only good thing about the Grand Prix Meetings held on June 22nd was the success enjoyed by the Worters stable for, this time, Chris was partnered by Bernard Hieatt. Between them, they had a field day, setting the ball rolling by finishing first and second in the 350 cc Solo race. Hieatt, riding a 350 cc Cotton, then went on to take second place to Walters' 500 cc Sunbeam JAP in the 500 cc race and Chris countered by winning the 350 cc Sidecar class from Archer, dotting the 'i' to bring the same 350 cc outfit home in third place in the 600 cc class, behind Tucker and Driscoll, both on Nortons, although Pat's outfit was described as a Norton Driscoll Special.

There is no doubt at all that, over the years, J.S. Worters was the most successful man ever to be involved in racing motorcycles at Brooklands because you have to take into account the fact that he had a long successful span as a rider before retiring to manage. Quite apart from the many race wins and places he and, later, his riders notched up at nearly every Brooklands meeting, the number of long and short distance records broken by Woolly and, later by his team, far exceeds that of any other participant – it is enormous.

On to the 200 Mile Solo Race Meeting of 1929 and some surprises in the bigger classes. The Worters equipe notched up a One-Two success in the 250 cc class with Staniland and Hewitt's Excelsiors heading Fernihough's similar machine home – race average 79.26 mph – there being only twenty yards between first and second man.

A huge retirement rate occurred in the 350 cc Race, so big that at one point Secretary George Reynolds was heard to call to the lap scorers in the score box 'There are enough retirement cards for all of 'em if you need them'. But Denly led it

Eric Fernihough (246cc Excelsior) later riding Brough Superior, to become first to lap Brooklands at over 120 mph on two wheels.

throughout and averaged 89.20 mph without trouble on Spring's lovely AJS, and was cruising towards the end. Viewing's Zenith and Ashton's Chater Lea were second and third respectively.

One had come to think of long distance races in the 500 cc class as the special preserve of Horsman, Denly or Lacey but this time it was Ernie Nott's Rudge that put the cat among the pigeons. Ernie led from the start while Bill played a waiting game until there was a lap between them, whereupon he turned it up and, for some time, they circulated together. Bill came in to refuel at half distance and, a few laps later was in again, this time to retire with a broken steering damper anchor plate. From then on it was Nott's race and he went on to win at 100.07 mph – a great average for a race of that distance in the late twenties and a very well deserved success.

The 1000 cc Race was alternately dull, comic and rather sad but never exciting. There were five starters, the race being led at first by Wright and Baldwin, followed by Reg Barber's 598 cc Matchless. This was the form until half distance, the three being followed by Pat Driscoll's Norton. Wright dropped out with a sudden silence at 41 laps and Pat became rather more interested, passing Barber and getting to within fifteen seconds of Baldwin, where he stayed for some time before taking the lead. There was a bit of place changing between them and then Baldwin came in on the 68th lap with a bent exhaust valve. He took off his crash helmet to retire but was urged by his pit to 'finish on one' so, replacing his hat and removing the front plug, he completed the last three laps to finish second. Not second to Driscoll, though, for poor Pat had had to pull out with a seriously injured foot, smashed by a lump of flying concrete, so that Barber was victor, averaging 90.64 mph to Baldwin's 89.02 mph. Yes, one never knew what was going to happen in these races, particularly among the 'big 'uns'!

A fortnight later, Spring and Denly took the 500 cc AJS to Montlhéry for records, returning with:

1 Hour	104.51 mph
2 Hours	101.26 mph
100 Miles	104.52 mph
200 Miles	101.23 mph

A worthwhile trip.

The September Brooklands meeting was very hot indeed and very unexciting, to the extent that many of the spectators just couldn't decide whether to be spectators at all, preferring to sit it out and listen to the broadcast of the Schneider Trophy Air Races, under the pine trees on the Members Hill. 'Bemsee' Secretary George Reynolds, even, was an absentee for, as one of a very few qualified timekeepers in the country, he was roasting down at Ryde, timing the air race.

To keep the record complete, we must chronicle this meeting but the only highlight about it was the reason for F.C. Kirby's Sunbeam retiring in the Private Owner's Handicap. Many many different reasons were given for retirements at Brooklands but Mr. Kirby had a new one here. It was the truth and I never heard it quoted as a reason for retirement again. A wasp settled with its forelegs on the terminal of Kirby's plug and its bum on the body of the plug. Effectively, it earthed it and it stayed there for proof. Beat that if you can – it happened on the right day and gave everyone something to talk about.

The racing? Hewitt won the first one on Worter's 250 cc Excelsior at 86.46 mph, with Archer and Cobbold second and third respectively. McCudden's 350 from the same stable was second to Werts's Rex Acme and ahead of Archer in the 350 cc race, and these two races were followed by three more unthrilling ones.

Then came the two Passenger Handicaps, the first being won by McCudden, with Cobbold second and Archer third, and the second by Horsman, followed by Baragwanath and, again, Cobbold.

Apart from the fact that it must have marked Cobbold as the 'eternal placeman', for he was third again, the last handicap, won by Lones's Morgan, was on a par with the rest. Not much of a day, really, apart from the social side.

The October 5th Meeting was better, for it was two meetings, Championship and Cup Day, rolled into one, the former being run off in the morning and the scraps for the Cups taking place in the afternoon.

Staniland made a bright start to the meeting for, as reigning Champion, he retained his title, putting the speed up from 78.31 to 84.27 mph. Lacey, Denly and McCudden were the favourites for the 350 cc Championship and this was the order in which they finished, Bill's average being the splendid one of 102.69 mph, but Bert reversed this in the 500 cc race, winning it from Bill at 106.72 mph with a best lap of 111.42 mph. Much, much better.

The bookies were laying three to one on Lacey for the 1000 cc and must have caught a cold because Bill won it at 106.19 mph after Wright faded so, at least, there were some happy punters around!

Sidecar Champions? Staniland won the 350 cc race at 77.93 mph with Denly and Cobbold supporting. Denly won the 600 cc at 82.59 mph chased home so hard by Tucker and Driscoll that he made it by only ten yards. Tucker won the 1000 cc race from Driscoll by 250 yards at 84.13 mph.

An afternoon of handicap races followed a morning of scratch races. The 250 cc event went to Viewing, Reynolds and Staniland in that order at a speed of 83.00 mph. In the 350 cc Race it was Viewing again, McCudden and Werts at 88.62 mph. The Private Owners Race was won by Packman, Howell and Welch at 85.87 mph and the 90 mph Handicap by P.M. Walters, Denly and Barber at 91.89 mph. The Five Lap Passengers Race went to Tucker, Johnston and Baragwanath at 84.84 mph.

This left only the Wakefield Cup, the first heat of which was won by Barber and the second by Hieatt. For a long time it looked as though the final would be won by Fernihough, whose 250 cc Excelsior had started from the 2 mins 30 secs mark but, on the final run in, Eric was swamped by Hieatt, Barber and Clifton, Hieatt's winning speed being 91.72 mph. Poor Eric. Small bikes were horrible things to ride in handicaps. You led to within inches of the finish and then, when convinced that you've made it, this sort of thing happened. It was far more fun catching them up on a 'big 'un' – at least you could see the problem that confronted you.

Four rather run-of-the-mill handicaps preceded the Hutchinson '100', always a classic but also a difficult race to follow. In fact, this one was more than usually difficult because while Lacey's Grindlay Peerless was on the scratch mark, the limit man, Jack King riding a 172 cc Zenith Villiers, was receiving from him no less than 42 min 33 secs start. Jack King, incidentally, was an employee of Pat Driscoll and was Pat's number one passenger in short and long distance sidecar races. He stayed almost constantly on the motor racing scene and subsequently became a valued maintenance man and pit member of the post-war Aston Martin motor racing team. I think this must have been one of his first races and certainly the first long distance ride.

As with previous 'Hutch's' there were numerous pit calls for plug changes and fuel bothers and quite a lot of troubles that were more serious, but it soon became obvious that three fast bikes were coming up well from among the back markers. They were Gibson's 350 cc Sunbeam, A.R. Quinn's Triumph and Hieatt's 498 cc Zenith and, even at this point, it became clear that if all three kept going, there would be nothing else to beat them. Hieatt, in fact, won his 'Gold Star' in this race with a lap of over 104 mph and this must have been some consolation for having to retire later, with victory almost in sight. Even in the nineteen thirties a 'Gold Star' was much coveted and was awarded, in each class, to riders who had lapped at over the 'magic century'. Treasured as it was, the star wasn't gold – it was a very thin tiny brass star enamelled on the front with the figures '100' and with the recipient's name engraved on the back and it attached to the ordinary BMCRC member's badge at the base. In the 1920's it was rewarding to win a Gold Star on a 1,000, good to get one on a 500 and very good indeed to win it for a three figure lap on a 350. In the thirties, not many people were riding 1000s so this list didn't get much bigger. 500 cc stars became two a penny just before the war but 350 cc laps at over 100 mph were still few and far between. Although my own '1000 cc' Star came along in 1934 and the '500 cc' Star in 1936, I did numerous 99 mph laps on different 350s, including one or two at 99.99 mph but never one at over the 'ton'. There was also a 'Double Gold Star', a more elaborate affair for a bike lap at over 120 mph of which, I think, only two were awarded, one to Noel Pope and one to Eric Fernihough, both Outer Circuit lap record holders of their periods and both Brough Superior mounted.

The outcome of the 1929 Hutchinson '100' was that Gibson won it with his Sunbeam at 85.33 mph, Quinn was second and F.L. Hall's little New Imperial third. That concluded the 1929 season and we now enter the final year of our story.

A.L. (Lance) Loweth (498cc Norton JAP), a consistent performer. Lapped the track at over 90 mph on a 490cc side valve Norton.

Chapter 7

The 1930 Season

The 1930 season of motorcycle racing at Brooklands came in not with a bang, not with a roar, but with an ear splitting crash. Nothing, in fact, had ever been seen like it at the track before and it certainly was never seen again. True, it was the usual wet weather and rather depressing day but the opening meeting of 1930 was sponsored by *The Motor Cycle*, one of those two wonderful weekly journals that has done so much for motorcycling in all its forms right back from the very early years.

This was a clear demonstration of the power of the press for, taking this one meeting under its wing, *The Motor Cycle* made a pre-meeting offer to its readers of admission to Brooklands at very special rates. The result was that, instead of the usual spectator attendance of some hundreds or possible a few thousands, Brooklands was literally swamped by the most gigantic crowd ever seen at any meeting held there, car or motor cycle, before or since.

The offer was admission for 1/3d, half the usual admission fee and free admission for his machine to every motorcyclist who came to watch and who presented a coupon that could be clipped out of the 'The Motor Cycle' dated 3rd April 1930. The same applied to sidecar owners who produced a second coupon for their passengers. Cycles were free and cars 3/- each. All this was heavily publicised in many issues of the magazine prior to the meeting.

The result was that almost the entire British motorcycle movement must have turned up – 25,000 people it was believed, although no one ever really knew how many for, long after the car parks were filled to bursting point, the roads inside the track and finally, the approach roads to Brooklands itself, became a solid static mess of vehicles and humanity. The entrance gates quickly ran out of tickets and shut up shop but the crowd still streamed in throughout the morning. When traffic stopped moving, they parked their vehicles at the roadside and walked. They couldn't be refused admittance – they all had their coupons but there was nowhere – literally nowhere – to house that number of people. When they could no longer get into the enclosures, they jammed the link roads and when these were filled there was only one other place for them and it was there they went so – pulling down the railings they climbed up behind the bankings and sat and stood there four deep.

Nothing like it had ever been seen before and such a reaction caught everybody with their pants down. The Weybridge residents must have been close to heart failure for – to give just one example – the one mile journey from Weybridge station to the track was taking, throughout the day, two hours by car. Complete chaos.

The only surprise to most people was that the meeting was held at all, so great was the risk of an appalling accident involving the spectators on top of the bankings for those at the front, as it were, were being pushed off the edge and some were involuntarily sliding down, all the time, fighting for a foothold so that they could get back.

Fortunately, most of the riders were experienced hands and didn't need to be told of the risks involved – the merest amateur could see them. So, crossing their fingers, the Club, watched by trembling officials of the ACU, went ahead and ran off the meeting.

One lap sprints opened the programme and resulted in –

	250 cc	*350 cc*	*500 cc*
1st	C.S. Staniland (Rex Acme)	B.L. Hieatt (Rex Acme)	A. Denly (AJS)
2nd	E.C. Fernihough (Excelsior)	C.S. Staniland (Zenith)	L. Hawthorn (Cotton)
3rd	L.J. Archer (New Imperial)	A. Denly (AJS)	B.L. Hieatt (Excelsior)
Speed	78.43 mph	83.14 mph	90.88 mph

This was a good start because no one needed much banking on a standing lap, and the crowd was, perhaps able to get some idea of what racing was like at the track for a lot of them must have been seeing it for the first time.

Next, a Three Lap Handicap up to 350 cc which Chris won at 95.59 mph and then a Match Race – car versus motorcycle – between Jack Dunfee's Ballot and Ernie Nott's Rudge, won by Ernie at 99.61 mph.

Next, a complete innovation for Brooklands, a Relay Race between the Red, Blue and Yellow Teams which consisted of –

Red   W.J.C. Hewitt, 348 cc Zenith, B.L. Hieatt, 498 cc Zenith, C.S. Staniland, 498 cc Excelsior sidecar

Blue   C.B. Nickell, 348 cc, Chater Lea, Gus Grose, 499 cc Rudge, G.H. Tucker 588 cc Norton sidecar.

Yellow   H.G. Birch, 348 cc Chater Lea, R.R. Barber, 498 cc Matchless, E.C. Baragwaneth, 998 cc Brough Sidecar

This proved to be the success of the day. Hewitt, Bickell and Birch fought the first lap, all three overshooting the finish line and losing time in the process.

Hieatt, Grose and Barber took over and, although the Red (Worters) team held its slender lead, Grose gained a lead over Barber on this lap, making a perfect pull up, although Hieatt overshot slightly which put the three teams almost level.

The Yellow team was now out of it but there was a great scrap between Tucker and Staniland, ending in victory for Woolly's Red Team by a machine's length, at an average of 77.33 mph. A really good idea and the crowd loved it.

There followed a rather mediocre handicap and, after that, a Match Race for the 600 cc sidecar outfits of Horsman and Tucker, which was perhaps the best event of the day, for both contestants decided not to wait for 'Ebby' but to start, anyway. They did so and what appeared to be a very good match race ensued, Tucker winning at 76.97 mph so presumably someone in the timing box was sufficiently 'with it' to click a watch on seeing the runners leave the line.

By now, the whole thing was taking on rather a circus atmosphere, which nobody minded, and it was announced that Joe Wright would make an attack on the Outer Circuit lap record on Claude Temple's supercharged OEC. A van went out, bearing the machine and stopped on the Railway Straight, disgorging a machine which subsequently turned out to be, not the OEC but a supercharged Zenith which, in the event, did a few laps, misfiring badly before returning to its base, the van.

At this point there was some delay, followed by an announcement that the record attempt had been abandoned, and saying that a 3 Lap Passenger Handicap would be run off. This was done but, in the middle of it, Wright suddenly appeared, travelling fast, apparently with the idea of having a go at the record after all. Some lack of liason here and it must have been a surprise to the sidecar boys, providing a bit of light relief too.

Finally, the meeting ended with a Match Race between Baragwanath, Loweth and Staniland which was won by Chris at 99.90 mph, after which the huge crowd did its best to get unravelled and leave for home.

What it all proved, as far as Brooklands was concerned, was anyone's guess. Certain it was that a better day's entertainment had been enjoyed by more people than ever before at the track and in the words of today's maxim 'that couldn't be bad'. It wasn't Brooklands but, in many ways, it was better.

Later, it was announced by the track authorities that since many more thousands had had to be turned back without gaining admission, they really didn't know how many people had turned up and, later still, Percy Bradley, Clerk of the Course issued the following apology via the columns of *The Motor Cycle*.

Sir,

If you would be so good as to allow me a little space in your valuable journal, I would like to take the opportunity of making an apology to your readers for any inconvenience they were caused through the delay that took place in getting through the gates at Brooklands last Saturday. Although I know that **The Motor Cycle** *is a very widely read journal, I must confess that the Brooklands Authorities were not quite prepared for such a colossal number of visitors, especially on a wet day. The power of the Press, particularly* **The Motor Cycle** *was underestimated so that a certain amount of congestion occurred. I am sure however, that the skill of the competitors as shown at this meeting repaid any inconvenience that was occasioned. I must congratulate* **The Motor Cycle** *on the keenness of it's readers and also for the very sporting instincts they displayed during the wait outside the entrance.*

Yours faithfully,
A. Percy Bradley

There was another amusing half page item in the same issue of *The Motor Cycle*, headed 'The Brooklands crowd seen from the air' –

'Originally, it was with the idea of making a bird's-eye study of riding tactics that a member of *The Motor Cycle* staff took the air in a Moth from the Flying School. It was an interesting idea but was, unfortunately marred by the necessity of flying on the outside of the track at about 500 feet (low flying round the track during a meeting is, of course, neither desirable nor encouraged).

But, if it failed in fulfilling its original object, it succeeded in another direction. Mist-shrouded glimpses of the amazing spectacle of crowded Brooklands and its parking facilities so hopelessly overtaxed made a memorable sight. The inadequate entrances were still endeavouring to unleash a traffic block extending nearly quarter of a mile up towards Weybridge Station. And this at 4 o'clock, or nearly two hours after the first race. Motorcycles, sidecars and cars could be clearly seen parked anyhow on the grass verge at the roadside all the way up the road from the main entrance to the station, their owners seemingly having given up the idea of getting them through the jam.

And then there were the cheery crowds which lined the track, two and three deep on top of the Members Banking right down to the Railway Straight, waving encouragement to those who were endeavouring to climb the banking in between the races: the Fork with its dark mass of humanity crowding on to the track by the start; the Member's Hill, normally one of the quietest spots, black rimmed with people; and finally the long line of folk who were watching the racing on the stretch towards the Byfleet Banking.

The 350 cc – 1000 cc Handicap was watched from the air and it was amusing to note the way in which the riders' heads bobbed mechanically up and down. The Moth was badly beaten down the Railway Straight by L. Hawthorn (498 Cotton Blackburne) and A.L. Loweth (490 Norton) who, as they streaked along, made the smaller capacity machines look as though they were standing still. Brooklands seems to infect the upper regions, for, as the little Moth nosed towards the landing ground, three lovely bumps reminded *The Motor Cycle* man that the Fork was immediately underneath.'

So, just where did all this get us or, rather, where did it get Brooklands? The answer, I'm afraid, was – nowhere. Nothing seemed to be done to follow up this clear indication that there were crowds ready to come to Brooklands if Brooklands wanted them. What should have been done to get them there again?

In the first place, I think two things had been learned. First that the public would come to Brooklands if the conditions were right and, second, that if Brooklands did want bigger crowds they would have to do something about traffic and crowd control.

One has to bear in mind that the BMCRC adminstered and ran the motorcycling racing side on behalf of the Brooklands authorities who, themselves, were only really interested in the car side. But the lessons learned here could so easily have been applied to the car side and since *The Motor Cycle* was owned by Iliffes the publishers, and Iliffes also owned *The Autocar*, the way was open for the Brooklands management to approach Iliffes via *The Autocar* and come to some arrangement to do something similar car-wise. Not, necessarily, the same thing again but, since the power of the press had been so clearly demonstrated here, some long term plan to publicise Brooklands and make it more attractive to people who would go there if the programmes and circumstances were right. But nothing was done on these lines and one can only assume that the authorities didn't really want big gates but preferred to stick to their old, outdated, and almost snobbish slogan 'The Right Crowd and no Crowding'.

Once again, the 200 Mile Sidecar Race programme was run off on May 4th and with it came tragedy, J. S. Worter's entry in the 600 cc Class – Bernard Hieatt – being killed when, just after half distance, he had been leading the race.

It was a bad day for the Worters stable. Particularly bad since, at half distance in both races, the equipe's entries headed the field and, in the 350 cc race, occupied second place as well.

In the 350 cc race, Staniland led all the way and, at half distance, was followed by Hewitt and Hicks, the latter riding an AJS for the first time instead of his now familiar Velocette.

With the halfway mark passed, Hewitt went out with a seized engine and this put Hicks in a secure second place. With twelve laps of the race still to be run, Staniland come in to have a loose silencer fixed, when still in the lead. The repair was made and he was away again, only to drop out a few laps later with a broken exhaust rocker. This left only four runners in the hunt and meant that Hicks could cruise home to win, which he did at 73.12 mph followed by Evan's Cotton and Packman's Zenith, both well astern of him.

At first, the 600 cc race was led by Tucker, followed by Denly and Hieatt but, at the 30 lap mark Tucker, who had refuelled early, came in with a flat rear tyre, which put Bert in the lead. Hieatt then began to put on the pressure in weather conditions that had been bad throughout the race and were steadily worsening. He caught him and led the race at half distance, averaging 82.13 to Denly's 81.75 mph. Bert went out with trouble that was unspecified, putting Hieatt in an undisputed position ahead of Horsman, who was a lap to the bad. Tucker had got going again and was now third but soon he, too was out of it with engine trouble, his place being taken by L. G. Emerson's Norton outfit.

Hieatt who, like everyone else in the race, had complained about visibility when at his pit, now left the track on coming off the Byfleet Banking, the outfit hitting the fence and its rider being killed instantly although his passenger, Matthews, miraculously escaped with minor injuries.

Horsman now took over and led to the finish, averaging 75.33 mph, with Emerson second and M. E. Davenport's Excelsior third. It was a tragic ending to what had been, till then, a good race, despite the appalling weather conditions.

Hieatt's death, despite its tragedy, was only the second motorcycle fatality since Brooklands had opened in 1909 and the first since 1912. I may be wrong but I do not recall another fatal accident to a motorcyclist at Brooklands after this and, if that is the case, the track certainly had a wonderful record from that point of view.

In the 1000 cc class of the 1930 200 Mile Sidecar Races, four singles and four twins came to the line and it was Driscoll's 588 cc Norton outfit that led for the first twelve laps before retiring on the thirteenth. J. M. Waterman's big twin Coventry Eagle then took the lead with Brewster's Norton second and P. M. Walter's 996 cc Zenith third. Baldwin, who had been riding Spring's giant single cylinder AJS – the first and only time, I think, that he ever rode a single – went out with 'things wrong generally' and, at half distance Waterman still led ahead of Walters and Baragwanath.

There were one or two changes in the order of these three between half distance and the end of the race but this was the order in which they finally finished, Waterman's average for the race working out at 74.50 mph. Quite something to have big twins occupying all three places at the end of a 200 Mile Race.

Poor fields, stylish riding and one good finish were the order of the day at the 1930 Grand Prix Meeting on June 1st.

In the 250 cc Class there were no non-starters and, for the first time, Fernihough headed Staniland for 16 of the 22 laps before hitting a sandbag and putting a spectacular end to his ride. Eric must have been wild about this. He hated 'parting company' more than anyone and loathed damaging the machinery. And he always rode with his head, too, much preferring a secure second or third place to having a prang when trying to stay better placed in a race. No doubt Chris was pushing him hard and enjoying the sight of him hurrying, although he would have been just as sorry as anyone to see his ride end 'on the floor'. Anyway, it was Chris's race and the New Imperials of Archer and Jones filled the places.

Eric, when asked for his reasons for non-starting in the 350 cc race said 'The Dear Firm, when it lent me the models, which are to go over to the Island for the TT on Monday, implored me not to bend them; Well, now I have bent the 250 and I'm not taking any chances with t'other'. So the 350 cc race became a battle between George Rowley on an AJS entered by Nigel Spring and Staniland's Worters-entered Excelsior, George finally getting it, Chris finishing second with Ben Bickell's Chater Lea third. Surprising in a way because Chris was so good at everything he did. But so was George. A much much better rider than anyone realised as I found to my cost in the 1935 Brooklands Grand Prix. On this occasion I was riding Les Archer's Velocette in the Junior and was pressed for third place for the whole hundred miles by George, whose works 'Ajay' was much slower than Les's privately owned Velo so that, in the end I only managed to scrape into third spot by a margin of one second – with Les on the works machine winning – and five minutes before we arrived, too.

Little wonder, then, that George also pulled off the 500 cc race in 1930, still aboard his 350 and at an average 2 mph slower than he put up in the 350 class. Yes, he was shrewd, too. There was no point in going faster than one had to.

The 600 Sidecar Race became a duel between Driscoll and Staniland, which ended when Chris retired although Pat nearly lost it before that when, overshooting a turn on the first lap, he all but found himself minus his passenger who, probably didn't think much of that. But they won it, in the end, from Archer and Freddie Brackpool's Matchless. The day's racing was ended with a Three Lap Winner's Handicap, which Bickell won from Rowley and Brackpool.

A small meeting, consisting solely of handicaps, was run off on June 16th, but most of the bright lights were in the Island by now and it produced nothing of excitement although the Worters stable did well, Staniland getting a first and a third and McCudden a first and a second. Archer, too, got a first and a second and, after only two seasons at the track, was now a name to be reckoned with.

By now it was clear that the spectators liked watching Grand Prix type racing and the Club put on another of these events in August, well supported by both riders and with quite a big crowd and good weather as well. The racing was good but one would have thought that, by now, the viewers would have liked to see the boys performing on another permutation of circuit, which could have been done with no alternative whatever to the sandbagged turns but simply by routing the runners to turn left at the end of the Finishing Straight and taking them anti-clockwise down the Railway Straight and round the Byfleet Banking, rejoining the Finishing Straight at its start. It would have given a much longer circuit and speeds much higher than the rather pathetic sounding '50' odd mile an hour of the winners to date.

But the same old circuit was used again, the highest winning speed being Hicks's who won both the 350 cc and 500 cc events, the latter at 60.31 mph, and the lowest, Archer in the Winner's Handicap – 49.68 mph. To see these speeds in cold print gave really no idea of how different it all looked in the flesh and must have done nothing at all to get new spectators to come along and have a look. Staniland won the 250 cc and 600 cc Sidecar and, this time, there was a race for three wheelers which Maskell's Morgan won from Lones.

As if to make quite certain that nothing whatever should go right for poor old Brooklands, the Weather Department laid on a show on September 13th that positively ensured that the programme of 200 Mile Solo races, if started, should certainly not be allowed to be completed. No doubt with the thought of the fatal accident in the 200 Mile Sidecar race still in their minds, the authorities did start the meeting, but wisely abandoned it after the 175 cc, 250 cc and 350 cc races had been run, postponing the 600 cc and 1000 cc events till September 24th.

The Committee of the Club probably had a double problem on their hands this time. They were certainly faced with the problem of insufficient entries and they will possibly have been racking their brains to think of something on the lines of an innovation to make the motorcycle racing scene more interesting at Brooklands.

The bright idea they had at this point – to include a class for 175 ccs – may have done something to solve the first part of the conundrum but it did very little towards the second for only five 'Tiddlers' turned out and while they probably gave their owners a day's fun, they can have done nothing for the poor spectators and could well have been a bit of a nuisance to the faster machinery circulating at the same time. For the first half hour, they were alone on the track while the 250s and 350s waited their turn to join in.

To begin with, Deller (Baker Villiers) led the buzzing procession followed by Jack King on Pat Driscoll's Zenith Villiers and by Meeten's Francis Barnett. Meeten, of course, was and always had been the Villiers king and, at the time, held many long distance records on Francis Barnetts so it was logical to assume that when and if the end came, he wouldn't be far away. Deller retired with a broken fuel pipe and Horsman (G.E. – not Vic) filled third place and he and Meeten began to eat up King's lead. They finally managed to do it so that, in the end, the Francis Barnett won at 54.36 mph with Horsman's Zenith Villiers second.

Staniland played a crafty waiting game in the 250 cc race, sitting behind Longman and Archer and content to stay there and let the New Imperial make the pace for as long as it took or until he felt it was time to take over. Longman was out of it before the race reached the half way mark and it was at this point that Chris began to stir things up a bit, catching and passing Les and slowly pulling out a lead which, at the end of the race amounted to nearly twelve minutes. Speed 78.02 mph.

The 350 cc race marked both the first appearance of the new radial four valve Rudge ridden by H. G. Tyrell Smith and also the return to the concrete of Rex Judd who, after an absence of three years, was riding Worter's Excelsior Blackburne, while J.A. Baker was standing in for Denly on Spring's AJS. After a slow start, the Rudge went into the lead, pursued by Baker for many laps until, soon after half distance, the Rudge began to drop back and finally disappear out of the picture. The rain was taking heavy toll of ignition systems and, at the finish, only Baker was left to win at 91.58 mph. Even he cannot have enjoyed his day much for when he came in it was found that the rear tyre had rubbed a hole in the saddle. A nasty thing to happen and if it hadn't been raining it would have been nastier.

At the re-run of the bigger classes there were three non-starters in the 500 cc class, Johnston, Gibson and Quinn, the last named having a good reason for he was riding for Horsman in the 1000 cc race – and won it.

Denly set the pace in this race and was hounded by Nott's Rudge. McCudden, a Worters entry, occupied third place for the first part of the race but then went out with a broken frame, letting in Lacey who, nevertheless, was quite a long way behind. When Bill retired, the position became AJS in the lead followed by three Rudges for, in addition to Ernie's works bike, there was a 'privateer' scrap going on behind him between Gus Grose and Jack Levene. Levene got the better of this and when drama entered into it in the form of Nott's rear tyre disintegrating, it was Jack who moved up to second place, followed by H. Clifton's Excelsior JAP and this was how it finished, Denly coming in first at 97.26 mph and the Rudge 1 min 38 secs behind. Lacey's retirement in this race is of interest for, apart from the fact that his departure was shrouded in secrecy, there was a reason for it since this was his first ride for Norton's and marked the end of his spell with Grindlay Peerless. Needless to say the new bikes were turned out exactly as in the past and would soon become just as great a menace – or greater.

Although there were no non-starters in the 1000 cc Race, it was unexciting, despite the fact that quite a lot of place swopping did take place. Quinn, the eventual winner, riding Horsman's Triumph, was slow off the mark and for a long time Driscoll was pacemaker. Many changes went on behind Pat before Quinn got near to him. At 44 laps, Quinn passed Driscoll and following them were C. T. Atkins (Douglas) and E. C. Thomas (Brough Superior) but soon afterwards, Pat disappeared from the picture and the final order was Quinn, Atkins and Thomas and the winning speed 94.32 mph.

Polar weather marked the running off of the Hutchinson '100' on October 25th and marked, too, the end of the season's racing.

Two scratch races, the first for 350s and the second for 500s were won by Hewitt at 88.62 mph and McCudden at 94.46 mph respectively, which added up to two wins for the Worters equipe and not at very high speeds either – alcohol and polar weather never did mix. Lacey was second to McCudden, his first notch cut for Nortons, and Staniland was third in the 350 cc race. A poorly supported non-trade Handicap was won by Dussek's Norton at 92.94 mph and then came the 'Hutch' itself.

For the first half of the race the unfortunate spectators – both of them – sat freezing for, with these long distance individual handicap affairs, you never could get the race pattern till the halfway mark had been passed. Then it became clear that as usual, the faster bikes had once again been asked for too much and that the race looked a likely one for Horsman's little 172 cc Zenith Villiers which was using its forty one minute start to the best possible advantage, although it would be a close thing between him and Hurst Mitchell's 350 cc Velocette.

The answer to this didn't come, in fact, until the very last lap when the Velocette caught and passed the tiny Zenith, winning at 94.68 mph so that, in this respect, the handicapping was good. Fernihough's 175 cc Excelsior did well to take third place at 75.23 mph but what the fourth man Williams – average 103 mph – and fifth, Quinn – 98.82 mph thought about it isn't recorded.

For better or worse, that is the greater part of the story of motorcycle racing that

C.T. Atkins (596cc Douglas). Second place 1000cc 200 Mile Race 1930.

H. Mitchell (Velocette). Winner of the 1930 Hutchinson 100 at 94.68 mph.

took place at Brooklands in the nineteen twenty to nineteen thirty period. Personally, I enjoyed every bit of what I saw and I think that the chaps who took part in it were just as great as those who ride today. But I am a self-confessed enthusiast, not only for Brooklands but for the type of machine that ran there during the period so it is, perhaps, natural that I should also rate highly the men who rode there at the time. In writing about it, I have tried hard not to see it clearly through my rose tinted glasses and couldn't possibly deny, that at times, both the racing and the standard of machine preparation was simply deplorable although, somehow, I never realised it at the time and it is sad for me to have to set it out in cold print.

Summing up, I feel that the riders left nothing to be desired but I feel, too, that this is the best that can be said of the general picture. Looking at the aspect of machine preparation, it seems to me that four participants, Worters, Horsman, Lacey and Spring, really stood out in this respect although there were others very nearly to the same standards, Hicks, Driscoll and Tucker among them. The machines of Lacey and Spring I would include in view of the almost showroom condition in which they appeared and those of Worters and Horsman because of the extremely high percentage of finishes they obtained in long race after long race – and this doesn't happen by accident Brooklands was an absolute killer where cycle parts were concerned and anyone who got even one machine to the finish in a 200 mile race – particularly a sidecar outfit – didn't achieve it by accident but by very careful preparation indeed. To do it more than once was excellent but to go on doing it again and again, year after year, showed conclusively that the problem had been fully understood. It would be interesting, if one had the time, to look back at the record and make an analysis of the reasons for each of the regular Brooklands riders' retirements, year by year, in the long races. Already, from what I have dug out myself, one thing stands out. It is that almost always, when the big professional rider dropped out of a race, it was for one of two reasons, tyre trouble about which very little could be done or serious mechanical bother.

Others did retire for these two reasons but, far more often they retired through broken cycle parts, silencer stays, exhaust pipes, fishtails, petrol pipes, magnetos falling off, fuel blockages, tanks that sprung leaks, bolts that sheared and numerous other similar troubles. This can only have added up to the fact that these components were in situ at the start of the race and weren't expected to give trouble whereas the professional's approach was that everything would give trouble if it had been doing its work for too long and if that was thought to be the case, it was renewed.

By today's standards, many of the machines were not too good and a few were bad and since it was the era of the rigid frame, combined with the Brooklands surface, that really constituted the problem. But some of those bikes, while they may have given very uncomfortable rides, were not bad from an engineering point of view and it was exactly this that the professionals demonstrated to the public – which was what the manufacturers paid them to do. So it seems to me that the professionals deserved every penny they earned because, from the moment one of them became contracted to a manufacturer, that manufacturer knew that the machine would be demonstrated to the public in its best possible light.

Very few of the buying public ever rode on Brooklands. Many, who went there regularly as spectators, did know how bumpy it was and knew, therefore, what sort of punishment the bikes were taking. Some, who went there less often, probably came away with the impression that it was smooth. This could happen if, for instance, one

A successful 'regular' in the 1920's and 1930's. Ben Bickell on his copper-plated 498cc Bickell JAP.

always watched from the grandstand down at the Fork or, where many people enjoyed watching, from the enclosure behind the pits. It certainly did look smooth there and it was, I suppose, about the smoothest part of the track. Only those who trundled their TT Replicas down the aerodrome road and kept round it till they nearly reached the Byfleet Bridge, parked the bike, jumped the ditch and took a close look at the boys at ten foot range really had an idea of what good bikes they'd bought. You had to get a close look to see what was happening. The Home Banking was, I always thought, the worst part of the track for bumps but you couldn't see it from the Member's Hill enclosures. The only way to see it was to break all the rules and climb up behind the Member's Banking, to stand on the top – and then you saw it.

I remember once doing this with Noel Pope, who then held the Outer Circuit Lap Record with his supercharged Brough Superior at over 120 mph. Noel was a very tough chap indeed when it came to the Brooklands Outer Circuit and it was his idea to do this because he wanted to watch Eric Fernihough who was, at the time, going out to practice, prior to making an attempt on the record.

Eric came past on his first lap and Noel watched him disappear over the big bump and down the Railway Straight, then turning to me with one word 'Crikey'. Next time round, all he did was to look at me and shake his head. Third lap and with Eric only two hundred yards past us, he turned away. 'Come on, that's enough. What the Hell made us think this was a good idea. Never knew it looked like this. Two more laps and you'd never ride round the bloody place again'. Much later, when we talked about it, he told me that he really meant that. If you watched it at close range for too long, you wouldn't want to do it, he felt.

Some of the better close range photographs of the big twins at Brooklands demonstrate this. Shots of them right at the top of the Member's Banking and, momentarily, on full lock after hitting a bump just couldn't be believed by the riders concerned when they were shown them.

Even much later than this I can recall something to demonstrate the bumpiness of the Home Banking. In the mid-thirties, *The Motor Cycle* offered a cup for the first British multi-cylinder machine to cover a hundred miles in an hour. One of the aspirants was the New Imperial firm and S. (Ginger) Wood rode the bike, a beautiful little 500 cc vee twin which, to be fair, hadn't been designed for Brooklands but for road racing. It tended to be short in the wheelbase for the Outer Circuit but it had the speed and, after some initial modifications, it became the first British 500 cc 'Multi' to cover one hundred miles in an hour.

But during the 'sorting out' period the vee twin New Imperial was quite terrifying to watch and one of the things that mystified its rider for quite a time was an eerie 'yelp' that he used to hear from time to time when the bike was high up and on 'full song' on the Home Banking. For quite some time the existence of the 'yelp' was doubted by many who found it hard to believe that any sound except the roar of the wind could be heard by a rider of a bike lapping at over a hundred. But, in the end, it was found to be true. The 'yelp' was caused by an agonised front tyre reconnecting with Brooklands concrete when the steering was on full lock. That really was bad handling.

Not only frames, but tyres and cycle parts took a hammering at Brooklands – engines sometimes did as well and not in the grinding way that a 200 mile race would take its toll on an engine.

Engines running on alcohol based fuels like PMS2 and RD1 ran cool and tended to lose what heat they had built up in the pre-race warming up period very quickly, and in an individual handicap race like the 'Hutch' the scratch men were often on the line for up to half an hour with engines dead, waiting while the limit men built up their leads, for the starters flag to fall. When it did, there was no time to be lost in a few easy laps – it was flat out with an almost dead cold motor. This didn't apply in the 200 mile races which, being scratch events, showed the race pattern right from the start.

No one, except possibly the irrepressible Freddie Dixon, treated a '200' as a flat out blind – there was always a lot of 'watching and waiting'. In fact, when I was talking to Pat Driscoll, he told me that the first half of nearly every 200 miles in which he ran wasn't really a race at all, his view being that no race of this length really began to be contested until the halfway point had been reached. Once half distance refuelling had taken place, Pat felt that all concerned could sit back and have a look at the situation as it then stood, then proceeded to plan their tactics accordingly. His own plan was to run the first half of the race at a pre-determined speed and then to see where it had got him. He might find himself a lap or even two laps behind the leader or might just as easily find that he was the leader. He wasn't dismayed if it was the former or elated if the latter – a great deal could happen in that second 100 miles. But only at that point did he bring the race tactics into action and he believed that most runners did the same.

1930 was my last season as a spectator of motorcycle racing at Brooklands and my

Wal Phillips, Le Vack's nephew, won the Private Owner's Handicap at the BMCRC Meeting in June 1930. Speed 80.85 mph.

first of involvement. Great as it was to be involved in competing, one had no doubt, even then, that one had to come in at the end of one era and the beginning of another.

To me, those great races of the 1920's and the men who competed in them had enormous glamour and excitement. As, during the part thirty-five years, those events have faded into the background, I have always felt that not nearly enough has been written about them to perpetuate their memory and I regard myself as immensely lucky to be the one to make a contribution towards this. I am very grateful indeed to my publishers for letting me do this book and although I know that any of the professional motorcycling journalists could have made a better job of it, I feel that with whatever shortcomings it has, it is, particularly from the point of view of the second half of the book 'straight from the horses mouth'. In this respect, at least, I don't know of any other book on the motorbike side of Brooklands that can better it and I think this is good because, while sheer history is important, it is nice, sometimes, to get 'behind the scenes' and to know why this happened or why that didn't. My aim has been, in this first half, to make my reader feel that he has been standing beside me as I watched these races and that, in the second part of the book, some of the questions I have asked the riders would have been questions that he, too, would have wanted to ask them at the time, even though we have both had to wait thirty-five years before being able to do so.

BMCRC Brooklands 200 Mile Races, 1925 to 1929

Solo Races

1925

250 cc	WORTERS (Cotton), 69.24 mph, Briggs (OK Supreme), Colgan (Cotton).
350 cc	HANDLEY (Rex Acme), 78.37 mph. Hopkins (Chater Lea) Kaye Don (Zenith)
500 cc	DRISCOLL (Norton), 82.80 mph. Hough (Norton), Guyler (DOT).
1000 cc	LONGMAN (Harley-Davidson), 69.56 mph Wright (Zenith)

1926

250 cc	WORTERS (Excelsior), 69.56 mph Balazs (Zenith), Couper (P & P)
350 cc	LACEY (Grindlay Peerless), 81.20 mph Handley (Rex Acme), Hamilton (Velocette)
500 cc	EMERSON (HRD), 84.22 mph, Worters (344 cc Excelsior), Walters (Sunbeam JAP)
1000 cc	ASHBY (Zenith) 85.06 mph, Longman (Harley-Davidson), Humphries (Brough Superior)

1927

250 cc	WORTERS (Excelsior), 71.18 mph, Edmunds (OK Supreme JAP), Hall (New Imperial)
350 cc	STANILAND (Excelsior), 83.42 mph, Hamilton (Velocette), Himing (Zenith)
500 cc	GIBSON (Sunbeam), 79.98 mph, Walters (Sunbeam JAP), Fernihough (HRD)

1928

250 cc	STANILAND (Excelsior), 74.34 mph Fernihough (Excelsior), Taylor (OK Supreme)
350 cc	PHILLIPS (Grindlay Peerless), 86.69 mph, Hopkins (Chater Lea) Bickell (Chater Lea)
500 cc	Le VACK (New Hudson), 94.85 mph Lacey (Grindlay Peerless), Nott (Rudge)
1000 cc	DRISCOLL (Norton 588 cc) 87.07 mph, Baldwin (Zenith)

1929

250 cc STANILAND (Excelsior), 79.26 mph. Hewitt (Excelsior), Fernihough (Excelsior)

350 cc DENLY (AJS), 89.20 mph, Viewing (Zenith), Ashton (Chater Lea)

500 cc NOTT (Rudge), 100.07 mph

1000 cc BARBER (Matchless 598 cc), 90.64 mph, Baldwin (Zenith)

Sidecar Races

1925

350 cc BAXTER (Zenith), 58.64 mph, Greening (Zenith), Worters (Excelsior)

600 cc STANILAND (Norton), 68.88 mph

1000 cc ASHBY (Zenith), 72.71 mph., Le Vack (Brough Superior)

1926

350 cc PRESTWICH (Coventry Eagle), 63.52 mph., Worters (Excelsior) Johnston (Zenith)

600 cc HORSMAN (Triumph) – *Only Finisher*

1000 cc TEMPLE (OEC Temple), Knight (Zenith), McEvoy (McEvoy) All outside

1927

350 cc HANDLEY (Rex Acme), 69.00 mph, Miller (Zenith), Hicks (Velocette)

600 cc LE VACK (New Hudson), 68.90 mph, Tucker (Norton), Harley (Zenith)

1000 cc BALDWIN (Zenith), 73.97 mph, Walters (Zenith), Baragwanath (Brough Superior)

1928

350 cc HICKS (Velocette), 70.84 mph, Ashton (Chater Lea), Longman (New Hudson)

600 cc DENLY (Norton), 78.43 mph., Tucker (Norton), Driscoll (Norton)

1000 cc BARAGWANATH (Brough Superior), 73.95 mph., Walters (Zenith), Edwards (Brough Superior)

1929

350 cc HICKS (Velocette), 70.70 mph, Staniland (Excelsior)

600 cc TUCKER (Norton), Dussek (Norton)

1000 cc DRISCOLL (Norton 588 cc), 77.78 mph, Baldwin (Zenith)

If one puts these results into tabular form with the aim of arriving at the most successful riders and makes of machine, on the basis of awarding 3 points for a win, 2 for a second place and 1 for a third, it works out as follows:-

BMCRC Brooklands 200 Mile Races 1925 to 1929 (Analysis of riders' Results)

	Wins (3 points)	2nds (2 points)	3rds (1 point)	Total
Worters	9 points	4 points	1 point	14 points
Handley	6	2	–	8
Driscoll	9	–	1	10
Longman	3	2	1	6
Lacey	3	2	–	5
Emerson	3	–	–	3
Ashby	6	–	–	6
Staniland	12	2	–	14
Gibson	3	–	–	3
Phillips	3	–	–	3
Le Vack	6	2	–	8
Denly	6	–	–	6
Nott	3	–	1	4
Barber	3	–	–	3
Baxter	3	–	–	3
Prestwich	3	–	–	3
Horsman	3	–	–	3
Temple	3	–	–	3
Baldwin	3	6	–	9
Hicks	6	–	1	7
Baragwanath	3	–	1	4
Tucker	3	4	–	7
Briggs	–	2	1	3
Edwards	–	–	1	1
Hopkins	–	4	–	4
Harley	–	–	1	1
Hough	–	2	–	2
Bickell	–	–	1	1
Wright	–	2	1	3
Taylor	–	–	1	1
Balazs	–	2	–	2
Himing	–	–	1	1
Edmunds	–	2	–	2
Hall	–	–	1	1
Hamilton	–	3	1	4
Walters	–	6	1	7
Humphries	–	–	1	1
Fernihough	–	2	2	4
Hewitt	–	2	–	2
Viewing	–	2	–	2
Greening	–	2	–	2
Johnston	–	–	1	1
Knight	–	2	–	2
Miller	–	2	–	2
Ashton	–	2	1	3

Dussek	–	2	–	2
Colgan	–	–	2	2
Don	–	–	1	1
Guyler	–	–	1	1
Couper	–	–	1	1
McEvoy	–	–	1	1

On this basis Worters and Staniland emerge as clear leaders on aggregate, with Driscoll a good third, Baldwin fourth and Handley fifth, despite the last having won two races outright, Baldwin's points being scored with one win and three thirds. Had he been around today, Chris would, I feel sure, have been the first to acknowledge that quite a proportion of his points were largely due to Woolly's preparation and tuning of the Excelsiors he rode under the latter's management.

Applying the same formula to the machinery, the picture becomes –

	Wins (3 points)	2nds (2 points)	3rds (1 point)	Total
Cotton	3 points	–	1 point	4 points
Rex Acme	6	2	–	8
Norton	18	8	1	27
Harley Davidson	3	2	–	5
Excelsior	15	10	2	27
Grindlay Peerless	6	2	–	8
HRD	3	–	1	4
Zenith	12	22	4	38
Sunbeam	3	2	1	6
New Hudson	6	–	1	7
AJS	3	–	–	3
Rudge	3	–	1	4
Matchless	3	–	–	3
Coventry Eagle	3	–	–	3
Triumph	3	–	–	3
OEC Temple	3	–	–	3
Velocette	6	2	2	10
Brough Superior	3	2	3	8
OK Supreme	–	4	1	5
Chater Lea	–	6	2	8
DOT	–	–	1	1
P & P	–	–	1	1
New Imperial	–	–	1	1
McEvoy	–	–	1	1

Zenith a clear leader this time with Norton and Excelsior quite a long way behind but still way ahead of all the rest. One reason for this is, of course, that Zeniths were so versatile when it came to laying out a range for they used every size of JAP engine from 250 cc to 1000 cc and, for good measure, also marketed a little 175 cc powered with the well loved Villiers 'Brooklands' engine.

But this doesn't detract at all, rather the reverse, in fact, because although not one of the biggest manfuacturers, the Zenith firm supported most branches of the sport at the time and had done so for years. If they hadn't, there wouldn't have been so many riders wanting to own and compete on them.

These 'statistics' are little more than rule of thumb, of course, and statistics can be made to prove anything. But it seems to me that, when it comes to the 200 Mile Races in this period, they are at least a fair indication of where credit lay.

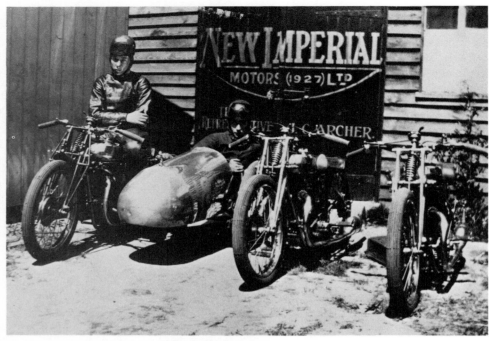

New Imperial's Brooklands 'base'. **Les in charge.**

Back at Aldershot. 350cc New Imperial sidecar outfit, 350cc and 250cc solos.

Chapter 8

Introduction

Most of the riders who starred at Brooklands in the twenties were idols to me when, as a schoolboy, I stood transfixed behind the tall iron railings that separated the spectators' enclosure from the track itself. Later, they grew in stature when, for the first time, I was able to amass the few shillings necessary to transfer to the Paddock so that I could rub shoulders with them, as it were, for the first time. With the exception of the 'baby' of the cast, Les Archer, they remained as they were in my mind for the rest of my life.

Idols remain idols so long as you never come to know them personally. They are seldom forgotten and throughout one's life on wonders from time to time what became of them in later life. From being an idol in the late twenties, Les Archer became a friend when I came to find myself on the start line of Brooklands races with him but if, in the twenties, anyone would have told me that within a few years I would have been astride one of his lovely bikes competing on a race at the track, I would never have believed it. He won the race. Neil Christmas was second on the other works Velo and I finished a rather poor third. It was a day I have never forgotten and I think it could have been the only time that anyone other than Les rode one of his machines in a race at the track. Bert Denly also became a good friend, mainly because he continued at the track with cars during my period of the 'thirties', and also through our mutual friend Charles Brackenbury.

So, although I knew all about their achievements at Brooklands and had seen many of them from behind the railings, I was quite literally meeting them for the first time when I set off with my tape recorder to see how life had treated them in the aftermath of Brooklands and to find out, if I could, what their racing recollections were.

Every one of these visits constituted a day out for me and wonderful days they were. In more than one case, I found the character of the man so interesting in that we kept wandering from the subject of Brooklands and racing to something entirely different. In that sense, this book has been, for me, the most enjoyable of any I have done, and the fact that their ages ranged from my own – the mid-sixties – to close on ninety, made it all the better.

LES ANSTEAD

For no particular reason, other than it seemed one way of doing it, the individual stories of the Brooklands participants are set out in alphabetical order for the second part of this book. So it's strange, in a way, that the first to come out of the bag concerns a man who never rode in a motorcycle race at Brooklands or, for that matter, drove in a car event. Despite that, his name was a household one to nearly every competitor at the track on two or four wheels. His memories of the track went back further than anyone else in the cast.

Born in Weybridge, and having lived all his life there, Les Anstead's recollections of Brooklands went back to the time when it was under construction. That alone would have made him a 'must' for inclusion in this book, but it so happens he had an even greater claim.

A skilled sheet metal worker for all of his working life, Les it was who made silencers and exhaust systems, bodies, fairings, cowls and every sort of fitting for both the car and bike people who raced at Brooklands. If something fractured and required welding, Les was the chap to get you out of trouble. There was always a frantic rush down to his yard alongside the Ship Hotel but, when you got there, the rush ceased, for Les wasn't a man to rush or be rushed – in fact I would describe him as 'unflappable'. Nothing every surprised him or ruffled him and I never recall seeing him other than good humoured except on the occasions, not altogether infrequent, when, having put down a job in order to get someone 'out of trouble' the customer sometimes forgot to pay. Even then, Les' stock phrase was 'Never mind, I'll get him one day. Wait till he's in the same boat again and see what happens'.

He had another stock phrase for the rider who would rush into his shop with a leaking fuel tank half an hour before the start of a race. 'Has it been steamed out? That's all right, I'll weld it for you – you just hold it.'

Whatever the problem, one always had the feeling that it would be all right once Les had seen it but, even so, he knew exactly what he could or could not do. I recall once being disconsolate when the front down tube of my Brough Superior pulled out of the head lug on the morning before a race. It looked bad but someone said 'Les'll do that for you' and I thought so, too. Woolly Worters stood looking at it and said 'He won't, you know'. When I queried his reply he said 'I know he won't in the time he's got. There's only one place for that – the Works.'

Nottingham! In a 1934 Austin Ten. Brooklands on a Friday morning, the bike to be stripped out completely, taken to Nottingham, brought back, rebuilt and tested by midday on Saturday! Yet aided by his foreman, Ike Webb, George Brough did the job for me himself.

Just before the start of the race Les came up to the line shaking his head 'Woolly told me. He was right. I wouldn't have wanted that one.' If anyone other than Woolly had given me the same advice I would have chanced it and taken it to Les and, thereby made it impossible to get to the Works and back in the time. Outside Les's own trade, Woolly had a better knowledge of what could or could not be done than almost anyone when it came to Brooklands machinery.

Like some others in the story, Les is fortunate in having a son who has followed in father's footsteps so that the wonderful little firm still goes on. On the day I went to see him, the 'Guv'nor' was there and taking an active part. I asked Les what he was making.

Slowly turning, holding a giant object in copper, the well known Anstead grin appeared. 'A hood. A copper hood. For a fire. Reproduction. If I'd had this contract years ago, I'd never had bothered with all you Brooklands lot.' We left the shop and went to his house, where he sat with his dog, by the fire, after I had been introduced to Mrs. Anstead for the first time since the Brooklands days themselves. It was good to see Les looking so fit and still taking an active interest. Going back a bit, I suppose that, complete bodies apart, he must have built more sheet metal bits for both bike and car people at the track than anyone else. How early, I enquired, did his recollections of Brooklands go back?

It seems that he started in the shop in Weybridge in 1924 and the first recollections he had were of when he was doing work for Zeniths who were then in Weybridge High Street.

Going back further than that, I asked whether he started in 1924 with his own business? It transpired this was not so, because the firm was O.R.D. Engineering then. They specialised in sheet metal work and this was the only profession he followed throughout his entire career.

On enquiring whether he had any earlier recollections prior to starting with O.R.D. Engineering I said I had been led to believe, for instance, that he had relatives connected with the Brooklands Estate even before the track came into being. This was indeed so, for his Father-in-law had been Dame Ethel Locke King's chauffeur. His Grandfather had been employed on the Estate and took part in the building of the track.

Les himself had been born in Weybridge in July, 1900. He first went to the track as a schoolboy, and was there a lot. He had friends – the Boxalls – who lived and worked on the Estate. They used to go moorhen hunting when there was a pond there. The Boxall's house was close to the bungalow that Parry Thomas had. They were a big family, another section living at Boxalls Lodge.

As a schoolboy Les used to visit the track often, to see his Grandfather, whose house was on the Brooklands Road – it still stands, by the way. He used to get rides on the trucks that the navvies were using to move soil to make the bankings, for at that time the track was under construction. They formed a sort of light railway and the navvies used to push them. They had a steam crane working there too, and that was something he always liked to watch. The whole project was very unpopular among the local people because all-Irish labour was employed. The latter lived on the Heath in shacks. The first job they did was to fell trees to get timber to build their shacks. Then they built the shacks, most of them wood and corrugated iron, and most of them were on the Heath just outside Weybridge Station. Any youngster was afraid to pass by there after dark. It looked eerie because they did all their heating and cooking on open fires. And the noise! It is alleged they drank the pubs dry – the opening hours were different then. They used to go to the pubs two at a time and bring the beer back to the huts in quart pots hung upon a long pole. Beer was cheap then and they were paid daily.

Les was not apprenticed to O.R.D. Engineering because he had served his apprenticeship at the Itala Motor Works on the Brooklands Road – as a sheet metal worker. He started at half a crown a week – twenty two and a half pence today. The hours were six in the morning until half-past five.

He worked there for about eighteen months, before Vickers bought the business in 1915. While he was there, the cars were being raced. That was his first connection with racing. The cars were there in order to test tyres for Dunlops. When he left Italas, Les went to Vickers. Then from there to the Bleriot Company, who were interested in air navigation. And from there into the army in 1918.

When he came out of the Army Les went to Canada, to the Pacific Sheet Metal Company in Victoria, in March 1920. He remained in Canada until 1924, when he came back and joined O.R.D. Engineering, at the premises he had owned ever since, for fifty years. He went there through a man he had known in Vickers, who was one of the partners.

The business became his in the early thirties but he was not working there on jobs for Brooklands people as an employee of the business before he actually became the proprietor.

The first Brooklands rider he got to know was Dougal Marchant. He was the first customer from Brooklands and he knew him well because, at the time, he was also living in Weybridge. Les believed he probably had a ride, at that time, on one of the first loop frame ever made, which Dougal Marchant had built for Chater Leas. He also did a bit of work for Victor Horsman, mainly pipes and Brooklands silencers. He came to know him and his mechanic, Quinn, quite well.

Tony Worters was another customer. But although he also lived in Weybridge and they were good friends, he didn't do a lot for him. Worters liked to do as much of the work on his bikes as he could himself. Les did a bit for him soon after he started with the Toronda, mainly on the sidecar. And he built the first fully streamlined shell that ever ran at the track, for Worters later on.

It was, of course, the shell for the 250cc Excelsior JAP that later became all-time 250cc lap record holder at the track, ridden by M. B. Saunders – the first and only 'Gold Star' 250 ever to run there. And lest there be confusion about J.S. Worters' Christian name, perhaps it had better be cleared up now. Many people, including Les, always referred to him as Tony. I knew him as Willy, in company with many others. But in recent correspondence he wrote to me saying that Willy is wrong, even though Chris Staniland always called him Willy. Woolly is right and it came about through the woolly teddy bear coat he used to wear at the track in the winter. He became Woolly from the first time he wore it and it stuck.

Worters prepared the streamliner for Chris Staniland. Les made the shell and it was quite tricky because in addition to the recesses for the rider's legs, the cooling vents proved a bit of a problem. He did not ever recall seeing Chris ride it. He thought it must have been just before they all pulled out because the bonus money had gone. He knew Saunders had got the 250cc record with it later but he was not sure whether it was that bike or another fitted with the shell he had made. Les was sure it was the first full streamliner although he had previously done quite a lot of fairings for front forks and other odd 'clever' gadgets to improve drag. But most of the track work was repair – and always in a hurry. It consisted of almost everything bar the engine or gearbox. Frames, forks, silencers, fishtails, saddle stays and, of course, tanks.

It took Les about an hour to steam a tank thoroughly, and even then, if it was well baffled, vapour would hang in the joins of the baffles. As an afterthought, he considered he must have done a bit more for Tony Worters that he thought originally, because when he and Chris switched to cars, with the Multi Union, Tony did all the mechanical work, but he did quite a bit of the bodywork. It was all coming back as he reminisced about the past. He could recall both Chris and Charlie Brackenbury having Bugattis at the same time and they carried out some experimental work on Charlie's car to try to find speed by raising the engine temperature a bit. Les thought it must have been the only Bugatti ever to run at the track with a cowled radiator. He did the cowl for it and he and Chris conducted the experiments. They consisted of having the cowl built with a small aperture and cutting the aperture bigger after each run until they'd got it right. A bit primitive when he looked back on it but not so many people attempted to experiment. Charlie and Chris also fitted fairings to the front axle. That idea must have come from the bike days. He could not recollect whether it made any difference or not, but they looked good and he remembered making them. He tried making up fairings for the dumb irons as well and he remembered that all of the fairings, when fitted, had resulted in an improvement of five miles an hour. But it was all by trial and error, of course, which was almost the only way to do it at the time.

The most important work Les did was making tanks for Sir Malcolm Campbell's record cars. He did that for him, working with his mechanic, Leo Villa. But the biggest job in actual size was the Brooklands silencer he made for Alastair Miller's 21 litre chain-driven Benz. Because the silencers had to be in proportion to the swept volume of one of the cylinders, and that amounted to more than five litres, since the engine was a four cylinder, he knew he was going to end up with a bigger box than he had made before or was every likely to again. The problem was to make it strong without making it too heavy. When it was done, he could hardly get the thing through the door of the shop. But he could not recall it ever giving any trouble. He was pleased about that because that old car used to lap at around a hundred and ten and he remembers people who'd ridden in it telling him that it was a roughish ride. He often used to take a good look at that great dustbin underneath it to make sure it was still all right, particularly if he was thinking of putting a bit on with the Bookies. He remembered that the car used to break the shackles on the front springs until he made new bolts with special plates to strengthen them. Those big old cars were a worry to the Scrutineers and they were to him, too, when he had done work on them. He used to keep notes of all he'd done to them and take the notes with him whenever he went up to the track. He always used to take a close look at the work he'd done on each of them – the vibration from an engine, and usually a four cylinder one of between twelve and twenty litres, was worrying. But he thought the vibration was as bad with the bikes.

It was not the cars or the bikes that caused him the greatest worry. The Morgans were worse than both of them. He never used so much gas and welding rod as he did when there were several Morgans running. They used to run a team of Morgans in the Relay Race, driven by Lones, Rhodes and Laird. After the first year they took a garage in Ship Yard, next to his place so that they could save time journeying down to see Les. He never used to take on much outside work the week before the Relay Race. But the chaps who drove them were heroes, he thought. He found the Morgans quite frightening, even from where he watched, positively dangerous.

The nicest and most beautifully finished cars on which Les worked were the team of Delages that came over in the late twenties or early thirties, for the Grand Prix. They were 1.5 litre straight eights and the drivers, he thought, were Benoist, Divo and Senechal. He believed it was the first time they ran at Brooklands and it may have been the first time they ever ran at all because they had a cockpit overheating trouble that was too big for him to correct in the time available. Seaman had one of the cars later on, he recalled. Ramponi rebuilt it for him and it showed the ERAs the way home. They were beautiful cars.

Being privileged to receive bits of useful information, Les used to have a bit of a flutter with the bookmakers, but like me he got the same treatment from them in the end. When they saw him coming, they used to make a sign which meant 'don't bother'. So he did what I did – got a mate to put it on. The best one he ever had was with one of the Delages, after the works had finished with it. They sold it to a private owner, a Captain. He had the car in Les's place all the winter while he was skiing in Switzerland.

Unfortunately, he lost an eye in a skiing accident and when he returned, there was some doubt as to whether he'd be allowed to drive it. But they let him practice and he took it steady and only lapped at about a hundred and five. He told Les what he thought about it after the practice and when, on the day, they were offering 8 to 1 on him, Les staked all. The Bookmakers never saw which way he went. Les chuckled at the memory of it.

The bulk of his work was repairing the ravages of Brooklands concrete, but he would always build bodies if people wanted them. He did one on an MG, a K3 that belonged to Manby Colgrave. He got married to a lovely lady and then gave up racing. Very wise of him. Les would have done the same! Colgrave sold the car to Billy Cotton. He was slightly built and Bill wasn't. Bill must have bought the car without trying it because he came rushing down to Les saying he couldn't even get into it. He'd got his young son, Bill Jnr., with him and, as soon as Les looked at the job he knew he'd got a problem and that Bill never would get into it and be comfortable if the standard K3 body was to be retained. So Bill asked Les to re-body the car as quickly as possible and he did just that. Bill was a very nice chap indeed. He never once came down to see how Les was getting on without taking him into the Ship for a drink afterwards.

He was always doing work for Thomson and Taylor, of course. One job he did was for the Honourable David Tennant on one of the big Leylands that had belonged to Parry Thomas. The car had been rebodied with rather a pretty road two-seater sports body and it had overheated when running in the Hour High Speed Trial although Les thought it had put more miles into the hour than anything else running. There was talk of cutting louvres in the bonnet but he had a look at it and it seemed to him that if louvres were going to be cut anywhere, they'd be of more use in the tail because the new body had no exit for the air and there was no flow. This was agreed and he cut louvres in the tail, which solved the problem.

On enquiring whether Les did much work, either through Thomson and Taylors or direct for Campbell on the big World Record cars, he recalled that he was not personally involved. He lent Thomson and Taylor a panel beater for that, and it was Eddie Cox who went. He did more work for Robin Jackson, who ran the other tuning and maintenance place at the track. In fact, he had worked for him before he was in the business. He had made a body for his racing Morgan when Jackson was still at Cambridge. He saw a lot of Robin. He had a lock up just round the corner from Les's own shop – in Elmgrove Road. He thought Robin's business really started there. The lock up grew into a workshop and he took on Bob Hubbersty as manager. Unfortunately Bob died soon afterwards.

Another body Les made for Robin was the offset single seater for the eleven hundred Lagonda Rapier that Mr. and Mrs. Eccles used to race. He made the body, the tanks, the exhaust and silencing system, in fact all the sheet metal work on the car. It was supercharged and was really quick, particularly round the Mountain. Marjorie Eccles was one of the best lady drivers around at that time, he thought.

Another car Les often worked on was the big twelve cylinder single seater Delage that held the lap record when John Cobb and later, Oliver Bertram, had it. That car was maintained by T and T when Cobb had it but, later, Robin looked after it and Les often went up to do odd jobs on it. Later still, Klenantaski had it and then the Junior Racing Driver's Club and he still kept working on it from time to time. The 500 Mile race always produced a lot of work both before the race and afterwards. The work after the race was no problem but the practice period could be a headache – everyone used to leave it to the last minute.

And so it went on. A great life to have lived and a store of memories. Les Anstead was, if not the 'idol of the crowds', at least the 'idol of the competitors' at times and had it not been for him, many a runner would have failed to make the starting line in all those years.

Although I have known and loved Brooklands myself, back to the nineteen twenties, his memories go back far further. Further, in fact, than anyone I've known. I doubt whether there can be anyone living who has earlier recollections. How could there be – he was born on the spot, saw the great dream come to fruition, saw it dawn, blossom, wither and die.

I found Les' recollections of Brooklands, particularly the early ones, vivid and accurate and on reading back over the story could only pinpoint one thing I wanted to check with him. He had mentioned one of the Grand Prix Delages passing into the hands of a Captain who had won a race with it on whch he, Les, had won money. I wasn't able to find any record of this and went back to Weybridge a month or two later to check it with him.

To my sorrow, I learned from his son that Les has died only the day before, after a sudden and short illness. At first I couldn't believe it. No words of mine can adequately express to his wife and family my sorrow at hearing the news. In terms of the things that matter in life, he was the wealthiest of men for he lived for his home life and was a master of his craft. He had a keen sense of humour equalled only by his energy for work and capacity for enjoyment. One only had to look for the twinke in his eye to see whether he'd noticed something amusing – and he always had. He was one of the kindest and most generous men I ever met and was unbelievably tolerant. During the ten years I spent at Brooklands, I never once heard him say an unkind thing and only ever heard other people say nice things about him. There was a lot of paddock 'gossip' in those days and like all of us, he enjoyed it, but if he ever mentioned that he'd done a job for someone who hadn't paid, he never said it with rancour, usually adding with a chuckle 'He'll cough up when he's got it I expect' adding as an afterthought 'If he remembers'. His recollections of Brooklands were by far the earliest of anyone's and they had to be because you can't go further back than seeing the track built and riding on the trucks that carried the materials. Everyone who knew Les will feel an enormous sense of loss. I am more than grateful to have been given the opportunity to record his contribution to this story on Brooklands.

L.J. ARCHER

Despite the fact that he started racing at Brooklands in 1926, it would be wrong to describe Les as an 'old' Brooklands rider for he was, in fact, competing at Brooklands right up till the mid, and late, thirties. We talked, Les and I, at his Surrey home not far from the family business in Aldershot where, for years, he has been engaged in motorcycle activities with his father.

Always Velocette or New Imperial mounted, Les had a long and successful career at Brooklands with both solos and sidecars. I asked him first, not about racing, but about his early introduction to motorcycling itself.

His interest started because the Archers, as a family, were in the business of cars and motorcycles at Aldershot, where his father came to live in 1902. Les began to ride on the road at the age of fourteen, having won his first motorcycle from his father who promised him a machine should he become top of the class. The machine was a small two-stroke Cedos and the year 1921.

Les joined the family business in 1923 and went through the ordinary gamut of motorcycle sport in all its styles, trials, grass track racing and long distance events with the MCC. In fact it was with the MCC that he had his first introduction to speed, which was at Brooklands.

Les's first ride was in the MCC High Speed Hour event and that was in 1926, when the MCC held their annual event at Brooklands. He borrowed a New Imperial which was a replica of the 1926 TT model. It was a splendid little machine and it won him a Gold medal.

Les has always been associated with New Imperial and Velocette. Both he and his father obtained agencies for both makes.

Following his run in the High Speed Hour, he immediately told 'Pa' that all the riding he had been doing was not for him any more and they must acquire a racing machine and go to Brooklands, which they did in 1927.

The 1927 season wasn't all that brilliant in as much as the first machine New Imperial provided, after loaning him that splendid little ex-TT model, was nothing more than what they called a Model 5 Replica. It was only because of the good work of such kind fellows as Hopkins of Chater Lea, who let Les and his father into some of the secrets of how to reduce the weight of valves and increase compression ratios, that this little machine was made to be any good at all. It was not until 1928 that they managed to get some recognition, official that is, from the Factory. Then they were running not only 250s but 350s as well, both solo and sidecar.

Their New Imperials were on loan from the works and although Les was not absolutely sure of the year, they became established at the track with a fairly large workshop at the back of Tony Worter's premises in the Paddock, just at the rear of where a very dear friend, Freddy Hicks, was based. It was, in fact, seeing the wonderful performances of Freddy Hicks that made Les ambitious, some day or other, to own and ride a Velocette, which he did when poor Fred got killed on an AJS in the TT of 1930.

It is difficult to know whether the Archers brought any influence to bear on New Imperials to produce, much later on, their Grand Prix Replica model. They produced the engines up at their factory in Birmingham, whilst the Archers had a 'slave' frame, into which Les placed every engine, both 250cc and 350cc, so that they could be run at the track for a few laps and given a certificate of performance over the half mile and over the lap. These certificates accompanied the complete machine when it was sold to the new owner. In fact it was quite a step forward from the type of machine they sold Les in 1927. It represented a marked improvement too, for the firm was then spending money down at Brooklands in leasing premises and so on, with all the expense that entailed.

Bob Foster's unit-construction racing 250 was one of the many machines that came through the Archers hands much later in the thirties, when Matt Wright was with New Imperials as their engineer. Although Les had official recognition with Velocette in the thirties, the New Imperial people used his services only in the 250cc class. He also had had his own Velocette shed, after he took over for them at the track.

Matt Wright was associated even more with the New Imperial 500cc vee-twin. It always seemed strange that, while the first 500cc Hundred Miles in the Hour was done by Bert Denly on a single cylinder Norton in 1927 and, bearing in mind that this was done so long before, the 'Multi' hour seemed so difficult to achieve, and happened so much later. It will be recalled *The Motor Cycle* offered a cup for the first 500cc multi-cylinder machine to cover a hundred miles in the hour. So many people had a crack at it, Ben Bickell with the Ariel four, Tommy Spann with the vertical twin Triumph, Tom Atkins with the flat twin Douglas and 'Ginger' Wood with the vee-twin New Imperial that it seemed, almost, as though development had slowed, by that time. Was Les in agreement?

Les Archer (New Imperial 250cc) No 10 H.Le Vack (New Imperial 250cc) No 9 200 Mile Solo Race 1929.

Sidecar styling. Les Archer (New Imperial 349cc) No 4 C.B. Bickell (Chater Lea 348cc) No 7

Although this appeared to be so, Les considered the multi was a more difficult proposition. With regard to the New Imperial, 'Ginger' and Matt went down to the track sometimes with his father, and tried many, many times, having at least one nasty tumble due to tyre failure. All manner of shocking things happened to the machine during those attempts and it wasn't until the middle of 1934 that they claimed the Cup with a speed of 102 mph.

Inevitably, mention had to be made of Harold Willis, in view of Les's close association with Veloce Ltd. Les regarded him as an amazing man who twisted words. Wherever Harold Willis' name was mentioned, there seemed to be a new sort of alphabet, associated with the English engineering language. It is difficult to remember some of the comic names he had for things. The piston was the 'bung', the valves the 'nails', the flywheels became the 'spinners' and cams became 'knockers'. It was largely because of this that he was known and loved so. Apart from this, he was obviously very clever. His 'Whiffling Clara', a supercharged 350cc KTT, was loaned to Les. In fact, he believes he was the only rider to have the loan of that machine and actually work on it, which he thought was a great honour.

When questioned about his experiences with this machine, Les explained that most of his riding on it was, of course, when it was in road racing trim. It was extraordinarily heavy but he recalled the classic occasion when he rode it to victory twice on the same day, in two Grands Prix. The same bicycle won the 350cc race and then, after refuelling, went on to win the 500 event. This only thing 'clapped out' on that day was not the bicycle but the rider!

Certainly it represented a successful experiment. It was brilliantly designed but a very difficult machine to handle under certain circumstances, particularly when rushed into a fastish corner after having been ridden hard for a fair distance. It used to build up 'rich' on the over-run and had a most amazing contraption which used to operate a little valve which squirted raw fuel out of the great big receiver box onto the track to get the mixture right – and one hoped for the best. If the track was wet, and the bike suddenly came in on correct mixture and really started to forge ahead, the rider had to be somewhat of a tightrope walker still to be on the bicycle as it came out of the corner.

It was alleged that when Les rode the first 500 cc racing Velocette to appear at Brooklands, in the Grand Prix, he took it out and tested it, only to find it didn't like its Brooklands silencer. His words when he came in were 'Well, it's not frightening me yet'. He was asked how its performance compared with that of 'Whiffling Clara'. His reaction was that because it was a normal machine, with none of the silly characteristics he had mentioned about 'Whiffling Clara', it didn't frighten him, although it was much faster under certain circumstances. Years later, he had many frights, particularly in the Isle of Man, on the 500s.

When asked about preparation and tuning in the twenties, Les explained that he and his father were responsible for this. What used to happen was that they would finish a day's business and then go out to their little track shed at the back of their own garage and work on the bicycles. If there was anything that wanted doing they jumped on their piece of transport which, in itself, was quite interesting. The first vehicle they used to cart their machine to Brooklands in 1927 was a four and a quarter hp side valve Quadrant, a three-speed model with belt drive. There was a bulldog in Byfleet who hated them. He used to hear the machine coming from the Woking direction and would wait poised at a certain hill where they used very nearly to come to a stop with belt slip. Hardly a day went by when he wasn't there to pursue them. In consequence, Les arrived all ready to shake plenty of speed out of the poor little New Imperial after warding off the aggression of the bulldog.

The standard of preparation carried out by Les and his father was, generally, very high indeed. There were few retirements, even with the 'works' bikes that could have been avoided by better attention. In his opinion it would be a very good chap, with his hand on his heart, who ever suggested that, by his own carelessness, he didn't have an involuntary stop. It was bound to happen sometime.

The competition in those days, viewed in retrospect, was as tough and demanding as it is today. When we had an English industry which was going reasonably well, as it was in those days, there were a number of well-supported riders on very good machines. He considers it applied particularly in the field of records, a side of the job in which he and his father were deeply involved. In the 250cc class they were continually trying to beat the long distance on a New Imperial. It was hardly good enough for really high speed although, as can be recalled, he did, in the thirties, become the first rider to achieve the landmark of 100 mph with a 250cc New Imperial. Once again, of course, it was Matt Wright tuned, for during that time Les was, officially, a Velocette rider.

When asked how much help top riders were able to give each other in emergencies, especially in view of divided loyalties to different manufacturers, Les agreed that if a rider was in trouble, he was able to give help up to a point. This particularly applied in the sphere of Velocette and especially with regard to long races. Being officially with Velocette, if anyone was in trouble, he had the material available at the track. He and his father were able to give quite a lot of help to the boys who came to Brooklands and were Velocette mounted.

This co-operation extended to the professional, shed-based Brooklands living types too. He found them splendid folk. They had a very happy relationship with each other and when he looks back on that time, Les considers that aspect of his life at Brooklands as being most enjoyable. He cannot remember one nasty incident where one could say 'well, that wasn't much of a thing to do'. These sentiments would apply equally well today.

With regard to financial arrangements with manufacturers, most of the big companies, such as those who provided tyres, chains, fuel, oil and the like, had a standard bonus scheme in operation. Les and his father were lucky, in the case of fuel and oil, to get a retainer fee, and he thought that probably the largest sum he received was through the good services of Reg Tanner of Esso. It amounted to about £300 for any one year, and it went straight into the business.

The big money, and it was big for those days, lay in record breaking. Needless to say it generated rivalry, not only between the riders themselves but also between the manufacturers of the machines they rode. Les confirmed that what used to happen was that when someone went for a record, the next contestant would attack it only after an interim time, so that the previous holder could be paid out. The period was usually a month, so that it gave the manufacturer and the accessory people time to advertise and make what use they could of the achievement. If it was broken sooner, it was of less value to riders and no payment was made. So riders always waited the full month as a rule. One may think that this was rather an unsporting thing to do. But it was business. And, often, after the full month had elapsed, the person from whom the record had been taken would go straight out and break it again. And, in the same way, the other might then retaliate. This was an accepted business, which led to friendly rivalry.

The busiest time for record breaking was at the end of the season because this would interfere less with racing, and also because the annual Motor Cycle Show was held around this time. Les could remember an instance at Brooklands, with 'Ebby' and George Reynolds, when they were so busy at the time of the Motor Cycle Show because all of the sponsors were anxious to produce something that would bring kudos, just at the time of the Show itself.

Thinking about the problems associated with long distance runs, Les recalled the situation when there was need to set off at eight o'clock in the morning. If you started your machine up at ten minutes to, someone rang up from Weybridge and there was a row. You couldn't even warm a machine up before the magic hour of eight at Brooklands because of the injunction that was levelled against the track. But he remembered that when motorcyclists went for records at that time, there was a marvellous cameraderie between them and the car folk. All they had to do, if it was going to get dark and they were still going, was to ring up Lagonda at Staines. Out would come one of Lagonda's best test drivers with one of their lovely Le Mans cars and he would light up the track for them as they went round. He can still recall the eerie sensation of riding in that wonderful light with the rabbits scuttling in all directions. This is one of the things that will always stand out in his memories of Brooklands and long distance records.

I was able to bear that out because on the only long distance record ride I had, with Eric Fernihough, on a 250cc Cotton in October 1935, we went for all records from six to twelve hours. By ten hours we had broken them all, including the eleven and twelve hours. We had only to leave the machine leaning against the pit counter for the remaining two hours, in order to collect, but I wanted to go on. Geroge Reynolds was the timekeeper and he agreed to let us be lit with Eric's Light Sports Railton, but he insisted that the front wheels of the car must at no time be ahead of the front wheel of the bike. And it did bring the rabbits out too. Millions of them.

I raised the question of how the big twins tended to be temperamental and, as a breed, less efficient over long distances than the big singles. Although Les concentrated on the 250, 350 and, occasionally, 500cc classes, I sought his views on this aspect, even though he had never ridden a big twin at Brooklands. The record of big twins finishing in the long races was appalling and when they did finish, their speeds were often poor. To some extent one could understand, in those days, the problems of keeping two cylinders firing for a couple of hours or more. But the specific question was, need their record have been as bad had any one rider stuck to a big twin in the longer races? So many different people rode them every year in, say, the 200 mile races that apart from Baragwanath, who rode nothing else, they all dropped out and were replaced the next year by others. No one seemed to stick to them in the way that, for example Horsman, stuck to his Triumphs. Was one experience of riding a big twin over that sort of distance enough for most people?

He considered it was largely a question of economics and that some people tended to underestimate the cost of preparing and running a big twin. He didn't agree entirely about their unreliability for he could remember, years earlier, one big twin, possibly a single geared Harley. It turned out only occasionally because of the reason he'd given, but when it did, and once the rider succeeded in getting the clutch home, it just went round and round and invariably finished at quite a good speed.

Another question that arose was that of some riders keeping their machines from the previous year's racing until the new bikes had been proved. Did Les ever adopt such a policy or think it a good one?

He and his father did, after a few years, accumulate a collection of engines and there was sometimes a 'throwing out' of such things as frames and forks that they felt were time expired. So it is correct to say that, from the New Imperial time, the actual number of complete machines may have doubled. The newest components were built into the machines that he would describe as their first line of attack. Bits that might have been used, one season, on such a machine, were sometimes used much later to convert what had started life as a sprint machine into a long distance machine for, perhaps something over 200 miles.

Reverting to riders and their ability also as a tuner, Les considered that Bert Le Vack was the most outstanding, mainly because he had so much to do with the preparion of his own machines. He was the man who worked on them. As a rider he would put Chris Staniland next to Le Vack but, to the best of his knowledge, Chris had nothing to do with the machines he rode. All he would do was to put on a superb suit of white overalls and go out and achieve amazing results.

People like Dixon, Fernihough and Hicks applied themselves in exactly the same way as Le Vack, for they were all out-and-out riders and workers. Les would put all of them into one class. All had, he thought, a particular feeling for a machine, having put all those man hours into it. He recollected Sammy Davis, who was a great driver of racing cars, saying that it was preferable either for a racing driver to know everything about his car or nothing. In other words, it was better that he didn't know just a little about it. On reflection, he thought it was, perhaps, more correct to put Chris Staniland in the middle category.

Throughout his racing career at Brooklands Les was associated with only two makes, New Imperial and Velocette. An obvious question was whether at any time there was a point when he might have become associated with another make. On this point he was quite emphatic in responding with a firm 'no'.

It can be imagined that it was necessary, for financial reasons alone, for most of the big names at Brooklands in the twenties to ride both solos and sidecars. Did Les have a preference for solo or sidecar; did he think the hazards of one were greater than the other and did he consider either to be a greater test of the rider?

His reply was non-committal because he liked them equally well. He thought his successes all along were equally shared. In fact, if he checked back on the World Records he achieved, he would expect them to be fairly representative, percentagewise and successwise.

An important factor to be taken into consideration was that of tyres. By the time Les had started, the tyre problem had largely been solved, on the medium size bikes at least, but presumably some of the long rides with which he was involved would have necessitated a change of a rear tyre. Les confirmed this was so. At that time he used what was called the 'rib' long distance tyre for records and he never set off on a long ride without being well supplied with spare wheels and tyres in readiness for any emergency. One had to remember that Mac and Co. of the Dunlop Rubber Company were there constantly, to render every possible assistance.

Wheel removal had to be undertaken with care because there were no knock-out spindles in those days. When the replacement was fitted, it had to be carefully lined up and the job not rushed too much, although it was important to effect the changeover quickly. Tyre wear was abnormal, particularly with sidecar outfits.

Les got to know just how long a tyre would last and, on long rides, the outfit would be brought in, the tyre change being synchronised, if possible, with the refuelling stop. Dunlop Mac would often be there with the replacement wheels and tyres and would set off back to the Depot in the Paddock with the old ones.

Today, two-strokes form the hardcore of the race machinery.but, at the time Les was racing at Brooklands and even later, they were considered a spent force and unworthy of further development. An interesting question arose as a result. Had the engine designers of the 'twenties' and 'thirties' overlooked something?

He tended to agree. When he thought in terms of two-strokes the name of Tommy Meeten and his Francis Barnetts came to mind, and the achievements of some of the very early Dunelts. Even then, it was nearly always long distance stuff, never shorts or sprints – they just hadn't got it.

It seems strange that the designers should have overlooked the potential of the two-stroke for so long and that the two-stroke should, in the end, become an entity. Now, of course, it is predominant, at least in classes up to 350cc.

Les considered the achievement began with the German DKW. They made such progress and became so well able to equal the performance of the British four-strokes that there was a ban imposed on the three piston DKW. It was, in fact, then rated as supercharged.

Whilst still on the subject of racing engines and despite the fact that the modern racing engine is much more complicated and sophisticated than those of the 'twenties' and 'thirties', it would be interesting to know whether it was still the life of the big end that determined the life of the engine. This may have been the case whilst Les was racing, but perhaps there were other components, in his day, that needed most frequent replacement apart, obviously from tyres. Clutches, for instance?

Les found that clutches were very good tempered. The main problem related to engine design, especially with regard to the valves and guides. They were, at that time, out in the open and they had a wretched time. But he agreed that it was the big end that, in the end, decided the engine's life. The different designs of big ends were, at that time, countless. There was, for example, the 'geared down' type, which had double rows of rollers, one running on top of the other. Designers were groping in the dark a bit at that time. They tried all sorts of 'sneaky' things to try to achieve a longer life. In early racing a wear- resisting material such as Stellite was unknown. That came later, with Harold Willis. He had so many thoughts and new ideas that this is why the Velocette came to be so outstanding from about 1927 until the very early thirties.

Everyone grumbled about Brooklands and its bumpiness yet, in retrospect, its existence seems to have been taken for granted. So many of the people who grumbled about Brooklands and its shortcomings were the very same people who were so outraged when, suddenly, it was no more. This was another area in which it was hoped Les may be able to comment, especially with regard to whether he considered the old track would still be useful today.

It was Les's opinion that even today, Brooklands could have been used for testing and development purposes, such that its demise proved a great loss to the trade. For example, suspensionwise, a lot more could have been learned a lot faster. He recalled that on a sprint 350, lapping at 100 mph, it was customary to use a 26 x 2.375 front tyre, which is comparable to a moped tyre today, and of course, only a 2.75 section tyre on the rear. It was amazing that with a rigid frame plus what amounted to only a slightly sprung front fork it was possible to get any sort of adhesion at all. The rider definitely suffered.

Asked whether he encountered Col. Lindsay Lloyd at the track, in his capacity of Clerk of the Course, he confirmed that everyone knew him and a more charming man couldn't be imagined. The person he had more to do with was the chap who used to open the track at eight o'clock in the morning. He was known to all as 'Taffy'. And he knew all the riders and knew not only if they were pulling a fast one on him, but how they were planning to do it. He recalled with some amusement how riders sometimes used to try to cheat on silencers. He once ran a pipe through the box, direct to the fishtail – but was caught out.

One of the more outstanding personalities at Brooklands was A. V. Ebblewhite, known affectionately as 'Ebby'. He always seemed to be a man who had a terribly difficult job to do yet did it very well. He was quite 'unbendable' on the handicapping side, for he had to pit his wits against a lot of very wily people. Les had encountered him, but only in the sense that, as the Archers were residents, so to speak, he knew everything about them. Whenever Les won, he won, he thought, deservedly. Ebby realised that every race had to have a winner and that, in nine cases out of ten, the winner deserved his success. He never felt, in the case of 'regulars', that a fast one had been pulled on him.

Another personality he remembered with the greatest affection was George Reynolds. Les could recall one occasion when he was at the track with the little New Imperial – it was when he was trying to be first to record over 100 mph with a 250.

Above Record Breakers, early 1930's. Les Archer (right) with co-rider E.G. Bishop and the track 350cc Velocette sidecar outfit.

Below Historic 'Certificate of Performance'. L.J. Archer. October 12th, 1932 First to record over 100 mph on a two fifty.

George had been busy timing car record attempts all day, while Matt Wright of New Imperials had been working on the 250 for Les to ride. When it was nearly time to go home and just as they were starting to pack up, George came round in his car and said 'I think that if you want to have a shot at your 'century' record, boys, conditions could be nearly ideal within the next half hour. If you can be ready by then, I think on the times I've noted for you today, we might just make it. If you'd like me to, we can have a shot at it and if you don't do it, I won't charge you'. That was just one example of his real kindness and help. He had been taking times at the same time as his record runs and, like Les and Matt, was ready to go home. Les went out and got the 5 Kilometre and 5 Mile records at 100.41 mph – the first time it had been done with a 250. They had been so involved with the bike, all day, that they had hardly noticed how the conditions had improved as the afternoon wore on. But George had and, much as he would have liked to be on his way home, he came all the way round to where they were. As it turned out, he was able, to a great extent, to share in the credit.

Inevitably the question of Les Archer's son, Les Jnr, must arise and his involvement with another sphere of motorcycle competition. The question was, did he decide to take up motocross of his own accord or did Les Senior swing him from road racing, having raced himself?

The question of Leslie's involvement was easily explained. He left college and had a little MOV Velocette which was arranged so that alternative wheels, handlebars and exhaust systems were available for general competition use. He would load the bike up on a Saturday for a road race meeting, and then go on to a scramble on a Sunday, making whatever changes were necessary with this machine. It was done for one reason, because Les wished him to make his own choice. The Velocette was his first competition motorcycle. Later, Gilbert Smith of Nortons, who was always looking for someone he thought could be of some use to the Company, came along and offered a choice of Nortons. Les Jnr. had wonderful 350cc and 500cc road machines which he rode, and then he acquired a 500 scrambler, which was modified at the Archers own expense, in their own workshop, by Ron Hankins, who was their resident engineer. It was he who had been largely responsible for their success immediately after the war when they scored in the Junior TT with Bob Foster on an Archer- sponsored Velocette.

Les Jnr soon proved he was very adaptable and was quickly among the winners, having done a lot of riding on the road when he had a 350cc Triumph when he was at College in Petersfield. He reached the very top in motocross, to become World Champion in 1956.

We continued talking late into the evening and many were the memories that came flooding back so that, at times one could almost see that lean Outer Circuit Velocette with its workmanlike sidecar, its body functional but not, perhaps, the prettiest of the bunch, its lissom rider draped along the long black and gold tank as it rounded the Fork on its way up to the Home Banking. There were many Velocettes racing at Brooklands but two of them always looked very much alike to me, those ridden by Les and the late Freddy Hicks. Both had a certain slender 'Outer Circuit' look that spelt track racing, pure and simple, rather than a KTT set up to run on the Outer Circuit. Their record of speed and reliability was outstanding and when prepared and ridden by men like these, they were, barring accidents, almost certain placemen and very often were outright winners.

It's strange how two superb bikes of equal capacity but of different make can feel so

Les Archer and 'Pa'. All New Imperial 'Grand Prix' model engines were tested individually at Brooklands before the new machines were sold.

totally different. The only ride I ever had on a racing Velocette was when Les lent me his Mark VI to ride in the 1935 Brooklands 100 Mile Grand Prix. Two works machines had been allocated for the race, one for him and the other for Neil Christmas and, hearing that my own 350 cc Norton was below par, Les generously came up with the offer. It was a gorgeous little bike, quite a bit faster than the Norton and with a totally different feel. While everything about it was great, it felt, to me, slightly lighter at the back but with an engine that revved and revved – it was so willing. Within the first mile, I felt that it was a certain finisher – everything was right and the motor had that wonderful feeling of being unburstable. True, the Norton had that feeling as well, but I think the engine of the Velo has a certain willingness and sparkle that wasn't a characteristic of the smaller Norton. To ride it was a responsibility and great was my relief to be able to scrape into third place at the end, miles behind Les and Neil but, at least, inches ahead of the leading works AJS.

A success story like that of Les's, aided by his father, doesn't happen by accident. And when the next generation tops it there must be a moral in it somewhere.

GORDON COBBOLD

One of the great aspects of Brooklands was the unyielding loyalty it received from what could be described as the 'supporting' rider, the chap who, while not a winner, at meeting after meeting was always in or near the centre of the picture.

Chaps like this were the cream, for they could be relied on to put up a good show nearly every time and when, as sometimes happened, the big stars met with trouble in practice and were unable to get to the line, it was the good supporting riders who found themselves in the running. Even when the big names were competing, the supporting runners were never far away. Their machinery was just as well prepared and, in many cases, externally identical to the works bikes.

I never really knew whether to class Gordon Cobbold as a works rider or as a supporting rider, for the Sunbeam firm themselves never did include Brooklands on their list although they stood squarely behind the TT and many of the European races. They were represented by Charlie Dodson although he never rode for the firm at Brooklands.

So it was Gordon who came to be known as the 'Sunbeam man' at the track. There were others, Ron Gibson and Kirby among them, and all had their successes. But there is no doubt that if one talks of Brooklands and Sunbeam, it is the name of Cobbold that comes first out of the hat.

One always rather wondered how riders like this got into the game. According to Gordon he had no encouragement. It just happened. He was motorcycle mad when he was a school, yet he didn't know where it came from because motorcycling was never in his family. But while not actually supporting him, his mother just let him do as he wanted – and that was what he wanted to do. His first machine was a Douglas – 1911 or 1912, with the engine set high up in the frame. But quite soon it became Sunbeam. He bought his first Sunbeam, a long stroke, around 1923 and that was the first bike he raced. He just struck a Brooklands 'can' on it and went to Brooklands. He enjoyed the experience, but the long stroke, being a side valve, wasn't fast enough so he went over to an overhead valve Sunbeam in, he believes, 1925. It must have been one of the first – he didn't think the overhead valve Sunbeams came onto the market until the end of 1924. He knew that A. G. Williams and himself had the first two – they were delivered in London. It was good fun at that time. He used to ride the bike on the road during the week, usually with a girl on the back, and then, after taking off a few bits here and there, set straight off to Brooklands at the weekend.

It was questionable whether he found those early 1920's were the most enjoyable or whether he enjoyed it more when he became the unofficial rider for the works later on. He simply enjoyed it all. He enjoyed it the whole time and every time he went to Brooklands. There was nothing to beat it. It was a wonderful place. If a rider was in trouble there was always someone to help. They did have troubles, of course. But they occur today too, just as often.

Sunbeams generally, had a reputation for reliability. But although the old long stroke was very reliable, it wasn't so fast. The Model 9 was just as reliable until the rider began to look for more speed. Then he could strike trouble. It was the old story really, a question of balancing speed against reliability. It wasn't easy with the overhead valve Sunbeam. It was happy and reliable up to a lap speed of about ninety. But if an attempt was made to push up the speed another five miles an hour, everything happened. Pistons blew out, flywheels came out of the crankcase – everything.

Gordon got little help from Wolverhampton until 1926 and only a certain amount after that. But it was not a great deal even then because he preferred Brooklands to road racing, which was what they liked. He never rode in the Island and only did a few European races, but he can not remember which ones. He was fourth in the French Grand Prix one year and he remembers the Belgian Grand Prix at Spa because his bike caught fire. He thought the French Grand Prix must have been in 1927, when Alec Bennett won it, two Frenchmen were second and third and he was fourth. The Belgian event was run on a terrifically hot day and Gordon thinks the tank must have been overfilled before the start. At any rate he found the bike on fire when he was travelling at about 95 mph, so he stopped and had a fine old job trying to put it out. There was quite a lot of damage and he can remember the walk back to the pits in the blazing sun. He remembers his arrival there too – they filled him up with milk. Not what he wanted at all!

Asked whether any of his Brooklands races contained any heart stopping moments Gordon recalled just one incident that really stands out in his mind. It occurred during a short handicap with the big Sunbeam in 1928. The bike was lapping at around 100 mph and the incident happened at the Fork. The lap scoring box was on the outside of the track at the end of the Vickers sheds. He had started in the race and if not actually on the scratch mark, he was at least near to it and was entitled to be well over on the right-hand side at the Fork, almost clipping the box. All he could recall happening was a sort of a flash – something shooting out of the door of the box. He didn't know what it was and was too busy, really, to give it much thought, but apparently it was a young lady who'd never been to the track before and probably shouldn't have been in the lap scoring box anyway. She'd seen enough of the race at that point and had suddenly decided to cross the track and watch from the other side, so she stepped out smartly – right under his front wheel. She was a lucky girl – and so was Gordon that day for, at the time, he had no idea what it was he had seen. He must have been less than six feet from the box at the time and she must have been about the same distance ahead of him when she decided to cross the track. Grimes did a cartoon of it in *The Motor Cycle* that week. It was captioned 'I don't mind breaking my neck, but I do hate to be ignored – Gordon Cobbold.'

A great many of Gordon's successes were notched up at the track in private owners events, although he competed in all the open events as well. Looking back through the record and as mentioned earlier in this book, it will be recalled that in the 200 Mile Sidecar Race of 1926 he was using hairpin valve springs. That would seem to be about the first time that type of valve spring appeared on a Sunbeam at Brooklands and he was asked how this came about.

After he had won one or two races in 1925, Sunbeams offered Harry Weslake and himself three machines to keep down at Brooklands for experiment and racing. Harry, who was his entrant, did a lot of experimental work with them and soon they bore little resemblance, internally at least, to the standard product. Externally, apart from the Wex carburettor which Harry designed and manufactured, they were pretty well standard. Although the old Sunbeams gave a pretty rough ride, they never altered the frames or went in for a longer wheelbase as did Vic Horsman with his Triumphs. The Wex carburettor was a definite improvement. A lot of other Brooklands people used it although Harry didn't pay a bonus. The Wex was a very good carburettor for racing and on the road. Riders used it on trials bikes and it was good when using 'dope' as well. They did a lot of RAC and ACU tests with it and came it out on top every time. They even put one on a Morris Cowley – a good car but never a flyer – and it went down the half mile at 62 mph on an RAC Test and later the same day it averaged 35 mpg.

It was hard to recall what experiments were carried out for the factory because they were experimenting all the time, sometimes trying out ideas for the works and sometimes ideas of Harry's. They ran at a fairly high compression ratio on 'dope', about thirteen to one. They had no bothers at all with the big end; it was always pistons and valves. They used Martlet pistons but Gordon can remember trying out a magnesium piston for the works on the five hundred. Half way down the Railway Straight there was an almighty bang and when they stripped the engine down the piston had gone altogether! There was nothing there at all, not even the skirt or the boss. The same set up was used when they ran with a Martlet piston and the samething occurred. They didn't try it more than once or twice – it proved too expensive! Martlet pistons were good though, and they stuck to them. Sammy Lee and Brewster knew a lot about pistons. It is not generally known that Brewster was connected with Martlets, but Gordon confirmed this was so, Brewster had partnered him once on a World Record run, until he got cramp. He was a good rider, though.

Early in 1927, Gordon had appeared at a meeting with one of the Sunbeams which had the carburettor boxed in, and he was asked what was the idea behind that?

He said that they were working in the dark all the time, but it seemed right at that time, to try for a sort of supercharging effect. Douglases and one or two other people had tried it and they thought they ought to follow suit. Their scheme involved rather a complicated system of balance pipes, but it was difficult to know whether any real benefit was gained. In other words, the device worked if the wind was in the right direction. But since every rider went round in circles at Brooklands, the losses offset the gains – so they didn't proceed with the idea.

In 1929, Sunbeams told Gordon they intended packing up racing. So, as he wanted to continue he had a look around, talked to one or two people and finally came to an arrangement with Pellat to share his OK Supreme bikes. It was a difficult time for anyone who wanted to continue racing. The bonus had gone almost completely and, from the point of view of almost all the trade, the interest had as well. The arrangement he made with Pellat was typical of what two semi-private riders had to do if they wanted to go on.

He had a very good run in the 200 Mile Sidecar Race that year, one of the best he ever had, and it ended only when the mag packed up. It was a good bike and well prepared.

He also had a go at speedway racing because, at that time, there was a great shortage of riders. There was no question of having to make a decision; he just thought he'd like to have a shot at it, so he went to Greenford first – a half mile track – and later to the Crystal Palace. This was right at the start of the speedway era. He just took one of his own bikes, removed the mudguards and other odd bits, and piled in. They had practice days for people who wanted to ride on the cinders. Riders just went along and had a bash at it on whatever machine they had. Later, of course, special bikes were needed. Gordon got quite involved. He started, at first, with a cut-down Sunbeam,

Gordon Cobbold and his Sunbeams – always admired both at sprints and at Brooklands.

then he had a Douglas and a Scott, and he finished up with a Rudge. In the end he was riding on eight or nine different tracks in a season. There was plenty of opportunity – it was sometimes possible to have six rides a week in London if the rider wanted them.

With regard to the monetary aspect and whether it was worth it, a rider could get a fiver an evening to start with, which was good in those days. And, if he was moderately successful he could clear, say, another twenty pounds. It wasn't too difficult to clear a hundred pounds a week. The bright boys frequently doubled that.

Later on, speedway caught on all over Europe. Gordon went to Paris and rode at the Buffalo Stadium. Then the promotors went bust and the riders took it over. He made a lot of money there, but went to the South of France and blew it all, to come back after six months with only fifteen pounds in his pocket. The bikes had been sold too. But he considered it was worth it. Sunbeams had dropped out of racing at the end of 1928 as far as factory support to other than works riders was concerned. Then came the speedway, but in about 1930 Gordon packed it all up, opened a garage in Fulham, got married and that was the end of his riding career.

Or, to put it more accurately, the end of an era, for he went on to become a success-ful motor trader in his own right and, later still, went into partnership with Johnny Smith, the well known Brooklands driver of MGs. But even today Gordon hasn't lost his love of motorbikes and Sunbeams particularly. In comfortable retirement in Berk-shire he seems hardly to have aged at all. Still the same old chuckle when something, such as his jaunt to the South of France, amuses him, still the same laconic way of speech and still getting a 'kick' out of almost everything he does, particularly if it involves motorbikes. He is a leading light in 'Bemsee' and goes to many of their meet-ings, particularly Snetterton, which he likes. He is also a member of the Brooklands Society whose 'do's' he never misses and he is obviously enjoying life.

Riders like Gordon Cobbold were certainly the backbone of Brooklands at that time and it isn't stretching it too far to claim that without them there could well have been no bike racing at the track at all. True, it was the works-backed riders that notched up the big successes all the time but, at any one time there were probably only half a dozen manufacturers supporting racing at the track and for every one works-backed professional there must have been at least a dozen amateurs. Some, like Gordon, were fringe-backed by the manufacturer whose machines they rode.

Even to someone who saw it all happening, it's quite hard to believe that probably a third of the machines that competed at Brooklands at that time, cars and motorcycles, were driven or ridden from the homes of the owners to the track and, unless disaster had overtaken them during the contest, were driven ridden home afterwards, almost certainly with a stop at the local to recall the day's happenings. In that sense, one must concede that, when compared to today's racing, it was all very amateurish in those days. It was, but it had that certain something that really did make it better fun, I think, although all of it is enjoyable if you are an addict.

There is a wonderful spirit of cameraderie in today's motorcycle racing scene, among the riders. Just the same thing existed in the twenties but in a different way. I think it emanated largely from the small local clubs in the first place. Despite the acute shortage of money, it was an era of growth where motorcycling was concerned and clubs which, only a few years earlier, had sprung into life with no more than a handful of riding members quite quickly grew amazingly big and active. Many clubs organised runs to beauty spots all over the countryside nearly every week-end and if a local club contained among its members one who was going to race at Brooklands, it was certain that, on that day, the Club Run would be to the track.

Looking back on all this, one can not help feeling that the enthusiasm for motorcycling generated in and by local clubs at that time, contributed enormously to the success of Brooklands and even more so to the motorcycle industry itself. Another thing, of course, is – dare I say it – everyone was very hard up and so very unspoiled, at that time even to the point where a run to a beauty spot was something to be looked forward to and a run to Brooklands something very special indeed!

None of this would have applied to Gordon during the latter part of his racing at Brooklands and even before that he probably was receiving modest support from Wolverhampton. But he was one of the top flight amateurs right from the start and there were countless others who kept plugging away, meeting after meeting, sometimes with outdated or even unsuitable machinery, because it was all they could afford and because Brooklands was Brooklands and they wanted to be there. These were the chaps

G.C. Cobbold (493cc Sunbeam). Brooklands Opening Meeting 1926. Winner Race 6 at 86.62 mph.

one would see arriving full of hope and enthusiasm, with a bird on the back, and often one would see them returning home at the end of the day, centre piece of a club run, at the end of a tow rope, with the bird on the flapper bracket of a fellow member's much later and more glamourous machine. Sometimes, one could not help wondering just how many budding romances Brooklands broke up.

Every one of these chaps many of whom never won anything at all, made a greater contribution to the success of Brooklands than they ever realised at the time and I just hope some of them are around now to know it. The sacrifices they made, just to be part of the scene, were enormous. They made up the field although, at the time, they had no idea at all just how important they were.

And they were modest. Gordon is typical, although he did have a lot of success spanning quite a period of time. But when I met and talked to him, he kept saying that he couldn't recall this or that success which is why his biography is so short. So it seems to me right to expand it to cover all the chaps like him.

Apart from the bike meetings sponsored by *The Motor Cycle* which drew enormous crowds in the early thirties, Brooklands spectator attendance at even the main meetings was comparatively small but what it lacked in numbers, it made up in quality for almost every rider had his following of fans among the spectators. I am going to tread on dangerous ground here and say that in one way at least I think the quality then was better than it is now. If, for instance, a spectator had come to Brooklands mainly with the interests of a particular rider in mind and if that rider had a bad day, his fan would be disappointed – but fully sympathetic.

I still go to quite a lot of bike meetings today and one of the things I enjoy is to get away from the Paddock and watch the riding at various points round the course. It seems to me that some of today's spectators are just as enthusiastic for their idols but much less forgiving if things go wrong. I recall, some years ago, listening to a spectator who was obviously a fan of Mike Hailwood's who, at the time, was in his heyday with MV. On this particular day, Mike was mounted not on the MV, which wasn't available, but on a very mediocre Manx Norton. His riding was, as always, superb but not even Mike could get such a bike up to the head of the field so that having expressed his feelings loudly to anyone willing to listen, that particular fan set off home in disgust. Strange, really, because he knew a lot about racing and had seen his idol running at countless meetings and tracks, so must have had quite a lot of knowledge of race machinery. Even today, I think there are quite a lot like him so perhaps we are justly called a nation of spectators – because there's nothing quite like having a 'go' yourself to appreciate the finer points of a sport.

Old Soldiers Never Die. A recent picture of a beautifully restored 493cc 'Sprint' Sunbeam.

I seem, in my enthusiasm, to have drifted away from the point a bit which was to divert the spotlight momentarily from the stars to the supporting cast who, at the time, were just as much Gods to me as the regular winners. As a schoolboy spectator I think I slightly preferred them because, for one thing, being almost constantly in trouble with their machinery, they were slightly more approachable and grateful for being handed the right spanner at the right moment. That doesn't go against the 'big boys' at all but one never, ever, saw them in trouble. If ever they were, the machine usually didn't leave its shed and the first one knew about it was when its number went up on the 'non-starters' board. If unexpected trouble struck suddenly, the offender was wheeled away so quickly and silently that one wondered it had been there at all or was just a mirage.

Before leaving the subject, a word should certainly be said in the same vein concerning the supporting riders at today's meetings. In pre-war racing the machinery was, at least, simple to work on and cheap to repair and replace. Now it is so sophisticated and costly that one wonders how beginners cope with their problems. Motorcycle racing has always produced an unending stream of keen aspirants and for every one who is forced to drop out, there always seem to be two more to take his place so that today's fields, while huge, are still oversubscribed, which just shows what a very good sport it is.

BERT DENLY

Throughout almost the whole of the 1920s no name was held in higher esteem at Brooklands than that of Bert Denly. In the same way that Leslie Archer remained faithful to two makes, New Imperial and Velocette, Bert remained true to two makes also, Norton and later, AJS. It is not easy to become to all intents and purposes a star overnight and still be liked by your rivals, but Bert achieved it, riding at first for wizard tuner O'Donovan, who had himself been a highly successful rider of Nortons. Bert's first big success was the winning of the 1923 200 Mile Solo Race at an average speed of 77.61 mph. Many successful race results followed under the patronage of O'Donovan, who at the beginning of 1927 handed over the Norton racing interests to Nigel Spring, and this was the beginning of Bert's successful attempts on the Hour Record. At that time the record stood to the credit of Vic Horsman on his Triumph at a speed of 94.15 mph, for since 1920 he had been holder of the 500 cc hour no less than eight times, three of which were when he was Norton mounted and the remainder with a Triumph. The first successful Spring/Denly attempt produced a speed of 95.02 mph for the hour and subsequently Denly improved on this in 1927 to become the first man to cover 100 miles in the hour on a 500 cc machine. Still later, the record was raised twice more by Denly, finally standing at 108.60 mph in the middle of 1930, the later runs both being made on AJS. Solo or sidecar – it made no difference to the Spring/Denly alliance. The year 1928 produced a win in the 600 cc class of the 200 Mile Sidecar Races at 79.93 mph.

Leaving Nortons in 1929, the equipe became re-tooled with AJSs, these machines rivalling only Lacey's in their chrome-plated finish and superb appearance. The first big AJS-mounted success came in mid-1929, when the team won the 200 Mile Solo Races on the 350 at an average of 89.20 mph. Success after success followed, both in races and in successful attacks upon records, and one of the most rewarding must have been the breaking of the 500 cc Flying Start Kilometre Record at Arpajon the same year, at an average of 118.98 mph. Later still in 1930, Hicks and Baker played supporting roles but somehow it was always Bert's name that one associated with AJS. One counts oneself lucky to be able to number such a man amongst one's friends and his visit to my Surrey cottage to talk about all these amazing events and achievements was one I never shall forget because, while I knew a lot of the story, there was a great deal that I'd never heard before.

When writing about chaps like these, its sometimes tempting to describe one of them as 'the most outstanding of the lot' but it's something that must be avoided because each was outstanding in a different way. Lacey, for instance, stood out for the superb way he prepared and turned out his machinery; Horsman for his trackcraft; Worters for notching up the greatest number of any of them in terms of records broken and places won, sometimes riding himself and sometimes as an entrant; Nigel Spring for his organisation, to mention just a few. But Bert Denly must surely stand out not only for having been the first to cover a hundred miles in an hour on a 500 cc machine, not only for having had an enormously successful record breaking and racing career on both two wheels, three and four, but also for having been associated with Captain George Eyston in what were probably the most outstandingly successful car record runs ever made prior to World War Two.

There is no doubt that, on at least two particular occasions, Bert had luck. He was very lucky indeed to have got into motorcycle racing through a chance meeting with his future boss, 'Wizard' tuner O'Donovan, then number one rider and racing manager for Nortons. At the time, Bert was a lad and was working, delivering meat for the local butcher, his mount being an elderly belt driven, two-speed flat twin Douglas. There was a lot of meat to deliver. The butcher was a good one and had a lot of customers, all of whom expected their joints delivered on time – so Bert had to ride fast! He knew the local roads in Byfleet and the best line to take in and out of each and was using every inch of the road when he came face to face with O'Donovan who, in his elderly Morris, was just setting out to do his shopping. At that time, the 'Wizard' was nearing the end of his career as a rider and, stifling his fury at Bert's impudence, he saw at once that here could be a solution to his problems because if the lad could ride a wreck of a machine like that on the road, what might he do on a well prepared track machine on Brooklands. So, tracking him down, he lambasted him and, having done that, proceeded to make him a Brooklands star overnight. Tell me, if you can, of another case where a young man, content in his work, but with no thought of or knowledge of motorcycle racing, finished his job of meat delivering on Saturday and started work the following Monday morning as Number One works rider to a leading and outstandingly successful motorcycle manufacturer – and I will show you a lucky man!

That, certainly, was Bert's first and luckiest break. He was lucky to have been living and working in Byfleet within yards of where O'Donovan worked inside the track. Lucky to have 'carved up' the old man and even luckier that O'Donovan had the perception to spot talent that he, Bert, didn't even know he possessed. Lucky that O'Donovan controlled his anger to the extent of being able to offer him the job. And luckier still that, having been offered an interview, he didn't bother to go and that, even then, O'Donovan came back and offered it to him a second time. It may not all have been luck, of course. For the 'Wizard' to have come back twice must have meant that the 'carve up' had left a deep impression on him – it must have been one of the best.

Secondly, Bert was lucky in his first chance meeting with Eyston. Again, it was pure chance and, again, it came at just the right moment of his life. But this time he recognised it so there was no delay in forming the association. So those were the two major slices of luck and, of the two, I suppose the first was greater because if that hadn't clicked, the second would never have arisen.

Telling the story, years later, O'Donovan was adamant that, at the moment of crisis, he was doing, at the most, fifteen miles an hour. For all his great skill on the track, he was by no means the fastest of drivers on the road and had he been, the story might have begun and ended there. Out of the corner of his eye, from a side turning, there shot a streak. His reactions were quick but brakes weren't what they are today and a big crash seemed unavoidable. Bert's version is that, in those days, traffic up and down Byfleet High Street was so light that he was accustomed to using all its width on exiting from its side roads and it was a shock to find this elderly rather frightening looking gent ambling slowly along and using that very area that he needed and had, until then, found available.

O'Donovan ground to a standstill, cursing. But, if he expected some sort of an apology he was doomed to disappointment because by the time his wheels had stopped

Early days. Bert Denly (on machine). **Racing Manager O'Donovan** (centre).

nothing was to be seen of the Douglas or its rider. Bert didn't feel that an apology was necessary or wise and hadn't time to give one anyway.

For a moment, the great master sat getting his breath back and then it dawned on him that if anyone could get away with a thing like that, what could they do on a real bike? Don wasn't in his first youth and although he hadn't finished with racing, the time was approaching when he would want to hang up his leathers and there would be a new Number One rider to represent the Norton factory. He had held that position himself, for years, and had done wonderful work for the company both in development and riding. If that young idiot could keep on riding like that and if it wasn't just luck that had saved him, he might be the very one.

In the heat of the encounter, Don had spotted the meat lurching about in the basket strapped to the back of the Douglas and, putting two and two together, he set off hotfoot en route for Byfleet's one and only butcher. Bert hadn't returned but, when he did, he was dismayed at the sight of the tall, gaunt, figure waiting purposefully outside the shop. He swung in on the Douglas, partly dismounting while still in motion and was about to put a bold front on it and run into the shop when a heavy hand fell on his shoulder. Don indicated he would like a word with him, asking whether he always rode his Douglas in that manner.

Bert feigned surprise that his riding was anything but normal, so Don recalled the incident that had prompted him to visit the shop. He went on to say that if that was Bert's usual style, how would he like to ride at Brooklands?

Bert knew about Brooklands, of course and had heard the cars and bikes running round it from the outside. He had always meant to go in one day and have a look but the entrance to Brooklands wasn't free, even on non-race days, and he had better use for his money. Who was the old chap and what had it all to do with riding at Brooklands? Amazing really.The only man ever to have been offered the job as Number One rider for Nortons, never having ridden a Norton, never having been on or even seen a racing track, and not even realising just what sort of a job he was being offered – or why. Understandably, Bert's reply was non-committal.

Don wrote his name on a grubby scrap of paper with a blunt pencil and asked Bert to call and see him as soon as possible. But it didn't sound like 'possible' to Bert who, after years of working with him, can still mimic the old man's broad Irish accent. It sounded more like 'parsable' and Bert can recall he used to call the throttle 'the tottle' too.

Bert didn't keep the appointment which, in itself must be another record because no one else, surely, can ever have been offered Norton's Number One spot and not even bothered to go to the interview. It wasn't that he wasn't interested. Bert thought he was some kind of a nut case. He didn't know who he was and Don didn't tell him. Jobs were scarce in those days and Bert didn't want to chuck over one that he liked, to find himself out in the cold. So he just put it out of his mind.

But O'Donovan didn't. He was round at the shop a few days later and, not for the last time, gave Bert a piece of his mind. And that time A. Denly did go and, in going, handed in his notice to an astonished and irate butcher just one week later.

That started a chain reaction. From at first working on the bikes, Bert then began to share the riding with the Master, later taking it over altogether, while O'Donovan concerned himself purely with development and preparation, aided by his rider. O'Donovan then announced that he was ready to give up his interest in racing and competition completely, allowing his mantle to fall on Nigel Spring. The latter and Bert continued together, Norton tooled, until the factory's interest in Brooklands began to wane in favour of road racing. But AJS, hearing of these developments and being far from disinterested in racing at Brooklands themselves, were quick to spot a highly efficient and successful racing and experimental department consisting of two. They signed up the Spring/Denly duet, who then proceeded to do as well for them as they had for Nortons. So well, in fact, that the liaison continued right up to the end of the decade, when the bottom fell out of it, the bonus system ended and nearly everyone who was anyone switched either to cars or retired from racing completely.

At this moment the Denly good fortune struck again, perfectly timed as usual, and led to the next phase. One day, when Bert was running-in one of Spring's track AJS's, he found he had company. The company consisted of no less a racing personality than Capt. G. E. T. Eyston who was also running-in, but his mount was the latest 2.3 litre supercharged Grand Prix Bugatti. Together they went round, side by side, their running in speeds identical until, having done his stint, Bert came in, stopping at the pits opposite the Vickers sheds. At that time he had never met Eyston although both knew each other as masters in their own spheres. A few minutes later, Eyston pulled into the next pit and came along to compare notes.

For a time they talked about racing bikes and cars and then Bert said it was time to set off for home as his task had been completed. Eyston was quick to point out that his own running-in stint had not been completed. As he had some 'phone calls to make, would Bert like to finish running-in the '2.3' for him?

As he climbed into the lovely cockpit – and the cockpit of a Grand Prix Bugatti really is lovely – little wheels began to turn once again in Bert's head. Surely the same thing, the very same thing, could not be happening again. But it was.

Right from the outset, the Eyston/Denly partnership worked just as well as the two previous ones. While different types and with different backgrounds, they were in almost every way complementary. They saw problems in the same light, often having the same ideas as to how a problem should be tackled and each had a lot of knowledge in certain spheres which the other lacked. Although both were racing men, it was Eyston who was the business man and Bert the engineer. Their partnership, nearly always successful, grew from purely a business one to one of great warmth and respect and, very much later, when both were in retirement, to one of friendship. Both were countrymen and understood the language and both were fishermen. Not so long ago, when both were in their seventies, they were still going off together on occasional fishing trips.

And, if that were not enough, their chance meeting came at exactly the right moment for both of them, Bert knowing that the end of professional bike racing was near and Eyston at a time when he was thinking in terms of making the change from motor racing pure and simple into the realms of record breaking alone.

When Bert climbed out of the cockpit of the Bugatti that day – the first time he had ever driven a racing car – his report on its behaviour to Eyston was concise and constructive and George realised, at once, that here was a man he could use. There was a discussion between them and before very long, Bert Denly was working in the capacity of Chief Engineer to Eyston who, in turn was closely associated with Wakefields – and Castrol.

In retrospect, Eyston must have known a lot more about Bert's engineering qualifications and experience than Bert himself realised. The start of the liaison coincided exactly with the departure of Eyston's Bugattis, which had been maintained by Papworths who probably knew as much about Bugs as anyone.

But the departure of the cars marked a new era in Eyston's plans. There was to be more racing but it was to tail off in favour of record breaking and I don't think that, from the moment of their association, Eyston ever owned and raced another car. Almost every drive from then on was on a works car of some sort, with the possible exception of the 1933 Monza type 2.3 litre supercharged Alfa Romeo.

One of Bert's first tasks was to prepare this car for the Mannin Moar 'round the houses' race in the Isle of Man, undertake the initial pre-race testing and then accompany Eyston as riding mechanic in the race itself. He did the same with the K3 MG Magnette and considered that by the time they had finished, he knew that course nearly as well as the 'Cap' did. He partnered the 'Cap' in most of the big long distance races at Brooklands, mainly with MG's, and it would be true to say that, barring misfortune, they were seldom unsuccessful. These races were fitted in with long and short distance record runs undertaken on behalf of a wide variety of cars and for many different manufacturers. To quote two very different ones, a 7 day record run for the Singer Company at Montlhéry which was successful and a 24 Hour attempt on one of the big single seater six cylinder Delages at the same venue which wasn't, a piston breaking down after fifteen hours running.

In 1934, Eyston won the British Empire Trophy race at Brooklands, driving the K3 single seater prepared by Bert, and he had his Chief Engineer with him throughout the Mannin Beg that was won by Nuvolari in a sister car. The first of their 'out and out' record cars appeared this year with Bert in charge — the big and rather pretty streamlined saloon powered by an AEC diesel engine identical to the type used in the London Transport buses. It was in this that Eyston scored immediately with Mile and Kilo records at 115.41 mph.

Then it was a run for Hotchkiss, shared between them, which lasted for two days and two nights resulting in —

4000 Miles	... ...	95.76 mph
5000 Miles	... ...	94.73 mph
48 Hours	... ...	95.36 mph

What a marathon. And, in doing it, they also broke the 1000, 2000 and 3000 Miles, the 2000, 3000, 4000 and 5000 Kilos, the 12 Hour and the 24 Hour records.

Then began the first of a series of record runs with 'Speed of the Wind', the huge specially-constructed single seater, front wheel driven and powered by a Rolls Royce Kestrel engine. Again, Bert was the man in charge and, after Eyston had taken the World's Hour Record with it at 159.30 mph, Bert and, later, Chris Staniland climbed into it and, in turn, the three of them powered round the Bonneville Salt Flats to take the World's 12 Hour Record at 143.77 and the 24 Hour at 140.5 mph, covering no less than 3372 miles altogether. Remarkable too, that Eyston should have chosen two top grade Brooklands racing motorcyclists to partner him on such a task. A moral somewhere, surely?

In 1936 Eyston and Denly returned to Bonneville together, with the same car, sharing all the driving between them with Eyston, as usual, handling all the organisation and administrative side and Bert in charge of the machinery again. The Hour Record went up to 162.5, the 24 Hour to 149.10 and setting the 48 Hour at 136.35 mph, 6544 miles covered in the 48 hours, two drivers only, in conditions of blistering heat in the daytime and biting cold at night. And that was in 1936 — forty-four years ago. They weren't satisfied even with that for, in September of the same year, the same car appeared, diesel-engined this time and re-named 'Flying Spray', when Eyston took the World's Flying Mile for diesel-engined cars at approximately 159 mph. They already had the diesel powered 24 Hours record with the saloon at ninety-five — that had been netted on February 14th and 15th. In 1937, they went again, this time with the diesel-engined 'Black Magic' averaging 97.05 for 24 Hours at Montlhéry. Afterwards, in an interview, Eyston claimed his co-driver, Bert Denly, fortunately had stronger arms than he to hold the shaking monster. He confessed that when he came off after a three hour spell, his body was racked and his arms quite ineffective. Being far smaller than Eyston, Bert had extra seat padding to insert, each time he took over, and as time wore on Eyston wished he could have shrunk himself to half size to take advantage of this cunning plan. Daylight never seemed to come and, unlike the daybreak in America, it seemed to them an eternity.

This comment is interesting. Bert's extra padding was, of course, essential on all their runs for he was half Eyston's size but it could well be that, of the two, Eyston did have the rougher ride on all their paired runs. Bert always has been enormously strong despite his pint size. That run took place on a Saturday and one report says that, after it ended, mid-morning, Bert drove the car back to Calais by road and then on to London next day.

If the cars they had been using for their record runs until this point had varied from midget to monsters, the one now under construction for the out-and-out World Land Speed Record – 'Thunderbolt' – was gargantuan. In Eyston's own words 'My experience of motor racing taught me that there were many ways such a car might be constructed and I had to decide which would be the best line to follow. After lengthy calculations and innumerable discussions with streamlining experts, the tyre makers, the brake people and all kinds of specialists, I realised that there were many problems to be considered. I decided to use the world's best engines, two Rolls Royce motors of the Schneider type – the most powerful petrol engines in the world. These were to be installed side by side to keep the chassis length within reasonable dimensions. Four rear tyres were necessary to transmit the enormous horsepower available, and an entirely new steering arrangement was designed consisting of four wheels, each sprung independently – a total of eight wheels in all.'

So, this time, Bert, probably the world's smallest motor racing development engineer, was to be in charge of the construction of the world's largest racing car and he did this job just as well as all the others. It had to go to America untried, of course, and it reflects enormous credit on all concerned that, among all that vast complexity of engineering, only one serious snag arose. Eyston says this about it after describing 'Thunderbolt's' torrent of power on the outward and return run 'But we were disappointed for a dog clutch disengaged behind the starboard engine and I had to shut off promptly. A week of work and we tried again but the same fault persisted. My men were on their mettle – it was always necessary to dismantle the car completely to put matters right, but they managed it.'

Indeed they did and the results spoke for themselves – Flying Kilometre 312 mph. exactly. Flying Mile 311.42 mph.

Then, just for good measure before going home, the two of them shared the driving of 'Speed of the Wind' again, putting the World's 24 hour Speed Record up to 163.68 mph. And that was it for 1937. And, in 1938, they did it again, 'Thunderbolt' jacking it up to 357.5 mph – for the second and last time before the war.

The story of Bert Denly's motorcycle race successes is covered in the first part of this book but, as can be seen and great though they were, they formed only a part of the whole.

Bert is an old friend of mine and we always enjoy chatting together about old times. But the trouble is that, in his life, he has done so much that it really is quite hard to recall the sequence so quite a lot of research was needed to establish even the highlights, some of which were a surprise to the subject himself. So, trying to ease him in gradually, as it were, we went right back to the very beginning. Bert had clear recollections of his first motorcycle, the one with which he delivered meat for the Butcher in Weybridge. It was a 1917 Douglas, which he owned whilst he was living in Byfleet.

It was, of course, while riding this machine that he met O'Donovan who was then the Norton Racing Manager and works rider.

Apart from the Douglas he had no other machines or machine he kept for racing. Indeed, he did not know anything about racing. He knew about Brooklands, of course, but although it was on the doorstep, he had never been there because you had to pay to go in. And, anyway, he wasn't all that interested. He ran the old Douglas on the road and it got him around wherever he wanted to go – that was all he wanted.

When he started the job with O'Donovan, they worked on the machines for a bit, or rather Don did with Bert helping – just so that he could get to know what they looked like. Then Don suggested he had better have a ride round the track and he sent Bert out with a mark on the throttle lever, telling him not to open it any further than that. But he didn't really tell Bert much about what to expect although he knew every inch of the track himself. Don was amazing with a stopwatch – he could tell the speed of a bike or a car over any point, no matter how short a stretch it was. How he did it no one knows. He could tell the speed of a machine at any point, even over a distance of a hundred yards or so. He must have had a good walk round at some time, on the quiet, and measured up some of the landmarks that could be seen from different places.

Bert went out and had a go, trying to keep the throttle where Don had said, but when he got back he received a severe telling-off from Don, who said he had gone too quickly. Bert considered his speed on this first run had been between sixty and seventy, although it seemed more. It was unlikely he had ever touched fifty on the Douglas, which was the only other machine he had ridden. Even at that speed the Norton gave a rough ride, with its rigid frame and small section tyres. The worst of it was that Don was half as big again as him. The bike fitted Don but Bert could hardly reach the handlebars. Looking back Bert thought it unlikely that he could have held the Norton if it had hit a real bump. He had his arms extended dead straight, even to reach the bars. If it had twitched, he would have lost one bar and that would have been the end of it. And probably the end of his career as a racer. Next time out, Don let him go a bit faster. Bert didn't think he would make it on that occasion. The bike shook and wobbled; he had a hell of a job to stay on it. Indeed, he felt scared stiff, but he wouldn't admit it of course.

Once he had been out for four or five rides and managed to stay on each time, he gained more confidence because he knew it wasn't only luck that was preventing him from coming off. He was all right then.

All this time, O'Donovan had been helpful and understanding. He wanted it to work out and he was helpful in that way. But it seems unlikely that he fully understood that because the bike fitted him at racing speeds, it would have been easier for Bert if it had been made to fit him whilst he was cruising. He would have got with it much quicker had this been so. His feet were only just on the rests but it was the distance between the saddle and the handlebars that made it hard. It really was a full stretch for him even to reach them. Don was better with a sidecar than he was with a solo, but it was his knowledge of the track itself that really impressed Bert. He knew every bump and every gradient. Apart from the track itself, he also knew how to use and to cheat the wind. If the wind was coming off the Byfleet, he'd take a line across the Fork well out from the Vickers sheds so as to get the most benefit from it on the run up onto the Home Banking. And, if it was against him, he'd tuck the bike so close into Vickers, it seemed he might touch the sheds, so that his line would slow him as little as possible.

Bert's first success came after a couple of months, when an attempt was made for the

'Hour' record. Jack Emerson had got it then at about seventy eight or nine and they put it up to 82 mph. By that time, Bert was obviously in control.

Although he had not liked to mention about the bike not fitting him he did so when they started going longer distances. He did a lot of riding that year because although they had taken the 'Hour' in June, the old man wanted to push it up as far as possible, so they went after it again twice in October. Bert managed about eighty-five on each occasion, from memory. But Vic Horsman took it off them less than a month later and it was the middle of the next year – 1924 – before they got it back again at 87 mph.

Bert's first big race success occurred during the 200 Mile Solo in 1923 – the same year. The problem that came up at the last moment on that occasion was the minimum weight riders had to be – nine stone six. Not even Don had thought about that. Bert managed to start in the end, with lead sheet screwed to the soles of his boots and sheet lead sewn into a cushion strapped round his waist. He only just made it, for, there was practically nowhere else to fix lead to him. He won the race, but at the end of it the inner tube could be seen poking through the rear tyre and there was not a single roller on the primary chain.

Don was pleased with the result. He showed when he was pleased, but certainly not otherwise, and it was mostly 'otherwise'. One of the first jobs he gave to Bert was to paint one of the sidecar bodies red while he went to do some shopping in Weybridge.

Denly's first big successs. Winner 500cc Class, Brooklands 200 Mile Solo Race at 77.61 mph. 'Hardly a roller left on the primary chain and the inner tube peeping through the rear tyre!'.

By now – made to measure – nearly!

That was all he told him. Bert looked around the shed and found a brush and went on looking for paint. In the end he found what he thought was paint – but it wasn't – it was rouge Don used for fitting bearings. Bert used it all on the sidecar body and when Don came back, he nearly went through the roof. He grabbed a primary chain that was hanging on the wall and slung it at Bert. If he had been taller and moved more slowly it would have cut his head off.

He retaliated by picking it up and slinging it back at him. Don then calmed down and was as nice as could be. One could never predict his behaviour; it was the Irish streak in him.

From that time on, Bert has few other vivid memories of how he spent his apprenticeship with O'Donovan or of the races in which he rode during the time they were together. But he recalls Nigel Spring coming into the picture to take over the Norton Racing Department from O'Donovan, particularly because by that time – 1927 – the 'Hour' was again the 'property' of Horsman, who had held it since September of the previous year at just over 94 mph. The fact that there were only six more miles to be crammed into the hour in order to be first to reach the magic figure made this a priority target for them.

The moment they were ready, the equipe set off hotfoot for Montlhéry but, once there, it was far from plain sailing. Although they were successful in the end, Bert got it on the fourth attempt. The first attempt lasted fifty-six minutes until the magneto went; on the second he did fifty-two minutes when the magneto went again. After something like about fifty minutes of the next attempt, the engine blew up. In consequence, they had to work all night because other people were after the record. Next

1926. Successes followed – but still on beaded tyres. Bert and 'Wizard' O'Donovan, pleased with a big win.

morning he went out again and they managed to scramble home.

Bert couldn't believe he was the first man ever to put 100 miles into the hour on a 500cc bike. They had been running almost all the week, and it was the fourth attempt they had made. He was beginning to think they would never do it in the time they had left. Nortons got a few shillings out of it, of which he had some.

He does, in fact, hold two other 'records' connected with this because he is the only rider firstly to have broken the 500 cc 'Hour' Record twice in one month (which he did in October 1923 when riding under O'Donovan's banner) and secondly, twice in the same week. He achieved this when trying to be the first to notch up the century on the 23rd June 1927 – the first of the four runs he describes as having lasted for fifty-six minutes. He didn't make the magic hundred that time but, nevertheless, he bettered Vic Horsman's 94.15 in his fifty-six minute run, averaging 95.02 mph. In other words, he put nearly a mile more into fifty six minutes than Horsman had put into the hour.

It will be recalled that Bert did that first hundred miles in the hour in 1927 – fifty two years ago. In the mid-nineteen thirties, about eight years after his run. *The Motor Cycle* gave a cup for the first British 500 cc multi-cylinder machine to put a hundred miles into the hour. A lot of people attempted to do so, Ben Bickell on an Ariel 'Square Four', Tom Atkins on a Douglas – a flat twin, Tommy Spann on a vertical twin Triumph and New Imperials with their wide-angle vee twin. New Imperials finally got it, with 'Ginger' Wood the rider. It proved a very difficult nut to crack and it does seem strange, that all those years later it should have proved so hard. Bert's own views were sought, in the hope that he could offer some explanation for the time gap.

In his days at the track, singles were the vogue up to 500 cc capacity. They had years of development behind them and the bugs were mainly ironed out. By the mid-thirties, small capacity twins were only just coming into the racing scene so they were probably still in the phase of having their problems sorted out. He was surprised they had not made better progress, but it was difficult to comment further because he didn't see any of the runs. By that time he was having his own problems with the cars, which kept him fully occupied. He knew there were a lot of unsuccessful runs – he thought the trouble with the Ariel was the hot spot that used to build up in the centre of the block with the four cylinders round it so that the head gasket proved to be the thing that kept failing. But he had no recollection of what troubles befell the others.

Some entrants at the track always had new cars or bikes each year, but never parted with the previous year's machinery until the new ones had been proven. But neither O'Donovan or Spring parted with any machines to other riders. It was a gradual process. They kept rebuilding all the time, and trying new ideas. In consequence a situation occurred where they started with a new machine and would continuously replace parts until they reached the point where, one day, they replaced the part which was the last of the original bike. Some of the parts fitted were, of course, experimental.

When the Norton era ended and Bert became works rider for AJS, still working with Nigel Spring, he started with a clean sheet of paper as it were. He had quite a stable

Unique success, under the mantle of Nigel Spring (centre). A. Denly – First man ever to cover a hundred miles in the hour on a five hundred. 28th June 1927. Speed 100.57 mph.

Back at Brooklands and another photograph. L to R. Bert, Nigel Spring, Monty Bird ('Jazz' of Discol) and George Pearce.

Practice day Paddock shot. Spring, Denly and passenger George Pearce.

comprising 350's 500's and even a giant single, a 750, all of which he rode, both solo and sidecar.

The 750 cc single was a terrible monster, although the idea behind it was good, because in the long distance Outer Circuit races at Brooklands, 500 cc and 600 cc singles often were coming home ahead of the 1000 cc twins and, of course, because there were records to be had in the 750 cc class. When riding it at Montlhéry, he managed to scramble round at nearly 120 mph, but the frame broke and the engine scraped along the ground. Bert thought he was falling off, but he didn't and that was the last time he rode it. It was a bored out five hundred, the extra capacity being gained by getting the crankpin as far out as possible on the flywheel so that the engine had an enormously long stroke. It was a terrible engine. It was rough and it vibrated, he thought. He recollects however, that he did manage to win one race or event with it at Brooklands.

Contrastingly, both the 350 cc and the 500 cc singles were very good to ride. The 350 in particular was a lovely little machine. All the bikes from the Spring stable were superbly turned out. They almost rivalled the Grindlay Peerless and Nortons run by Bill Lacey. Bert thought that Bill may have been a little in front of them. His machines looked lovely and they went.

The AJS engines, with their chain driven overhead camshafts, were not quite as easy to work on as the old push rod Nortons. But they were very good. Some valve spring trouble was encountered early on but once they had overcome it they had no trouble at all. If they were going for a hundred mile record or for the hour, they knew they were going to get to the other end.

Of his rivals, Bert considers Le Vack stood out the most, as a rider, above the others. He rode all classes of bikes. He built them, developed and tuned them and rode them and deserved all the success he had. Freddy Hicks was another who prepared and rode his bikes well. Bert remembers pairing up with Fred on one of the Ajays for some long distance records. Baker rode with them to make up the trio. Fred did well on an AJS in a 200 Mile Race too. And, of course, there was Lacey – he was always good. Of the other Brooklands personalities, he never came across Dixon very much, who was riding Douglas towards the end. Marchant was good, very good. He used to build and tune his own bikes and knew how to ride them. Chris Staniland was a very good rider but the machine didn't really interest him. He was test pilot for Fairey Aviation and didn't have the time. Worters used to do all his bikes and between them they made a good team. Each of them performed his role perfectly. He didn't know much about Fernihough because he was usually on the smaller capacity bikes during the time Bert was riding. He never contemplated riding any make of machine other than an AJS or a Norton.

He had no preference towards riding solo or sidecar. He just didn't mind at all. But sidecars were harder work and sometimes more exciting. He had more big thrills with sidecars. He had two handlebars break off on sidecars and one on solos. He did mean break off too. Each time it occurred on the left, so that he still had a throttle but no clutch. The one on the solo occurred during a two hundred mile race. Horsman, Le Vack, Rex Judd and himself were all up in a tight bunch when the bar broke off. It was definitely the left bar that time. It went just as he was leaving the Railway Straight to go onto the Byfleet Banking – the worst place it could have chosen. But he stayed on and got the bike back to the pits.

He thought he was carrying ballast in lieu of a passenger both times, although he could not be sure he didn't have Jack King with him on one of these occasions. He was his passenger for a lot of the time before Jack went on to ride with Pat Driscoll. Jack won a cup one year, a passengers cup, when he rode in one of the long races with Bert.

He holds no strong views about machines other than those he rode. The two-strokes are going well now, which suggests the designers must have overlooked something. Back in the early days O'Donovan had a little two-stroke Velocette going very well indeed, at about the time he started. He rode it only once and they were up in the eighties with it then. Rex Judd rode it several times and O'Donovan was really interested in it until it locked up one day and threw him off. After that he didn't care much about it. It would seem unlikely O'Donovan ever put it in a race.

He remembers having very few mechanical troubles. They used to have a bit of valve trouble now and again, but very little trouble with the big end. The Ajays were not much bother at all.

By 1927 Nigel Spring's track Nortons were shedding the 'spindly' appearance of O'Donovan's in the early 1920's. Wired on tyres, too!

Asked whether he considered whether Brooklands would have been any use today, his reply was typical. He could not see why not. It was a good testing ground. It was bumpy of course but if a machine could stick Brooklands it could stick any place.

With regard to personalities, chaps like Ebby and George Reynolds were both very nice men indeed. Ebby was all right if you didn't try to score over him. He had a difficult job to do and he did it well. He always seemed to want to help you if he could.

Reverting to the cars with which he had been involved, which comprised everything from a 750 to building the huge World Land Speed Record six wheeled Thunderbolt, Bert drew attention to the diesels they used for record breaking. The first diesel, a saloon, had an AEC bus engine built up in a Chrysler chassis. They had some fun with that. He cannot remember what the front axle was, but he recalls it breaking when he was lapping Montlhery at about a hundred and nine with it. That was exciting. He lost a front wheel and when it went, all the brakes went too – they were hydraulic. It was at night, just before he came off the banking. There was a big firework display. The car tried to run down the banking, to the inside into the sand, and if it had done so it would have rolled over. He had to use all his strength to keep it on the track and it finished up about a foot from the inside. He remembered that all right!

When Eyston asked him if he would like to finish running-in the Bugatti for him,

Big success, 1928. Nigel, Bert and passenger Jack King, winners of the 600cc Class 200 Mile Sidecar Race at 79.93 mph. Jack worked for Pat Driscoll and was his regular passenger.

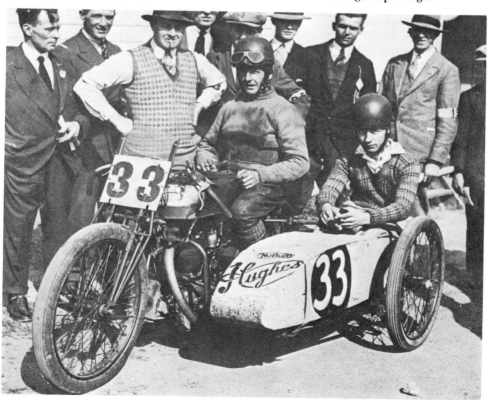

Bert didn't wait for him to change his mind. He'd never even sat in a racing car but soon he was in it and going round before Eyston had started on his way back to the Clubhouse. He told Bert the revs to use, left him to it and said he'd call him in when he got back. Bert just kept going and that was how it began. Whilst he was driving the car, one or two ideas cropped up in his mind which he could put to the Captain concerning the car, and that was that. Eyston seemed quite happy and, as he left, he said something like 'I'll be seeing you' or words to that effect. Later, he wrote, to ask him to go and see him, which he did. It seemed likely that with the steam going out of the bike side at the track, Eyston knew they were all on the look out for something to do. He wasn't a man to take someone away from a job that they were happy doing. All this was towards the end of 1930, when Bert was still with Nigel Spring and AJS. Even then, Pat Driscoll and he had been thinking about going to Nortons. They actually went to the factory but the money wasn't all that good so that was out. The meeting with the Captain came at just the right moment. Bert had no hesitation in starting straight away with him.

There was a lot of experimental work going on all the time as well as general maintenance. The first job he did was to overhaul the blower of the big 4.9 litre Bugatti that Kaye Don had been driving at Brooklands. When that was done, they did some testing with that car at the track, springs and suspension mainly. He did the testing of that. He recollects that he got round at nearly 130 mph. But the big car was a handful.

Same Team – Winners again. This time the 350cc 200 Mile Solo Race 1929. Speed 89.20 mph.

Again in 1930. Short or long distance made no difference. Winner of a one lap 500cc 'Sprint' at 90.88 mph.

It jumped about all over the place. But it was quick. It was not possible for the driver to keep his foot down all the way round. They were trying to improve the handling and the brakes – they did a lot of brake testing too.

Thereafter one job followed another. If a manufacturer wanted racing or record breaking advertising they just handed the problem to the Captain. So it never stopped. MGs, Rileys, Singers – and the big Panhard. On the last of these, the testing was carried out at Montlhéry. It was a giant and when Bert got in it he couldn't see over the top of the scuttle. He had to have a special seat made for him. He needed that always for the big cars. It used to fit inside the Captain's seat, so when he got out for him to take over on a record run, he just took his seat with him – and put it back in before he took over again. The Panhard was quick, though – 140 mph plus. But it was also heavy and hard to steer.

Captain Eyston was very good to work with. He used to take the problems over from the manufacturers, whatever they were, racing or going for records. They said what sort of advertising it was that they wanted and then left it to him. Sometimes he knew right away the best way to do it, sometimes he would talk it over with Bert first, but either way they invariably arrived at the same solution. From then on it was just a question of how to tackle the attempt. When the car was ready to go, he drove it if it was a short run or they shared the driving if it was a long one. The runs that stand out as being the most enjoyable are those in which they broke records.

Mention of the very long, fast runs they did with 'Speed of the Wind' on the salt, brought back some memories. Bert recalls how they had a nine mile circuit marked out, flat and unbanked. Sometimes the salt bed used to break up into rough patches after about 12 hours and these patches had to be avoided because they shook the car and would sometimes cause it to break away. When this happened they had to fight to get it back. It would lose adhesion and start to drift out wide. It had front wheel drive, of course, but it was necessary to get it back quickly because at 165 mph or more it would soon be a long way off course. Whilst this was happening the car had to be kept flat out. Getting it back on course was hard work because it was so big and heavy. It was hard work driving it too, if the weather was hot, as it often was. It was not unusual to have both hands on the same side of the steering wheel. Bert used to drive it like that quite a lot of the time later in the runs. He could not recall whether he ever mentioned it to the Cpatain, who may have done the same.

During the hot runs, they had the pit in a tent, open at each end for the car to run in and out, so that the chaps could work in a bit of shade. They had to be careful when coming in after an hour or two at speed. If they came in too fast, they could easily find themselves still travelling at 120 mph, wrapped up in the tent!

With regard to 'Thunderbolt', only the Captain drove that. It never ran until they got to the States. One memory that will always stand out is the first time they did a quick run with the car. They used a Dodge truck to start it, with a boom stuck out in the front which fitted into a dowel in the tail of the car. Bert drove the truck and the Captain told him to go flat out all the way and not to take his foot off until he met up with him at the end of the run, so that they could do a quick turn round for the reverse run. They must have been doing about sixty when the car's engines fired and there was so much black smoke that visibility was nil. It really was – Bert could see no further than the tip of the bonnet. He kept his foot down and just hoped that the car hadn't stopped somewhere in the fog. But it hadn't and, after what seemed a long flat out drive, he could see it in the distance. When he got there he climbed out and scrambled on to the car to get the hatch cover off. For a moment he thought they must have had the wrong driver because there was a black man sitting in the cockpit. It was the Captain, covered from head to foot in black dust from the brakes. That was the second lesson they learned. The first was the trouble they had with the clutches.

The problem with the clutches created plenty of work, but they had a lot of help over there. That was the only trouble they had, even though the whole project was experimental. The engines were the only known quantity. Everything else was, to some extent, experimental, at least until they had been out for the first time. Even second time round they didn't know what might crop up, but it was all right in the end.

Bert is well into his seventies now and enjoying comfortable retirement in Sussex. He enjoys seeing old friends and chatting over past events and the day I spent with him will never quite be forgotten. I asked him if he ever saw the Captain? His reply was very much in the affirmative. He had seen him only the week previous, when they had another day's fishing together.

Bert enjoys his retirement and has no complaints at all. He potters about. He drives the children to school and collects them in the school bus. His family and grand-children are nearby. Nice to be driven to school by a driver who, in his time, may well have touched nigh on a hundred and eighty! And that was forty four years ago.

L.P. DRISCOLL

In a sense, Pat Driscoll was one of my earliest Brooklands contacts because it was in 1932 that, having bought my first Brooklands 'racer' and put in my entry, I was detected in the act by my parents who, at the time, weren't keen on the idea at all. Thinking it better, at the time, to avoid direct confrontation, I contacted Duncan Ferguson, then Secretary of the British Motor Cycle Racing Club, explaining the position and asking if he knew anyone who would like to ride the bike for me. The bike, of course, was the 174 cc EF-JAP, a product of Eric Fernihough's fertile brain, two-speed and with belt drive, the very last belt driven racer to run at Brooklands.

I didn't really expect that anyone would jump at the chance much as I longed to ride it myself but, to my delight, I received a letter from Duncan saying that a Mr. Jack King, sidecar passenger to Mr. L. P. Driscoll, would be glad to ride the bike. That was how I came to know Jack and, through him, Pat.

In my capacity as the ever-present spectator, I had seen Pat ride many times, particularly admiring his style with sidecar outfits in 'Round the Mountain' events and wondering who his active and intrepid passenger could be. Later, I enjoyed seeing him race his supercharged TT Lea Francis on the same course and even recall one 'Bemsee' meeting when, driving the Lea Francis, he took part in a match race against another sidecar outfit on the same course.

I found Pat to be the friendliest of riders, so much so that since he was the only star whose acquaintance I'd made at that time, I haunted him to the extent that he must have reached the point of being fed up with the sight of me. Somehow, he managed never to show it.

Later still, when he switched over altogether from bikes to cars, becoming Number One man in the works Austin racing team, finally driving the lovely little supercharged 750 cc overhead camshaft single seaters, I envied him still more, listening avidly to anything he had to say and valuing his friendship very much indeed.

While Pat did ride solos, I always thought of him as a sidecar man, later wishing that I'd known him during the era in which he was riding regularly in all those wonderful long distance Outer Circuit races but finally accepting that as time had passed, I never would hear the story of them direct from him. So it was rather a special day for me when, at last having an excuse to go down to see him in Hampshire, I spent a marvellous day with him to get the story that follows.

I had written to him and subsequently spoken on the 'phone so that when the day came and having enjoyed his hospitality for lunch, I was delighted to find that he'd had a good think about things on which to talk. I had hardly to refresh his memory at all from the extensive notes I'd taken with me.

Pat's motor racing career ended with a very serious accident indeed in which one of the works Austins overturned. He was injured so badly that, after a long convalescence, racing of any sort was out, which made him turn to boats, allied to marine engineering which, to some extent, is obviously still an interest.

Armed with my tape recorder and sheaves of questions, I little realised the easy passage I was going to have because, right from the start, he was able to recall nearly everything I asked without reference to notes. Our talk just sailed ahead and all I had to do was listen.

Pat's motorcyling career started at the time when he lived at Ealing. There was a very famous motorcyclist, Billy Newsome of Newsome & Fletcher, who had a shop at Ealing, and he used to pass his shop on his way to and from school. Newsome was a friend of his father's and Pat used to go in there and look at the bikes and waste a lot of time. The Driscoll family had a very good driver named Charlie Lloyd, who drove Pat's father's cars, and who was with the Mercedes company before he came to them to do demonstration work and take parties on to the Continent.

There had always been engineering in the family. Pat's grandfather was Dennis O'Driscoll, Chief Engineer to John Fowler of traction engine fame. His father had dropped the 'O' from his own surname after the Irish troubles at the end of the last century. Pat's father was an architect and while he liked cars, and they always had a good number of cars, he liked horses more and they were all brought up to ride them. Through Lloyd, Pat was first introduced to Brooklands. He used to go to Ealing County School and when his father was away quite frequently at his masonic meetings, Charlie Lloyd used to write a letter excusing Pat from school so that he could take him to Brooklands. In fact on one occasion when they were there, he and his cousin, Cliff Lewis, whom most people will remember, met Baragwanath. To boys of about 13, as they were then before the first World War, he was a real man mountain.

He used to manage about six trips a year to Brooklands with Charlie Lloyd, all in school time and all unbeknown to his father. Their visits were made mostly in the week, on practice days, and as a result Pat got to know quite a number of people. Although he was young, the elder people seemed to be young too; they didn't appear to be as old as they would seem to today's younger generation so he didn't get turned away as in all probability children would today.

Right from the start Pat had the urge to race and he wanted to join a club. He got the address of George Reynolds, the Secretary of the MCC, from Mr. Newsome. The Club Headquarters were then at Leytonstone and he wrote to join, but he wasn't eligible for membership until he reached the age of 14. He joined the club on 5th December 1914, the same day as he had his first driving licence.

Pat's first race was in the 1920 MCC Brooklands meeting, when he rode a Power Plus Indian in a two lap event. He didn't do any good because he didn't know how to ride a bike properly, let alone how to sit on it correctly.

He found it a bit of a surprise riding at Brooklands. Although he was able to ride the machine flat out on the road he discovered that when he rode at Brooklands and hit a lot of bumps it was a bit disconcerting.

The MCC had only one meeting each year, which on this occasion proved more than enough for Pat. He didn't go very well and that put him completely off the Indian. He was rather a small lad, and not awfully heavy so he decided that he wasn't heavy enough to sit on a 1000 cc motorcycle. He advertised the Indian together with a sidecar he owned, in *The Motor Cycle*, in exchange for a Sunbeam or similar, thinking that he would then ride in trials for a spell, trials riding being good fun in those days.

Amongst the replies he received was one from a man named L. G. Williams of Shepton Mallet, who had one of the 1920 works Nortons that had been ridden by Noel Brown into 8th position in the 1920 TT. This was in January 1921 and the machine was a side valve. The overheads didn't go in for the TT until 1922, the first one of them being ridden by Tony Vandervell. The upshot of this was a few letters, because it was not customary to telephone long distances in those days. Pat was offered the Norton and an OK with a Villiers engine, which was one of the cheapest bikes you could get in those days, in exchange for the Indian combination. He went to Reading, after agreeing to the swap, with his father in the sidecar and Wally Loweth, who was the younger brother of A. L. Loweth who used to ride Nortons in later days. Both parties met at Reading station, as arranged, and made their way to the fast road on the London side of Reading where they could try the various bikes. Pat liked the Norton and Williams liked the Indian, but the former didn't look at the OK at all, because he didn't think much of it. A deal was arranged on a level swap basis and they went back to Reading to have lunch, Wally riding the OK and Pat the Norton. That was how he came to ride Nortons, simply because he had got a racing machine which he wasn't really looking for!

The Norton was entered for the annual meeting run by the Motor Cycle Club because Pat didn't feel sufficiently confident to go into the full-blown BMCRC races. He thought they were all too expert and that he would do better by adopting this approach. But it was a bit of a myth because when he got there, the races were more or less comprised of BMCRC members, so he thought he might just as well have gone in for the others. He rode the Norton and even had a bit of trouble sitting on that, but it finished its race, a short handicap of two or three laps. That was the end of Brooklands for 1921. Later, he rode the bike, with its close ratio gearbox and high gear ratio, in an MCC sporting trial that proved to be a bit of a miss, and from then on he raced it in hill climbs and speed trials, with reasonable success. His next visit to Brooklands was on the occasion of the Gypsy Motor Cycle Club meeting in 1922. By then he had put a sidecar on it, a very light sidecar which he used in some hill climb events, and he won that Gypsy race, which was his very first race win. The prize for it was a Wex carburettor. The Wex carburettor was supposed to be very very good but money was very short in those days and he couldn't afford to try it and make it second-hand because it was more valuable to sell and so get a few pounds to buy other things. He could not recall whether he ran that bike again at Brooklands in 1922, but he raced it in a lot of hill climbs and speed trials and broke the record at Aston Clinton. In two years he won over a hundred firsts in events of this kind, for there were hill climbs and speed trials held every weekend.

Pat continued to use the same bike up to 1924, for it was that year, some time between Easter and Whitsun, that he joined O'Donovan. The opportunity came about when Percy Chambers, who had been responsible for the repair and tuning of motorcycles at O'Donovan's Great Portland Street premises, decided to leave. Pat was asked if he would go and work there which he did, as he was glad of the opportunity. His 16H Norton, which had won a tremendous number of events, had been tuned by himself, and it was this that had made O'Donovan interested in having him work for his firm. Pat was also very interested in getting into the O'Donovan establishment as he thought there were probably a lot of secrets he could learn.

O'Donovan was an Irishman, with a Jekyll and Hyde temperament. Either he was most placid, or he was in a furious temper. There were times when Bert Denly and Pat had been working at Brooklands and something had displeased him or they had been for some long distance records and the bike had blown up. At one time, most probably during 1926, they had a particularly bad run on big ends. They were going out for long distance records and after covering about 200 miles the big ends were collapsing completely. As a result, his temper didn't improve. Pat can recall that when they came in

L.P. Driscoll. 588cc Norton and sidecar. Passenger Jack King.

and started taking the machine apart, O'Donovan had come in furious with rage and had picked up a hammer which he threw at them. Later, he came back and brought them some sandwiches, all placid again. But he was quite a nice chap to work for. He was extremely clever. He knew the speed of anything over any part of the track. Pat could not recall anyone who had that quite exceptional ability. It was a particularly valuable attribute because so many people would not do a complete lap for fear of being timed by stopwatch. Yet he would get them just the same.

Pat stayed with O'Donovan from early 1924 until eventually he left in the early part of 1927, to open Brooklands Service Station. In the meantime he had tried to buy a partnership in O'Donovan Motors because the firm wasn't very prosperous when he joined them. He wanted to buy a half share but they couldn't agree a price and the long and short of that was that O'Donovan gave him the sack. But Bert Beach, his partner, who had the biggest financial interest in the business, came round and saw Pat the next day. He said the financial aspects had nothing to do with Don, and so he couldn't sack him. Would Pat come back? So he went back. Later, he got out of favour again during March 1925, when Nigel Spring, Staniland and he went for some records. They got about 15 records, which in those days were Class Records, but there were some that were classed as World Records, which annoyed O'Donovan very much. He nearly got the sack again over that, but eventually nothing came of the incident. Pat rode a Spring bike that year and won the 200 Mile Race on it.

In the 1925 Hutchinson 100 race, Pat started as a reserve, but had to retire when the clutch lever came undone and the screws fell out. He held the lever in his hand until it made a tremendous great blister, about the size of an egg. In the end he could hold it no longer and had to retire. After that they used to tape up their controls. It was a safety precaution they learnt the hard way.

Brooklands would shake things to bits in no time at all, especially as the girder front forks they were using in those days were very rigid. They didn't provide much spring-ing, not like a modern fork, and of course they were used in conjunction with only a narrow section tyre. The tyres in use then were only of about 26 x 2 1/4 inch size, of the beaded edge type.

He won the 1925 200 Mile Race, with 41 laps of the 500 cc race covered. Denly's Norton was second and Hough's AJS third, Driscoll's Norton coming up through the field slowly and relentlessly. Horsman dropped out and Pat went on to win at 82.80 mph. According to Pat, Grogan should have won that race, but coming in to the pits, he skidded and fell off, cutting his nose very badly. He had to be taken to hospital to have it stitched. He was placed fourth in the end but he would have won the race otherwise.

In the report of the 1926 200 Mile Sidecar Race, it is recorded that the suspension of Pat's sidecar appeared to be slowly collapsing. Pat, however, claims this to be untrue.

Pat Driscoll and Jack keeping low round 'the Byfleet'. A practice run.

It didn't collapse at all. He started off with a fellow named Felix Thompson riding in the sidecar. Norman Thompson was his correct name, but he was usually known as Felix. He had ridden in Pat's sidecar in short races and sprints before, and was very good but for some unknown reason he became completely hysterical on this occasion after probably about twenty laps. He got into such a state that he was going to get out of the sidecar so Pat had to come in. Denly had already stopped with a broken gudgeon pin so he took Denly's passenger on board and they had done about two laps when he started punching Pat in the ribs and indicating to him that he wanted him to stop. So they went into the pits and stopped whereupon his latest passenger announced his false teeth had dropped out on the track! He wanted to go and look for them and he wouldn't continue, but whether he ever found them remains a mystery. Fortunately a huge chap, a spectator standing at the back of the rails behind the old pits, said he would take over and he climbed over the rails. Norman Thompson was sitting there with his red jersey on which was worn by those riding the 600s. The newcomer insisted he took this jersey off for him to wear and then he got into the sidecar, which was a little streamlined Watsonian affair. He was so big that he hung out about two feet at the back and off they went. They had covered quite a distance before the bolts that held the body down pulled out of the front of the sidecar, so they had to go into the pits and fit straps.

They climbed back to second place, but with something like 7 to 10 laps to the finish and the bike going beautifully, a gudgeon pin broke. Pat was credited with seventh place, even though he had retired several laps adrift. What displeased him most was that the special gudgeon pins he was using had been made by Vickers.

Pat rode in both of the 1926 200 Mile Races solo. He rode a Zenith-Chater Lea in the morning and a Norton in the afternoon, having the mag chain break along the Railway Straight whilst riding the latter.

The Zenith-Chater Lea ride came about because he had ridden in the 1925 sidecar TT on the Norton and had an engine that was a bit of a pup. He wrote to tell Spring about it and he brought over one of their own Brooklands engines which they put in. This annoyed Nortons very much because they were running a new dry sump engine which was giving a lot of trouble. When they put the Brooklands engine in, it went well and Pat managed a lap at 39 mins 50 secs which was about 20 seconds faster than Freddie Dixon's record lap.

It was this that made Nortons a bit cross with him but in the race a rocker standard broke at Ballacraine and so Pat went out on the first lap.

Nortons wouldn't let him have a bike for the 500 cc event the next year, but because Beach of O'Donovans was very friendly with Dougal Marchant and he realised Pat could ride reasonably well, he suggested that Zenith build a 350 frame to take a Chater Lea engine and that Pat should ride the finished machine. Unfortunately these machines were built at the time of the general strike, and because they had to get special people in, instead of the normal frame builders, both frames were overheated during brazing. In both races the centre section of the frame that held the tank and gearbox broke and although the bikes finished in both races it was a question of holding the tank and the gear lever with the knees for half of the race, which wasn't very entertaining.

In 1927 Pat started up from scratch on his own, running the Brooklands Service Station. He had done a lot of tuning for private owners. O'Donovan didn't touch any

Pat and Jack (490cc Norton). Fresh after a long ride.

private owners' bikes except the very special ones, like those owned by Grogan and Spring. The others used to come up to Great Portland Street where Loweth and Pat used to work on them. Pat considered he had got O'Donovan Motors round the corner financially because he knew what needed to be done to the bikes so that they could be made to go quickly with only a small expenditure. He also knew how to sell stuff, whereas nobody there had any idea. Soon O'Donovan Motors were getting quite prosperous and he realised that if he could do it for them in such a small shop, as they had there, he could do it for himself, especially if he could get some reasonable premises. So he went ahead and obtained premises in Ealing, whereupon he did very well right from the beginning. When the Labour Government came in to power, in about 1929, money became very short and things were difficult financially. By then Pat was employing about three people and it was a job to keep his head above water but he somehow managed. It was not until about 1930 that the pinch became very severe and he thought he may have to close because trade was falling off so much. It was then that he hit upon an idea that might bring things round. He placed a column advertisement in *The Motor Cycle* suggesting that Norton owners should bring their machine to Brooklands Service Station to have any repairs carried out. All they would need to pay for were the parts required, as all labour would be free. It produced the desired result and he was swamped with work. He made enought profit on the spares to tide himself over a troublesome time. The Motor Trade Association held a special meeting in London about this novel approach and Pat thought everybody was against him except old man Stevens who ran the London Velocette agency. He supported him and said there was nothing in any regulations to prevent him giving away his labour if he wanted to. He considered the MTA would only make themselves look stupid if they

Pat Driscoll rode Spring's 588cc Norton, and Denly the 490cc in the 1928 200 Mile Solo races. Bert retired before half distance. Pat won the 1000cc Race at 87.07 mph.

tried to take action, so the whole thing was dropped. In consequence, Pat conducted his business in this manner for twelve months, by which time he had got round the corner.

Some of the Norton engines with which he was supplied were far from satisfactory and needed much attention before they could be used competitively. For example, on the 16H side valve and model 18 overhead valve engines there was a cam lever that ran on the cam from the fulcrum and back, each end of the timing case, which lifted the ohv push rod tappet or in the case of the side valve engine, the tappet alone. An identical part was used in either case but a problem arose because the cam levers were not ground to shape against a jig. As a result they could be off-centre as much as 3/16ths of an inch. Consequently an inlet valve timed to open at about 20 degrees before top dead centre would be closing dead on bottom dead centre or the other way round. Experience taught him exactly where to look and what to check.

In the earlier account of the races at Brooklands during the twenties it will be recalled that a lot of model 18 Nortons in long races seem to have gone out through broken rocker standards. When questioned about this, Pat recalled that it was not until 1925 that this problem occurred. He had one go in the 1925 TT. The 1925 rocker standard had been altered so that it was possible to use a valve spring which was approximately 50% longer than the original. In consequence it was necessary to use a very hollow cap and a curved rocker lever that tucked down into it. The new design was brought out for the 1925 TT and through the practice and the race, half the bikes broke either a rocker standard or a rocker. When Norton Motors first incorporated

'Brooklands Grand Prix' events were held on the 'Mountain' circuit. Here, Pat Driscoll follows Chris Staniland's Worters entry.

1929. Pat with 'eternal' passenger Jack King, winners of the 200 Mile Race, 1000cc Class at 77.15 mph on Spring's 743cc 'single' AJS. Pat thinks it was the only race it won, but Bert Denly thinks he won one on it also, even if shorter!

the same modification in their production models, the same thing happened, but they soon altered the stamping of the standard and the rocker so that from 1927 onwards the problem had been overcome. It was almost unheard of to break a valve in a Norton. Some did go in France but they were special valves made out of KE965 from a batch of bad stampings. The whole lot broke but they were made away from the works and so it was no fault of the Norton factory.

In the 1928 200 Mile Sidecar Race, Pat had a carburettor stub break and had to change it. He made his way along the finishing straight, got a stub from some other machine, fitted it and still made third place, but he was 27 minutes behind the winner.

Carol Holbeach was his passenger in that race. In view of the trouble Pat had suffered the year before, Holbeach came to him and bet him £2 that he would stick it out, so at the end of the Race Pat had to give him £2. That's all he got for riding 200 miles in the sidecar.

In the 1000 cc 200 Mile Solo Race that year, which he also won, he had no trouble at all. He ran at a scheduled speed because he reckoned that in long distance races he didn't want to call at the pits until after about 100 miles. He would always run at his own pace because by the time the first 50 miles had been covered there would be about a dozen bikes out. As long as he had worked his way into the first three by about 100 miles mark, he considered that by depending on the Norton's reliability, he would be all right.

The retirement rate was simply enormous, because half the field set off as though they were in a 3 lap race. It was always the same. Half the field went flat out from the start. If you held back and waited for the retirements to occur, they always did. The Douglas entry was a good example. They would always spring off the line, yet all retire after the first 50 miles.

In the 1928 Brooklands Championships, a 'Round the Mountain' event with a little twist in between, there were nine starters in the 600 cc class. Tucker led all the way, Hicks was second and Pat finished third. There was, in fact, some controversy over the result with Ebby, because Pat maintained he had won. He reckoned the lap scorers were a lap adrift because Tucker turned over at the fork and he couldn't possibly have won the race. Pat reckons that while the Tucker mishap was going on, they missed him. Bemsee made amends by giving him a special award, a cigarette case with the club crest engraved on it.

He had an amusing story to tell about one of the mechanics who came down to Brooklands with Spring and Chris Stanland in 1924. He was a very good, trustworthy man, very careful, and he built the engine with which Pat won the 1925 200 Mile Race. He built most of the Norton engines and he was an absolutely first-class fitter, that is until 1928. In that year they went over to France for records, and he took a fancy to Advocat, that horrible French yellow drink. They couldn't keep him off it and when he got completely sozzled and they gave him water, it made him even worse. With the aid of Mrs. Stewart and Dougie Hawks, they locked him up in one of the car sheds that had been used for the Grand Prix and managed to get him sober in a week. He promised he wouldn't drink any more, so they let him out. Unfortunately he hadn't been out two hours before he started drinking again and it was just impossible to do anything with him. So Pat sent a wire to Spring and he came over to give him the sack. Pat took him back to London still completely sozzled, and parted company with him at Victoria after giving him some money from Spring. That was when his relationship with them ended.

In the 1929 200 Mile 1000 cc Solo Race, Pat rode one of his own 588 cc Nortons. He arranged a new method of engine lubrication. He had built an engine with a dry sump crankcase and had taken a feed out of the oil tank, straight through the timing side of the engine and into the crank. It was not a dry sump as far as the return was concerned as he was using only the pump of the dry sump system to direct oil to the big end. He had a separate foot control pedal to pump oil into the engine twice a lap, as he had done with earlier engines. This arrangement proved very successful and the bike ran beautifully. He was able to lap at about 98 – 99 miles an hour all through. It was on the last lap, as he came out from under the Members' Bridge, with the sun laying low on the horizon and shining into his eyes that he suddenly saw a huge lump of concrete on the track. He swung the bike down to the left to miss the concrete but swung it up a moment too soon so that he hit his foot on the concrete lump. It cut the footrest off as though it had been cut with a big hatchet, split the whole of his boot and broke the whole of the front of his foot. He shut off and it wasn't until the engine had actually stopped that he realised he could just as well have gone in to the pits, in which case he would have won the race. He knew Baldwin on the 1000 cc JAP was about six or eight laps behind him and that he was lapping slower than the Norton. Barber won, having averaged 90 mph as Baldwin had to finish on one cylinder. He had bent a valve and finished with no plug in the front cylinder.

It had been a simple modification to make to the Norton but he was able to lap consistently about six or seven miles an hour faster than he could before in long distance races because he was putting oil straight into the big end. Big ends were always a worry.

Just one interesting story remained – how he acquired the 172 Zenith Villiers mentioned earlier. The story started in 1927 when Pat entered for the Brooklands Grand Prix that year, which was run over the mountain course. He drove a Norton and sidecar and on the first lap was going like the clappers. When he arrived at the chicane outside the Paddock his passenger, Lionel Daniels, leaned the wrong way and they hit the sandbags. Bert Matthews ran into the back of him in the resulting melee, the front of his sidecar hitting Pat's rear wheel. Pat was using his 1925 TT bike with the offside rear wheel chain sprocket, which was cut at right angles by the impact. A bone in his ankle was cracked, too. So he was laid up for a bit. He had to visit Zeniths because he used to sell Zeniths at that time, his foot having healed well enough to be able to drive. He saw a little 175 cc trials bike and he asked Freddie Barnes if he could have a ride on it. The outcome was that he was lent it to ride in the London to Gloucester Road Trial, run by the North London Motor Cycle Club. He had an enjoyable ride too, being impressed by the bike, which was light and comfortable. It had the right gear ratios too, so that it just popped over all the rough hills. When he took it back to Zeniths, he found they had one of the first 175 cc racing Villiers engines, which they were setting up for dirt track use. When he showed interest in it, it was suggested he might like to purchase a similar model to play about with. The price was less than he thought so he bought one there and then. He thought that if he could get Jack King, who was his sidecar passenger, interested enough to ride it, it would make sure he didn't forsake the sidecar. Jack rode the Zenith Villiers in the 200 Mile Race and he led until about 5 laps from the end, when the piston collapsed. Later, Pat entered him in a five lap race, which he won at about 82 - 83 mph which, considering it was over forty years ago, was not bad going. All he did to that bike was to put on a carburettor with big choke and an 82 main jet, straight off his 588 Norton, and run it on RD1 fuel.

This took us up to the point where I came in and I can now see why Pat was happy for young Jack to ride my relic! Even now, I can recall that little Zenith with its purple and black tank – one of the prettiest of the 'tiddlers', I thought.

One or two things in Pat's story rang a bell with me. For instance, referring to his early visits to Brooklands he describes the older people as 'young', going on to say they didn't appear to be as old as they would seem to today's younger generation so he didn't get turned away as in all probability children would today. I would agree with him absolutely on this, particularly as applied to Brooklands because, when I first went there as a youngster, I received enormous kindness from older people, all of whom really wanted you to know and understand what was going on. I think that part of the reason was that young people, in that era, were much more diffident. It was an era of 'speak when you're spoken to' and, if 'spoken too' one was immediately grateful and anxious to learn. Age is no barrier at all where a mutual interest is concerned, particularly in a pioneering era.

I was interested to see that, on one occasion, Carol Holbeach rode with Pat in a 200 Mile Race because when I was at the track in the thirties, Carol was Sales Manager for Thomson and Taylor who, in addition to their tuning activities, were Railton Concessionaires. The Railton, of course, followed the Invicta as another of Noel Macklin's conceptions and when the war broke out in 1939 and Carol was out of a job, he went to work at Macklin's Fairmile organisation at Cobham. He was my boss when I joined the organisation, throughout the war years.

When talking of the £2 that Carol received for his 200 mile 'battering', Pat says 'It's different from today's money; they would want £200 today'. If he had been talking about industry, I would agree with him wholeheartedly. But, though I'm not sure, I don't think he's right when it comes to sidecar passengering – I rather think that enthusiasm is still as great and that there could still be a 'waiting list'. But I'm not certain about that, I agree.

VICTOR HORSMAN

Although I never met Vic Horsman during the time I was at Brooklands, I watched his racing with interest, marvelling at his knowledge and trackcraft.

Though his visits to Brooklands in the 1930's were probably less frequent that they had been in the twenties, I actually saw a bit more of him because, still true to Triumph, he was by then competing at BARC meetings with a beautifully turned out little 8 hp single seater which, although not as fast as its contemporaries, the works Austins, was obviously under development and was becoming faster on each appearance.

Even then, I didn't meet him and it wasn't until I began enjoying, as a guest, the TT Rider's Associations annual lunches in London that we met for the first time. We met again at the Brooklands Reunions put on each year by the Society and, by the nineteen seventies, I had the feeling that I had known him almost right from the start.

I feel sure that one reason for Vic's many successes must have been meticulous attention to detail and I don't think anyone would deny that, in every way, he is utterly concise and clear thinking when facing a problem. He is a splendid host and, in his ninetieth year, that seems to make no difference at all.

Without doubt, he is the 'Grand Old Man' of Brooklands in the literal sense because, successful as they all were, none of my subjects could have been old enough to compete at the track, as he did, before the start of World War One. This apart, he was certainly first in the field again when the track reopened in 1919.

As in the cases of the other subjects of this story, I was grateful to Vic for taking me 'behind the scenes' when talking of his arrangements with Triumphs during the time he was riding their bikes and I wasn't really surprised that, as he said, he found it preferable to be 'works supported' rather than 'works employed'. It isn't the first time I've heard it for I have found the same thing in my own life. There are many snags to being 'self employed' but one of the virtues is that no one has to be called 'sir' (except, possibly, the customer!) and one can take one's own decisions and stand by them.

In this connection, one can see exactly Vic's point of view during the time he was working for the factory and can see theirs just as clearly. If customer's racing machines, or even Replica road versions, required specialist attention, he was the chap to talk to about it. For his part, this was a boring diversion from the goals on which he'd got his eye. Very difficult, but you can't find these things out other than by trying them.

Each of the riders who became the stars in this story seem to have had a different entry into racing. Here, then is Vic Horsman's – different again.

Vic's interest in motorcycling started through reading. He was a mechanically inclined youth and he used to read technical books, the *Model Engineer* and things like that, which contained articles about building one's own motorcycle. He read these and it fired his ambition to own a motorcycle. By then he was 18 or 19 years old, with an interest in electrical and lathe work – indeed, anything that related to general engineering.

Eventually he saved up and bought a motorbike about 1905 or 1907. Exactly when he could not recall, but as he was working in Derby then and as his driving licence was No. 13, it must have been pretty early.

The first machine he tried was a front wheel drive Werner, with the engine bolted on the steering head but he did not buy it. Instead, he bought a 2 hp Minerva, with automatic inlet valve, surface carburettor and coil ignition, of course. Later on he bought a two and three quarter hp Minerva fitted with an MMC engine, which was quite a big machine in those days. He fell off that machine quite frequently and it cost so much to repair that because he was not well off, he sold it and bought a pedal bike and made do with that for a couple of years. Later, the longing for a motorcycle returned and he bought several machines, culminating finally in a Bradbury which was purchased around 1910. It was on this machine that he started doing a bit of competition work.

The Bradbury was a fairly hefty motorcycle of roughly 500 cc capacity and was one of the first to have a reasonably high compression ratio, which put a bit of pep into the engine. Vic rode mainly in short distance events, speed trials and hill climbs and occasionally in reliability trials. These were, of course, the single gear days.

In due course Singers brought out quite a good motorcycle and they started using it for racing at Brooklands, which attracted Vic's attention. He bought a Singer, which by then had become a fashionable machine. All his riding was as a keen amateur because he was then in the cinematograph business. He was the technical man with a firm that supplied machines and programmes to cinematograph theatres.

It wasn't very easy to get time off for racing but his job took him round and about a good deal, up and down the country, and this was often used as an excuse to get away. Also he had a very considerate gaffer, who probably knew about these goings on, but turned a blind eye to them. He was interested in supporting sport; a lot of his employees, for instance, were interested in rugby and got time off for it.

At that time there were a tremendous number of speed trials and hill climbs all round the country, to the extent that there was something on practically every weekend. But Vic confined himself as far as possible to local events.

G. E. Stanley was the Singer rider and tuner at Brooklands and he was a pretty good fellow. The secret of his success was that he discovered why occasionally a manufacturer had a particularly good engine, which they used to put in a frame and lend to people up and down the country. Now and again a particular engine would win all the hill climbs and when that engine eventually blew up, the manufacturer was often cut out of the running.

Stanley got thinking about this and he came to the conclusion that now and again an engine was turned out in which everything was plumb and square and fitted well. So they used to take everything to bits and do what they call nowadays tuning.

Vic prepared his own engines himself. He had the use of quite a good workshop and he was on friendly terms with Stanley. He was able to give Stanley a certain amount of information, mainly of a technical nature, because in all probability he knew more about the theory of gas flow and similar topics than Stanley himself. When he got interested in racing, he started reading up the theory of tuning.

Whilst riding the Singer it never occurred to Vic that he might attempt a record. He rode merely for the fun of it. He liked riding at Brooklands on a more or less standard machine which he himself had modified in certain limited respects. That was before the first World War. After the War he started his own business and began riding professionally.

During the War he kept the Singer stored away and when racing started again, which he believes was in 1919, he went down to the track with it. By then he had taken up the

Vic Horsman. First serious racing machine. Norton with chain drive and three speed gear.

Norton agency, and he had also bought himself a BRS 'Special' Norton, but he found that his Singer, although it couldn't be credited with the speed that the Norton certificate gave, would still beat the Norton. Eventually it paid to drop the Singer and work on and ride the Norton, which he did for about two or three years.

The manufacturer gave a certificate of speed with the machine, when it was sold. To get that certificate they used to take a rather high line on the banking before swooping down to the Railway Straight to record it. It was a one way speed, certified by an official time-keeper, so there was no jiggery pokery about that. But there could be no doubt that the speed was helped by swooping down the Railway Banking before passing through the timed section which extended for only half a mile or a kilometre.

The Norton was Vic's first serious racing machine at Brooklands because before the First World War there were few motorcycle races as such. The British Motor Cycle Racing club did exist, but he first raced in the car meetings, the BARC running two motorcycle handicaps at each meeting. At those meetings riders were issued with a coloured jacket, just like a jockey. There was nothing to go on from the racing point of view except to follow the procedure used for horse racing. Both car drivers and motorcycle riders had to wear a coloured jacket, and they included a couple of motorcycle races because it brought new interest and encouraged two classes of spectators. The Norton had a single gear with belt drive. Vic soon found that if he was getting enough power the belt could not cope. He was one of the first to turn up at Brooklands with a chain drive and three speed gearbox. He can remember O'Donovan taking a look and turning up his nose, asking Vic whether he thought he was riding in a reliability trial.

Vic found O'Donovan to be very decent, although a bit cantankerous and possessed with a mercurial temper. He was the official Norton representative at the track and that was why Vic changed his allegiance from that marque. Nortons were not a very big concern and O'Donovan had the first offer of anything that was going, including the pay. As a result, Vic switched over to Triumph.

When he took up racing a Triumph, he had to share the agency in Liverpool with the existing dealer. But the latter wasn't very interested in motorcycles and Vic took over the whole agency the following year.

When Vic arranged at the Motor Cycle Show to take up racing for Triumphs, he asked them to send him one of their last year's TT machines, the only machine they had in racing trim being a Triumph Ricardo 4 valve. They told him that they would have something new coming out later on and that they would send that along in due course. The works hadn't much of an idea of how to tackle racing for they seemed to think that if a wand was waved over the machine, and if the rider had some wonderful secrets, it could be changed over in a matter of minutes from a standard machine into a racer. Vic, of course, knew this was not correct, and he asked them to send him a machine, no matter what state it was in, so that he could work on it during the winter. He didn't like the 4 valve 'Riccy' and he told the works he may not turn out with that number of valves, there might be 4, 6, 8 or 10! Already he had made up his mind however, that there would be only 2. Fortunately Col. Holbrook, with whom he had made these arrangements, said he didn't care how many valves it had, a situation that suited Vic particularly well.

Looking back, Vic considers he was very fair with the Company. They more or less let him fix his own terms and he didn't take advantage of the situation. They were very alarmed that he might go for hundreds of records in a week and nearly break them, so he undertook not to do this and always to have a maximum amount he could win in any one day or during any one week or any one year, which he certainly wouldn't suggest if he had the chance all over again. Yet whilst he was an independent rider, working outside the factory, he got on well with everybody. They made any special parts he needed and did any of the things he was not able to do himself.

The first hour record to be broken by Vic was established very soon after the War, in September 1920, at a speed of 71.68 mph. It occurred during a 200 mile race but towards the end of the race he had a burst front tyre and for that reason he didn't get the 100 mile or 200 mile record. A few days later he went for the longer distance records and on the way broke the hour record again.

A report of this first hour record by Victor Horsman appeared in the *'Athletic News'* dated Monday, 20th September 1920. The report is headed, 'An Unexpected Honour' and it reads as follows:- 'The finest ride accomplished at Brooklands this year was that of Victor Horsman, the Liverpool rider on a Norton, when he beat the Hour and Two Hour records. There had been a crowded week of record attempts during which some fine rides had been made. Nobody expected world records to go during the pleasant afternoon of sport provided by the British Motor Cycle Racing Club. Horsman was fancied for the Hour Race. He got away very well and came round the banking a long way ahead of the next man. It seemed obvious that he would do something sensational if he lasted the full time. In the eleventh circuit he lapped the second man at about 80 mph and a little while later it was announced that the 50 mile record had been broken.

Vic – 'Initially I rode Nortons, but since O'Donovan had priority with the factory, I switched to Triumph'.

It still required three minutes to the expiration of time when Horsman came round on the 28th lap and passing the line he shut off his throttle and dawdled along at a touring pace. He knew the race was his but what he did not know was that he was in a position to secure the most coveted record in motorcycling, that of the unlimited hour which had stood for nine years. The spectators waved him on in futile efforts to explain the position to him. As it chanced he kept going and beat the hour record without knowing he had done it. He could have tacked on about two miles had he known the position. When he toured up to the Fork again, he was enthusiastically informed of the result of his wonderful ride and persuaded to attempt the two hours record. Again he sped round the track with his engine roaring healthily. With ten minutes to go, he was well inside time, but a little later his rear tyre burst. This time, however, he knew that he was running for the record, and despite the risk of riding at speed with a deflated tyre, he rode on, wobbling alarmingly, endeavouring to crowd every yard he could into the time. Again he was successful, although his time over the last two or three laps was necessarily slow. It is stated that one of the Midlands cracks is going to Brooklands with an eye on important records and Horsman has given him something to get on with. Horsman's Norton was a TT model, fitted with a Sturmey Archer 3-speed gear, so that by no stretch of the imagination could it be regarded as a track freak. Record breakers on specially tuned buses do not carry 3-speed gears round with them.'

He had, of course, broken the previous record, which was held by Emerson on the ABC. The old speed was 70.46 mph and his new one was 71.68. Vic's principal

Horsman's sidecar 'had a bad reputation' – but passenger 'Curly' Quinn seemed to enjoy it!

recollection is the very pleasant one of getting a very nice letter from Jack Emerson later, congratulating him on getting the record and promising to get it back again as soon as he could.

His immediate reaction was to make Emerson's reclamation of the record as difficult as possible because before the latter could get it back he had pushed it up to 72.48 mph. Emerson did try again, in 1921, and he got it back at 72.87 mph.

The reason why Vic had put it up so quickly after his first successful attempt was that on the way to the 100 miles he had missed some other records, which he had to pass during the hour in order to get the longer distance ones. It was for that reason he more or less had to break his own record.

Emerson raised the record again in 1921 to 74.26 mph and that record was subsequently broken by Halford on a Triumph at 76.74 mph. F. B. Halford was the designer of the 4 valve Triumph. He was employed by Ricardos and later designed the engine used in the Tiger Moth aircraft. He was a clever man, technically. The 4 valve Triumph was a very quick machine off the mark although it hadn't a high maximum speed.

The hour record was broken again and again, Denly raising it to 85.58 mph in the third of three successful attempts made in 1923. In those days the Hour record was very highly thought of and valued by manufacturers for advertising purposes and also it was the time when a change was being made from side-engines to overhead valve designs. Denly's later record was made on the ohv model. For some reason Nortons would not supply Vic with an ohv engine, which is, perhaps, one of the reasons why he changed over to Triumphs.

The increase in speed brought about by the continual breaking of the hour record in 1923 can be attributed largely to the advent of the ohv engine. It was in November 1923 that Vic regained the record at 86 mph, on an ohv Triumph.

It was the first of its kind from this stable, using a Triumph bottom end and a cylinder head of Vic's own design. He had the patterns made and had it cast and machined in his own shop. It was his way of proving to them that the 2 valve was superior to the 4 valve at that time.

His new 1923 Hour Record on the Triumph was no less than 13 mph higher than his previous one, but it was difficult to make a comparison and attribute the 13 mph increase in speed to the new cylinder head alone because his first attempt had been made on a side valve machine, which no-one would expect to be as fast as an ohv. Even so it was considerably faster than Halford's hour record, which was made with a 4 valve design. From then on, it was virtually Horsman and Denly, neck and neck, although in 1925 Dixon came on to the scene with his Douglas, raising the record to 89.92 mph.

Fred and Vic were very friendly. Fred was a very good-hearted man, in spite of a rough exterior. He was always up to some prank or other but he would help a fellow rider if he was in a jam. He was a very good mechanic and he was enormously strong. He could straighten wheels and frames with two hands and one foot.

It was during November 1925 that Vic regained the Hour Record from Fred, just before the Show. Such timing provided good advertising and on at least one occasion, Vic came off the track after taking the hour record, whereupon the gates were then

Vic with his 600cc Outer Circuit racing Triumph. 'Two valves and long wheelbase'.

closed for the whole of the winter. Then he could be sure his new record would be safe for the rest of the year.

Although Vic was the first man to cover 90 miles in the hour on a 500, a rider named Kenley covered 91.20 miles in the hour, riding a 350, in July 1926, a very remarkable feat. His machine used a Blackburne engine, prepared by Dougal Marchant.

Vic then took the record from Kenley at 94 mph and Denly subsequently took it from Vic in 1927, at 95 mph. From then on there was a great rush in the Norton camp to push it up to at least 100 mph, according to Bert Denly. He was under the impression that Vic was right on his tail at that time. They went to Montlhéry in June 1927 and made three unsuccessful attempts. They had a magneto fail twice and an engine blow up on the other occasion, but they worked practically non-stop, in the belief that Vic was not far behind.

Strangely enough, this belief was unfounded. Vic had gone to Montlhéry because the track was smoother and there was less loss of speed from wheel hop. Also, there was no need to have a Brooklands silencer, which undoubtedly slowed the machine and increased the risk of seizure through back pressure. But by that time he had joined

By 1927 the shapes of Vic's sidecars were improving but this one seems to have suffered some nose damage. Standing behind is A.R. 'Curly' Quinn, Horsman's regular passenger, who also rode his Triumphs on occasion.

Record breaking in 1926. Horsman with his sidecar outfit and Freddie Dixon (Douglas).

the Triumph works, which more or less put paid to any racing.

Although Vic still had his motorcycle retail business, he was not very interested in it. He was more interested in racing and fiddling about with motorcycles. But Triumphs were not terribly enthusiastic about racing because they considered it didn't impress the public, who thought they were different machines anyway. When Vic suggested to Triumphs that they should make a racing model, based on the much modified standard machine he had been using, they jumped at the chance and offered him a job in the works to supervise production. However, he soon found that there was a great difference in working for a firm when you are employed directly by them than when you are independent. In no time at all he found himself loaded up tuning machines for every Tom, Dick and Harry, so he had more or less to give up racing.

The 1927/8 500 cc TT model was his racing machine put into production form. It was first ready in 1927 but not very many were made and it was continued for about two years before it was dropped. It was said to be too expensive to produce.

It was a very nice looking bike but it did not handle very well. His own track bikes had a very long wheelbase, achieved by extending the rear half of the frame. This was mainly to enable him to adopt a flatter riding position.

Recollecting racing at Brooklands, Vic recalled that on one occasion Rex Judd came into collision or very nearly into collision with him. On one occasion he was hanging on and keeping his head flat down on the deck, only looking up now and again, when something went wrong with Vic's machine. He had assembled it in a hurry and he can remember how it had two petrol pipes feeding two float chambers. His mechanic, Bill Quinn, did one side and he did the other, each having thought the other had tightened up the fuel pipe unions. They came undone during the race and emptied the tank. As Vic slid over to the left side of the track whilst crossing the Fork, Judd, who was not looking where he was going, looked up and found himself bearing down on Vic. His footrest caught Vic's back tyre and cut it through, and caught Vic's left foot, cutting through the leather of his boot. Rex went through the railings and Vic just slid along the track. He was very lucky. He had one or two bumps and broken frames but never sustained any serious injury. He was thrown once when he had a burst tyre but he managed to hold the bike until it was doing about 30 miles an hour.

There was another occasion when several of the riders were not in a very good state of preparation and they organised a strike. When Marchant started agitating about something they didn't like, they went on strike and the meeting was postponed.

One incident that stands out in his mind is when Reuben Harveyson went out of the Paddock much too quickly and not being able to slow down enough to turn onto Banking, went over the top. Another rider, who was working alongside Vic, looked up, saw him going and said 'He's dead', then carried on working. Reuben was lucky. He fell into a tree and survived.

At the peak of his racing career, when he was running his own business, Vic did most of his tuning in the evenings and dashed up and down to Brooklands every weekend. That's where Bill Quinn came in. He was an enthusiastic mechanic and Vic could send him off on a Friday night and follow the next morning, knowing that he would have everything ready for him. Bill took part in some long distance races and he also rode in Vic's sidecar. On one occasion he was pulled out unconscious. It was at the conclusion of either an hour or a two hour race and when Vic pulled up he patted him on the back and said 'It's all right, you can get out now'. But he still lay there and Vic thought he was resting. When he grabbed him by the shoulders and pulled him out, he was very dazed and half gassed by either the fuel or the exhaust.

Questioned about the time lag before the first multi did a hundred miles an hour, Vic had difficulty in thinking of a valid reason, although there came about a big slump around 1931 when no-one spent any more than they possibly could on any projects that didn't look like having a quick return.

Although he rode in sidecar events, he infinitely preferred solo riding. A sidecar seemed to him to be a really unsafe vehicle at Brooklands. The tendency was to have very skimpy bodies with hardly any springing in them and also a very narrow track which reduced the drag, but made them painful to ride in. He didn't like them at all.

Although tyres were still quite a headache with big bikes in the 1920s, he had very few tyre failures or worries. Only twice was he forced to retire on account of tyre failure. In both cases he was thrown off his machine, but not seriously hurt.

A remarkably clear and concise account of events that happened forty years ago, from the lips of a man now entering his 90th year. It was interesting to see how his enthusiasm for anything technical provided the entree to the sport. Vic Horsman's racing record speaks for itself, so that little remains to be said except to express my grateful thanks to him for his kindness in receiving me and helping me with the story.

C.W.G. LACEY

When one has a series of characters in a story, all of whom were immensely successful in the same field at the same time, it isn't always easy to pinpoint where any one of them went ahead of the others.

In Bill Lacey's case, however, it really isn't hard and if one had to sum it up in one word, that word would have to be 'elegance' because there was nothing to choose between the elegance of Bill when he was racing and that of his bikes.

There were many fast bikes at Brooklands and I think Bill would probably be the first to agree that the engineering standards of his close rivals probably didn't fall behind his own at all because if they had, they would no longer have been rivals. But it was Bill who went just one stage further to make his bikes *look* beautiful in addition to being superbly turned out and tuned.

The first of Bill's bikes that I saw racing at Brooklands were his 350 cc and 500 cc Grindlay Peerless, both JAP-engined, and when I cast eyes on them I was spellbound. Spellbound, that is until I saw them in action – and that was even better.

To have turned bikes out like this must have taken countless hours of meticulous work for which someone had to pay and I confess to not knowing whether, in fact, it was Bill or the factory he rode for who looked after that part of it.

But this could be the reason why no-one else, except Nigel Spring with his team of AJS's, followed in the Lacey footsteps. Cash flow was restricted in those days even more than it is now and it may well have been that priority number one with many manufacturers was to have race results that they could advertise, even if the machine that provided them was not ultra-glamorous in appearance.

It's interesting to see how almost an identical pattern keeps cropping up in the leading riders' choice of race machinery. In one or two cases they start with either one or two makes and from then on, practically never change. Others, when only at the curious stage regarding racing at Brooklands, try one or two makes in the early stages. But, to a man, they seem to pick on one make and stick to it until forced by circumstances to make a change, then applying just the same principles with results that are equally successful. Bill's choice was Grindlay Peerless and Norton after a preliminary canter on his first mount, a Cotton.

Unlike most of the others he only rode solos and only on the Outer Circuit. With the exception of a short spell with a big twin Grindlay Peerless, it was always 350 and 500 or 600. Before talking to him I always imagined that sidecars must have been 'out' because they offended his engineering principles – but I was wrong.

Bill's first motorcycle was a 3.5 hp NSU with an overhead inlet valve and a side valve exhaust. It had belt drive and was manufactured in 1920.

When eventually he sold the NSU and bought a Rudge Multi he found the latter had a very low frame. He wrote to Rudges to ask if they could tell him anything about the machine as he did not know of any other Rudge Multi with such a small frame and with the gear lever in a similar position. They replied saying that it was a bike they had built for Cyril Pullin, after he had won the 1914 TT, to ride the following year, but then the war came along. Eventually they put a standard engine into it and sold it. Bill got very keen on the bike, knowing its history. His father bought him a Ricardo piston and they worked on the cylinder head, with the result that Bill rode the bike in some

The start of it all. Bill Lacey in the sidecar of his father's Rudge Multi.

of the Slough and District Motor Cycle Club events. He went on an outing to Brooklands. As he stood on the hill at Brooklands, near a woman named Mrs. Smith who had a big Norton and sidecar, he turned and said to her, 'You know, it's the ambition of my life to ride on this track'.

Funnily enough, he had made a similar statement once before, when he was a Kop Hill. He had seen George Dance put up the fastest time of the day on a 3.5 Sunbeam and he had said then 'By God, if only I could have a motorcycle like that'. The very next year he had acquired a 350 Cotton Blackburne and he made a time there, confirmed by the ACU, which equalled George Dance's three and a half record. That and this second incident made him decide to have a ride at Brooklands. He took his Cotton Blackburne and did four or five laps on it, before he came in to take a look at the plug and one or two other things.

He had entered for the Essex meeting on the following Wednesday because he was already a member of the Essex club and had ridden in hill climbs with them. He was sitting on the side of the carrier, because the machine had a sidecar attached, when a Brooklands official named Jack Cann came up to him and said, 'Have you been riding long?' Bill said 'yes', especially in hill climbs. So Cann enquired what he intended to do next. Bill said it was his intention to go out again and have another go, but Cann said it would be better to take the bike home. This dispirited Bill because he thought Cann considered him to be so slow that it wasn't worth taking it out again. He said 'Why take it home when I need to get some more practice in?' whereupon Cann asked when he would next be using the bike. 'Next Wednesday at the Essex Motor Cycle Club meeting' was Bill's reply, so Cann added 'Take my advice and take it home. It's going very very well and I wouldn't do any more with it, you'll only blow it up.' Bill asked how fast it was going but Cann replied that he never divulged information like that. He timed riders but never told anyone his findings. The advice Jack Cann gave him was good. He knew that if he went on belting round Brooklands, he would be likely to blow up the engine. He could not hope to appreciate the distance round the track or speed that could be attained down the mile.

Asked about the attitude towards racing adopted by his parents, Bill said that his father was very good to him. He used to say that he would buy whatever Bill needed to get going, but that he would have to pay him back. That was when he first started because he was a little unsure how he would adapt himself to racing. One interesting point emerged. When the Cotton Blackburne was purchased, Bill was afraid he might be tempted to use it on the road. It was brand new and he wanted to race it, and he knew that if he left the lights and mudguards on it, he would be sorely tempted to take it out on the road, perhaps in the evening, and pick up a girl and carry her on the back, or have a Tan Sad pillion seat put on. He knew you couldn't mix that sort of motorcycling with racing, so he took off the lamps, mudguards and various other pieces of standard equipment and sold them, to leave only the bare, stripped machine. In this way he could never use it on the road.

The engine was a 350 cc ohv Blackburne and this was the only occasion on which he raced a machine fitted with an engine of this marque. By the time he had started riding at Brooklands, the engine had been changed. This had come about when Vivian Prestwich came to him after he had got the record at Kop Hill. He suggested that he should fit a JAP engine in place of the Blackburne, to which Bill replied he was not sure whether it would be possible. Vivian offered the loan of a pukka racing engine, if he would like to try, so in due course a twin port JAP engine arrived. Bill set to and made new engine plates which he had to cut out with a hacksaw and drilled with a hand drill. He managed to fit the JAP engine and he returned with the re-engined bike to Kop Hill.

Unfortunately it wouldn't run at all well. At that time Bill's father used to accompany him and he always used to take a bottle of scotch, a bottle of gin and some cakes. He said he would go and see Bert Le Vack, who was at the same meeting, but Bill was convinced it would be a waste of time as Le Vack was a big man in those days and seemingly would have no time for the smaller fry. His father remained resolute and spoke first to Le Vack's wife, asking her if she would like to have a drink and then telling her what he wanted. She took him to meet Bert and he was able to tell him what had happened, adding 'Well, my boy's taken out his Blackburne engine and put in this JAP.' Bill knew nothing about JAP engines whatsoever. Bert came along to take a look at the bike and asked when Bill would be racing it again. Hearing it would be in a fortnight's time on Wednesday, at the Essex Club's meeting, he pointed out that Bill was using the wrong type of sparking plug and that on top of that he needed a better magneto. Bert wrote a brief note on one of his cards and said that if Bill went to Bosch's, they would give him exactly the same type of magneto as he used. When using it, he would need to keep the throttle wide open and if he needed to slow down, he should use the ignition cut-out. The magneto was specially constructed to allow this. So his father shot off to London with some money and went to Bosch's where he waited all day while they modified the magneto according to Bert's instructions. When Bill rode in the Essex Club's meeting at Brooklands he finished second.

Bill regarded Le Vack as the greatest rider of his time but did not consider him to be particularly helpful. The only time he ever told him anything direct was when he suggested he must have the modified type of magneto, presumably because thereafter he must have regarded Bill as a direct menace. Afterwards, whenever Bill used to talk to him, he'd say, 'Well Bill, now it's possible that if you did this, that might happen'. But he would leave him to find out for himself. He wouldn't say 'Do this and that will happen'.

A long while afterwards, when Bill was working with him at JAP's late one evening, Wal Phillips came in with a cylinder head on which he had been at work for weeks with hand files. Wal had always been in awe of Le Vack, his uncle, and he stood about the shop for some little time before he showed Bill the cylinder head that had received so much attention. He certainly had made a beautiful job of it, for it was shining like a mirror. Eventually Bert had a look at it and when he held it up to the light he said

Bill's Rudge Multi, 'a machine they had built for Cyril Pullin'.

'Very nice job, very nice job indeed, but you know I did that to my 250 engine and I lost four miles an hour.' This was so typical of him. In other words, he had opened up the port too much as an experiment, which just dropped the speed.

It was during a rained-out Saturday meeting at Brooklands that Bert Le Vack and Bill got talking about a previous meeting where Riddoch had ridden against Bert on a 500 and Bert had retired because he knew Riddoch was faster. The matter was discussed in the shelter of Bill's shed when Bert said 'Well, I can tell you this, Bill, the day that somebody passes me on a motorcycle of any size and I know that the man has genuinely beaten me, that I've done my best and I can't do any more, I'll never ride again.'

Bill said he should not talk like that but Bert replied he really meant it, because 'that's the best time to stop.' Since the meeting was rained out, and couldn't be held and it was postponed to the Wednesday. Bert was supposed to leave England that evening to go across to the Isle of Man, to look after the New Hudson team. He was working for New Hudson then and told Bill that he was going to wait at Brooklands to ride in the Wednesday meeting so he would just have to disappear into thin air. The firm would be tearing their hair out but they would just have to wait.

When the race started on the Wednesday Bert got away before Bill but when they reached the end of the mile, coming on to the Byfleet Banking, Bill passed underneath him and went way ahead. He must have beaten Bert in the end by about 100 yards. Bert never rode a motorcycle again, except the 1000 cc which he took to Arpajon to attempt the world record. And that was the end of it. Bill has a photograph of Le Vack

Bert Le Vack (New Hudson No 1). 'Well Bill, the day that somebody passes me, I'll never ride again'. Later the same day, Bill Lacey (Grindlay Peerless No 8) did just that.

His first 'real' racer. The 350cc Cotton JAP.

First Brooklands ride, July 1924. Winner 3 Lap Junior Handicap. Speed 81.91 mph.

on the banking showing every detail of his machine and underneath you can see Bill about half as long again as him, where the camera caught him as he shot through underneath, almost a blur.

He knew it might happen because when he came over to Bill that Saturday morning he had said 'I hear you're going very quickly' and Bill had replied 'Well, I don't really know, Bert, we shall have to wait and see.' That day it was Bill who foxed, for whilst he thought an awful lot of Le Vack, he just wasn't going to give anything away.

What set Bill on his feet as a racing motorcyclist was his decision to make an attempt on some world records and when he looked at the records book he found that there was a 350cc five hour record held by three Italians. By that time he had transferred his allegiance to the Grindlay Peerless marque.

His involvement with Grindlay Peerless came about at one of the annual Motor Cycle Shows when, having been quite successful on the Cotton Blackburne, he tried several manufacturers to get them to lend him a motorcycle. The first people he went to were OK Supreme. They were prepared to reduce the price of a bike but they wouldn't loan him one. In point of fact he needed a machine without an engine because JAPs were backing him with the latter. Eventually he arrived at the Grindlay Peerless stand and when he looked at the bikes on display he became interested in the low frame 350s they had on show. He spoke to Rowley Elliott on the stand who said he would get hold of Mr. Grindlay so that Bill could talk to him. After chatting to Reg Grindlay for some time about his plans, the former agreed to lend him a machine and if he needed any special tanks said that he would be pleased to make them for him, as the standard tanks might not be good enough for the type of work for which they were required. This was how he came to ride for Grindlay Peerless, on which he enjoyed a very long successful run.

Bill had decided he would like to attempt some world records and he prepared accordingly. His father accompanied him with his supply of cakes, buns and whisky, and Anderson of Castrol put in an appearance too. O'Donovan looked in and said 'It's a hell of a long way for your boy to ride, Mr. Lacey, I don't know whether he can do it, but if he gets into any trouble at all when he comes in to fill up, if he feels he can't go on, send across to me and I'll let the boy come over and ride it', the boy being Denly, because Bert was a little bit smaller than Bill, and would fit into the machine quite well. But Bill persevered and went on to establish the record that had been his target. He maintained 87 mph for five hours, to break the record set up by three Italians originally, taking it from them single-handed. But it was a very lonely ride.

With regard to machine preparation and tuning, Bill had no equal for he considered himself first and foremost as an engineer. He was accustomed to turning out his machines with a dull plated finish except for the wheel rims, the engine plates and the handlebars. Apart from the fact that they looked wonderful, it made them much more easy to clean. All that was necessary was to wash them down with benzole. If the frames had been enamelled, the benzole would have taken off all the enamel and a dirty machine would have resulted. One thing he swore he would never do was to use insulation tape or 'centre pop' any bolts. This was another little tip that Le Vack had given him. They were talking one day about holding nuts fast and he had said 'Bill, it's so simple. All you've got to do is make certain that the surface on which the nut beds is flat and the bottom of the nut is flat. Do this and pull all the nuts up tight onto their bolts and they'll never come undone.' It still applies today.

Bill's machine never let him down in a race, although as mentioned earlier one report alleged that the Grindlay Peerless did not handle during a particular race and he had to retire as a result when the back wheel was found to be out of alignment. This was not strictly true.

The incident in question occurred soon after Vivian Prestwich had called on Bill to say that his Company were going to give a cup for a 50 mile scratch race. He added that Bill was bound to win it, even if the latter considered it hardly fair. However, with the offer of the cup agreed, Bill had to get a bike ready. He took it out on test and was very happy with both its speed and performance. In the meantime he had some new wheels built by Dunlops. He had sent them some hubs and they had used them to build the new wheels which on delivery he took across to Mac to have the tyres fitted, along with Bill Davis, who was foreman in the toolroom at JAPs. This was the first time the latter had visited Brooklands and he came down specially to see Bill ride in the race, since it was for the Prestwich Cup. Vivian Prestwich said to him he ought to go across to the Postman's Bridge if he wanted to see Bill motoring close to the grass bottom of the banking.

With 50 miles to go, Bill was in no immediate hurry and he took it reasonably gently when the field moved off the start line. At the end of the first lap, when he got on to the mile, he saw Bert Denly was in front of him by a hundred yards or so and he decided to open up and go by him to take the lead. He opened up and ran in close to the grass at the bottom of the mile, but he almost lost control of the bike when it shot up onto the 50 ft line in a nasty snake, causing him to ease off and not take the lead. He opened up again getting in close to the grass again at the bottom, but once more the machine got into a very bad snake and repeated the performance under the Members' Bridge. He did about four laps like that and he thought he was going to break his neck. In the meantime Bill Davis had left, muttering to himself that he would rather leave there and then as Bill looked certain to kill himself if he continued in the same manner. But Bill decided discretion was the better part of valour and retired. Arthur Bourne suggested something must be out of line, so they went up to the shed where the bike was and got a mechanic to check the alignment. He checked the wheel alignment and all the fork spindles for side play but found there was nothing wrong. On the following Tuesday Bill went back to Brooklands and tried the machine again. It would still snake very badly the moment he tried to go near the grass. Brewster looked in and suggested that the frame may have crystallised, which would necessitate having it heat treated. So they stripped the bike out, took the frame to JAPs, put it on the oven, sand blasted it, heat treated it and then replated it. When the bike was rebuilt and tried again, it was no better. Eventually Bill went to the Grindlay works and built himself another frame. But when he rebuilt the bike and took it back to Brooklands, the same thing happened.

Whilst he was pondering over the cause of the mysterious trouble Brewster looked in again and suggested Bill should let somebody else ride the machine. At first this rather shook Bill because he thought Brewster must have thought he had lost his nerve. But as he sat on the bike talking to his mechanic the latter reminded him that the machine was all right on the day on which he had practiced with it and they had cleaned it ready for the race. He went on to remind Bill that the only thing he had done was to change the wheels. Brewster was still there and he made the observation that the spoke lacing must have been changed. So they went all through this aspect very carefully, only to find the spoke lacing was exactly the same. All they found was that instead of putting

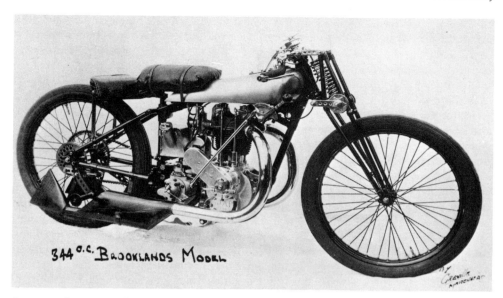

Cotton replacement – the 344cc 'Brooklands Model' Grindlay Peerless.

– But rebuilt to 'Lacey' standards and specifications.

on a WM7 rim they had put on another which was a quarter of an inch narrower. Bill said to his mechanic, 'Take those bloody wheels off, put the old wheels back on and I'll try it'. They put the old wheels back in and the bike steered like a dream, not causing a hap'orth of trouble. But Bill couldn't convince Dunlops that this had been the cause of the trouble, even though there could be no other answer.

It was the question of wheel support that made Bill discuss the problem with a technical man from Dunlops. He had seen the cars at Brooklands start to get bigger and bigger without the rims being widened, to get straight wheels. He knew that if the wheels were not almost straight, when riding close to the limit the stability factor would become very critical.

Asked how tough the competition was in those days and whether there was any money in it for the more successful, Bill found it difficult to draw a comparison with the situation that exists today. The money wasn't as great but he considered the competition was still just as keen. But it was more difficult to get established. It took quite a long time before any real help was forthcoming. A rider could obtain free oil and an odd plug here and there without too much effort but it was much more difficult to get any real money and to get free fuel, lubricants and accessories as well. The only thing that happened in the past that doesn't happen now was that a rider would not be paid a bonus, but he could always be sure of free oil, which he would still get even if he didn't get a bonus.

Bill broke a lot of records. Asked whether the money gained from these attempts generated rivalry, not only between the riders, but also between the manufacturers, the question was whether this rivalry remained on a friendly basis. For example, it is

Historic shot. Bill Lacey (Grindlay Peerless) right, and Knight (Zenith) left, in a match race with J.G. Parry Thomas (Leyland Thomas), shortly before Thomas lost his life in attempting to regain the World's Land Speed Record.

Above **First big Brooklands success. Winner 350cc 200 Mile Solo Race at 81.20 mph.**

Left **Mrs Lacey, also a successful competitor at Brooklands, receives her award from Earl Howe and Lady Campbell.**

alleged that there was an unwritten rule that if a rider broke a record, it had to stand for something like a month, and it then had to be broken by a clear mile an hour.

Bill considered this to be not always true. He could recall an occasion when Victor Horsman was annoyed with him. Vic was a past master at going out and averaging 99 mph for an hour and then going out a month afterwards to average 99.3 mph or so. When Bill raised the Hour Record from 100.06 to 103 mph, Vic, he felt was very disgusted with the result. Bill's first attempt was made at Montlhéry in 1928, when he raised the speed to 103 mph. Denly claimed it in 1929 at 104 mph and Bill got it back later in 1929 at 106 mph. All these attempts were made at Montlhéry, the only other time he attempted the Hour Record at Brooklands being when he did 100 miles in the hour for *The Motor Cycle* Cup.

Surprisingly he found that to ride at Montlhéry was a little more difficult than at Brooklands, the reason being that at Brooklands the front forks were in action all the time and the whole machine was constantly on the move, whereas at Montlhéry there were two distinct very bad bumps which, if the rider was unprepared, could give him a lot of trouble. The machine would seem to be static and all that could be seen by the rider would be a little tyre deflation, then all of a sudden a sloped-off step of about three inches would be hit, causing the forks to come into action and go on to full deflection.

One report had claimed that Bill parted company with his bike at Montlhéry, a point on which he enlarged. He had gone there with the 350 and 500 to attempt the Hour record and intended going to an Arpajon meeting had not the 350 started giving him trouble with unexpected vibration. When he arrived at Montlhéry with the 350 and found it was not going as well as he had hoped, he turned to his father and said, 'You know, if we were only back in England I could put this damn job right in no time. What the engine needs if about a millimetre off the cylinder barrel because the compression ratio isn't high enough. It's showing up reasonably well on the brake but the performance does not match up in practice.' His father knew of an engineer named Barault in Montlhéry but Bill considered that although Barault had an old lathe, it was unlikely he could handle such a job. His father said 'You get the barrel off and let me have it. How much do you want off it?' Bill said a millimetre would suffice, so he put his hand in his pocket and pulled out a shilling and said 'That's about it, isn't it'? Bill replied that if he could skim that much off, it would do the job. So his father went down to the town to see Barault and explained to him as best he could in a mixture of broken English and French. Barault went out into his orchard and cut off a lump of tree, which he chucked up in his lathe and turned down so that it would slide into the cylinder barrel, then skimmed off the desired amount. Meanwhile, Bill altered the gear ratios and found he got into a different scale of revolutions which created a vibration period. He therefore decided to try the rebuilt bike on the track the following morning and then strip the engine down and slip into town so that he could get the balance factor of the flywheels changed. He went out in the morning at about half past seven wearing a pair of grey flannels, a blue sweater, a pair of rope-soled shoes and a crash helmet.

There was one other bump at Montlhéry, which they called the Whipper Bump, on the bank farthest over by the Farm de Fey and whilst he was going down the back straight experiencing the vibration, he noticed that it had unscrewed the steering damper and that the damper rod was hopping up and down because the damper

Wind cheating. As low and narrow as possible.

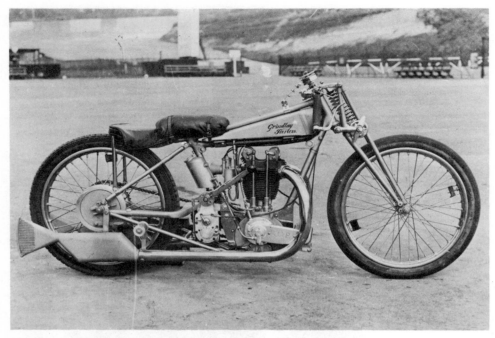

Bill's 1927 track racing Grindlay Peerless. Even more glitter. Offside view.

Same machine – nearside.

Front view. Note handlebar width.

Above **Bill, 1927 Championship 350cc Solo** winner at **94.15 mph,** with his father (in light suit).

Right **Menu** of the luncheon and presentation to **C.W.G. Lacey, October 15th 1928** to commemorate his breaking **Denly's 500cc Hour Record** at **103.30 mph.**

BRITISH MOTOR CYCLE RACING CLUB

COMPLIMENTARY LUNCHEON

AND PRESENTATION

TO

Mr. C. W. G. LACEY

(Holder of the World's One Hour Record for Solo Motor Cycles at a speed of 103.30 m.p.h.)

AT THE

ROYAL AUTOMOBILE CLUB

PALL MALL, LONDON, S.W.

ON

MONDAY, OCTOBER 15th, 1928

At 1 for 1.15 p.m.

TICKETS 10/- EACH (INCLUDING WINE)

Application, with remittance, should be made on the form attached and sent in the enclosed envelope to the Secretary NOT LATER *than* OCTOBER 10TH *owing to limited accommodation and arrangements.*

The man – and the machine – at Brooklands.

adjustment was at the top of the steering head. He let go with one hand to fiddle the damper rod into position, but by this time he had caught the Whipper Bump and there was no longer anything to restrict the lock of the machine until the two handlebar grips hit the tank. With only the sprint tank fitted, the handlebars swung right round on full lock, which bent the forks and the front wheel and chucked Bill off on to the banking. He rolled down the banking, but what made the incident worse was the fact that they were altering the inside of the track and putting in a lot of coarse rock as a footing, so that if cars ran off, they had something solid instead of just sand. He slid into this rock, which cut him badly. He had been travelling at over 100 mph when he was thrown off. The accident was never officially reported.

Although Bill had nothing against sidecar outfits from an engineering point of view, he rode only as a sidecar passenger, once for Marchant and also for Joe Wright. The latter was using a big Zenith and the occasion was at Montlhéry, when Joe was attempting a record. But the big twin outfits were never very efficient from an engineering viewpoint.

There was an occasion when he built up a big twin himself, using a Grindlay Peerless frame. He took the machine to Montlhéry for a record meeting when he set up new standing mile and standing kilometre times. Baldwin had managed to average 124 mph, over 200 km an hour, and the French people went mad. They thought it was absolutely fantastic to do 200 km per hour and they had a special medal struck for him to commemorate the occasion.

When he got back home and was talking to Vivian Prestwich, Viv said 'You know Bill, there's only one answer to this now and that's not to just break the record but to go for 130 mph. This is a round figure, this is something you can talk about'!. So they decided to try and build an engine and to assemble a bike that would meet this requirement. Bill gave a lot of thought to the problem and then went to Coventry to build the machine. In the meantime he had been working on the engine, finishing it off by using coil ignition in place of the magnetos normally used on a big twin. A distributor was made by the ML people and he had the distributor, firing two plugs per cylinder, supplied by two coils, which were wrapped in a little streamlined box underneath the second set of stay bars that came to the back wheel. The battery was built by Exide and was quite a small one for a battery of any power in those days. He had to extend the oil tank outwards by means of two sets of clips and slide the battery up on the inside, so that it was fully streamlined. It was a beautiful looking machine, with the high tension leads coming away from the coils along two chromium plated tubes.

Lubrication depended on a twin Best and Lloyd oil pump. One pump had a long feed straight to the big end assembly and the other pump fed to a distributor box which fed the backs of the cylinders, the rocker gear and the valve gear. But with one thing and another he had inadvertently put too much load on the drive because when he had gone down the kilometre at Arpajon at somewhere about 131 mph, the drive stripped on the pump and luckily the engine seized not when he was on full bore but as

The final switch – to Norton and the end of the decade. A photograph with C.T (Tom) Atkins (Douglas). Monty Bird ('Jazz' of Discol) on right.

he was shutting down. The engine locked up and it saved any serious trouble.

In 1928 Bill scored three second places at the Brooklands opening meeting, at the second meeting a first, and at the third Brooklands meeting, only ten days later, another first place. The reports in the papers said he had found a lot of extra speed in those ten days and the underlying reason is most interesting.

In the race at the second Brooklands meeting, which was a handicap comprising a heat and a final, Bill finished fourth in the heat. Reg Tanner came up to him and said 'Bill, you were mucking about a bit you know' but Bill said he had been flat out. Reg replied 'Well, do you realise you've only got fourth place. You frightened me to death, I thought you weren't going to get the sixth place that would qualify you for the final'. He went out in the final and his last lap proved to be considerably faster than any of his earlier laps in this event. Afterwards, Reg came to him again, expressing disbelief in his earlier statement. Bill had claimed he had nothing left, yet he won by about a hundred yards. Yet he affirmed that he had been really truthful, especially as Reg was a very good friend. He remained convinced he had gone flat out all the way. The reason for the extra speed on the last lap puzzled Bill. He asked the JAP mechanic who had been loaned to him to come in on the Monday morning so that they could take the engine out of the bike and go right through it and see if they could find out the reason, by checking the valve timing and everything else.

The first thing they did was to take off the cylinder head and lay it on the bench, before taking off the cylinder barrel to have a look at the piston, more as a matter of interest than looking for the reason for the extra speed. It was then that Stucking, his mechanic said, 'I've just noticed something Bill. Do you know one of your valve springs is bust, it's all in little bits lying down in the bottom. It's all curled up together'. When Bill had a look for himself he found the second spring had collapsed and had curled itself up, leaving only the outer and inner springs. So they fitted a new set of springs and took the bike out again on the track. The speed was now back to the original level, so they came in again, took the second spring off, and took the bike out again with only the outer and the third spring valve springs fitted. Up went the speed again so all he then had to do was to go to Terry's and get them to make him a new set of springs, the three springs combined poundage being equal to that of the two used for the test at the prescribed fitted length. The mysterious increase in speed had been due to the fact that the springs he was using were keeping the rocker under the cam. In other words he was getting better valve lift, because the rockers were floating. That didn't matter. He had found the extra speed and that was all that mattered.

He was reminded of the occasion when he averaged nearly 100 mph on a standing lap start whilst riding a 500. The occasion was soon after his accident at Montlhéry. His father had said it was a pity he couldn't ride in the Championship meeting and win the 500 Championship because although the 350 was badly damaged, the 500 was all right. Bill said he didn't think he would be fit enough but his father said they ought to talk to the doctor. So they had a word with him about this and he said, 'Well, it's not a very good thing really, but he's physically fit enough in himself. It's just a question of his wounds not having healed up properly. But I think we could do something about that if he wants to ride'. So he had them taped up, and so as not to make his injuries too obvious, he entered for the Wakefield Cup event as well as for the Championship. He told his father that he would ride only in the Championship and that he would slipstream Denly and take it as easy as he could until he got down to the mile, when he would open up and leave him. He was not boasting, for he knew his capabilities.

But when he arrived at the track in the morning Reg Tanner said, 'You'll have to go in the Wakefield Cup'. Bill said he didn't know whether he could, but Reg replied 'Well, you'll have to because I've got a bet on with Anderson for a £1 that you'll win his cup' knowing that Bill was on Esso oil at the time. Bill said he would have to wait and see how things worked out. It so happened that at the end of the 500 race he felt fine, so he went out in the Wakefield Cup heat and when he came in fifth Tanner said to him 'You left it a bit late, didn't you?' When asked what he meant, he said, 'Well you were in fifth place. You frightened me to death, I thought you'd lose the final'. He went on to say that there was a fellow going hellishly fast by the name of Mitchell. But, funnily enough, Ebby lodged an objection against him because he said his speed had increased so much over the previous time that he wasn't satisfied with the information that Mitchell had given on his entry form. When Mitchell was brought up before the stewards, he admitted that he was using one of Donovan's engines. So Ebby re-handicapped him. Obviously he couldn't base it on the speed Mitchell had done previously. He needed to give him a bit of leeway, so he re-handicapped him with reasonable margin. Reg Tanner suggested to Bill, who held the lap record then at about 107mph, that if he could break the lap record, he could still win the event. Bill was not easily convinced, especially as he was not all that fit. So Reg suggested that if he could carve quite a bit off the standing lap, that would help. He would organize two good strong pushers for the start line, which would be sure to help a bit. So Bill went off in the actual final and it afterwards turned out that he had managed a standing lap of 99.61 mph and other laps at 109.94 and 109.97 mph, to give an average speed of over 107 mph. As a result, he won the cup. It proved to be the fastest speed ever recorded in a race by a 500, to date.

Whether it was beaten or not, an average of 107 mph over a three lap race, for a five hundred with, of course, a three-speed gearbox and hand gearchange was quite something.

One interesting thing emerges from these rider interviews. The successes of these chaps were, of course, well documented in the motorcycle press at the time and most of these are described in detail earlier on in the story.

I did think, when writing that part, that these would be the things that would be remembered in the minds of the riders themselves but, strangely, they weren't – they seemed to have far better recollections of their few failures.

It was good to find Bill Lacey, now well into his seventies, looking as young and as dapper as he always had in the Brooklands days. When I met him he was hard at work in his neatly laid-out workshop at Silverstone, stripping a hideously complicated twelve cylinder Ferrari engine, aided by a tape recorder into which he was feeding a description of every dismantling operation.

Whatever great age he reaches, I know now Bill will never be happy without his 'shop' and the 'shop' will not be complete unless it contains at least one knotty problem.

From the 'shop' we went back to his lovely house where, for the first time in years, I met Mrs. Lacey, herself once an accomplished rider at Brooklands on one of Bill's bikes. She can lay rightful claim to be the only other person, I think, ever to have ridden one, bar the 'Maestro' himself.

My grateful thanks to them both for the hospitality they extended to me.

NIGEL SPRING

Despite his great contribution to the Brooklands scene I doubt whether, in 1939, after I had been at the track for ten years, I could have pointed out Nigel in a crowd. I knew all about him, knew what he had done, had seen his pictures and admired him in just the same way as the others but, somehow, he was to me an elusive and mysterious figure – a mystery man, if you like.

Having spent just one day as a guest at his home in Lincolnshire, I am wondering why. I think that it was because, when his work was completed at Brooklands, he really did drop out of the picture completely for he had other substantial business interests.

Many of the others went on to race cars or continued their business connections at the track. But sooner or later, it seems, everyone makes the TT Riders Association's Annual Lunch. When I heard someone say 'Hello Nigel', I turned and knew that one more gap in the story was filled.

At that time he was due to go into hospital for a major operation and a long time elapsed before he was able to see me but, in the end, a date was made and it was one which made my trek to Lincolnshire well worth the effort.

Although extremely successful as a rider in his own right, it was management of, at first Norton and, later, AJS racing interests that brought fame to Nigel Spring. Without his presence, an enormous amount of the glamour would have been missing at Brooklands.

His successes with Nortons were possibly greater than with 'Ajays' but it is for the latter that I particularly remember him. Barring Bill Lacey's, no bikes more beautiful than the 'Spring AJS' ever graced the track and had the steam not gone out of the industry because of the industrial depression at the turn of the decade there can be no doubt whatever that the equipe would have continued to go on from success to success.

Quite apart from my interest in getting the facts for this book, my meeting with Nigel was one which I enjoyed enormously and one I shall remember for a long long time.

Nigel first became acquainted with motorcycles soon after he left school at about 18. It had been suggested to him that he took up farming, so he went to an agricultural college. Like any other young man of that day he wanted to spread his evenings out so needing a convenient means of transport to get to London he bought a motorcycle, an elderly machine, purely for that purpose. He graduated from that to a Norton, as Nortons were very much in the picture in those days, this being during the early 1920's.

It was the Norton that led him to Brooklands because his attendance at public schools had brought him into contact with the then quite active Public Schools Motor Cycling Club. He joined and they held some meetings at Brooklands. In fact the first success he had at Brooklands was at a Public Schools meeting in 1923.

His first success occurred in August 1924 when he won the 500 cc scratch race at 83.84 mph but in the October closing meeting held on a very wet and horrible day, he lost a sidecar wheel. During the race he struck another machine, which dislodged one or two spokes, but proceeded without knowledge that he and his passenger were in any trouble. His passenger was virtually roped in to the sidecar, but when he began to see spokes fly and saw the wheel was getting dangerous, he stood this for about two laps and then gave his rider a slap on the back, just before the Fork. Luckily he did, because it enabled Nigel to be ready for what happened almost instantaneously when he saw the sidecar wheel fly off and go ahead of them. Although it was not compulsory, the machine had a skid fitted, which helped. It was a bit of a thrill at the time but he was perhaps fortunate for he had the space to use at the Fork and also on the run off from the Fork. He remembered the incident quite vividly and no doubt the sidecar passenger has an even more vivid impression.

Having acquired a reputation for increasing performance, it was fortuitous for Nigel that O'Donovan had reached the stage when he wished to play a less active role at the track. Nigel, on the other hand had got more and more enthused with Brooklands and now went to Nortons to meet Mr. William Mansell when it was arranged that when O'Donovan gave up, he would take over the Norton representation at Brooklands in his place. This came about in 1927 and when he assumed official duties on behalf of Nortons, his right hand man was still Bert Denly.

During the intervening years, Nigel had married and as a result did not feel that he should be quite so actively engaged in riding, although for some years he participated in long distance records, such as double 12 and 24 hours, and brought in other riders for that purpose. It was Bert Denly who showed him the way round Brooklands because they rode together the first time he ever attempted a record. They rode in a 6 hour bid so everything he learnt as far as Brooklands was concerned, came from

Nigel. 'Certainly struck another machine which dislodged one or two spokes' – much to the amusement of 'Dunlop Mac' (right).

Spring and Denly early on in the Norton alliance.

Denly. He was a very light-hearted man who really appreciated life. He quickly shared Nigel's outlook as far as the turnout of their machines was concerned. Nigel wanted everything to look bright and clean, not just on the inside of the machine, but outside as well, and they soon began to get a name for turning out their bikes in what they both considered to be the correct way.

By now, Nigel's thoughts were mainly concerned with tuning. As a young man he had been more than a little interested in mathematics and that stood him in good stead. He realised that to get the most speed, an engine had to turn over at greater revs and to do that it must have more fuel put into the cylinder head before it was ignited. In consequence he concentrated most on the induction stroke, working on the principle that the exhaust gases would find their own way out. Looking for more revs meant that he concentrated on the working parts. During the period 1925 – 30 the steel producers were learning almost daily and he obtained the very best materials that he could possibly buy for the manufacture of his con rods and valves, subsequently extending this to other items. He realised very soon that there was too much undesirable flexibility of the crankcase castings and as a result he had some crankcases cast in bronze. This gave greater rigidity and ultimately became general practice, only to be laughed at in recent years.

From the moment that Nigel Spring took over from O'Donovan, the successes started to mount. The first records broken were in April 1927, when Denly took the 50 kilos, 50 miles and 100 kilos at speeds of around 96 mph and at the second meeting, Denly beat Le Vack in a 500 scratch race – with a standing lap of 92 mph and a flying

Nigel (left) with Jimmy Guthrie in the Isle of Man. 'Now, for next year, overhead camshaft would be a change from pushrods'.

And with Handley (AJS) 'On the other hand, there's more than one type of overhead camshaft'.

'AJS made me a very handsome offer'. Denly (AJS) No 6 at 'the Byfleet' at Brooklands.

Record breaking at Montlhéry. Denly (AJS) and Hough, who sometimes partnered him on long rides.

lap of 104 mph, to average 100 mph for the race. By then, Norton Motors and the Spring team had their sights very much on the hour record.

The prospects had been discussed at Birmingham with Mr. Mansell, who was very keen indeed to have the first machine to do 100 miles in the hour and particularly keen that it should be achieved by a single cylinder model. With such a target firmly established, all Spring's work was pointed in that direction. Denly's efforts in the up to 100 km records provided the impetus he needed. He decided to make the record breaking bid at Montlhéry, because he knew the track and that it would be easier on the machine. He and his team drew up a programme to get over there as soon as possible, in an endeavour to forestall any others that might have the same thoughts, such as Triumph or Rudge.

The record was obtained on their first trip to Montlhéry, on 28th June 1927, although they did have various troubles. Indeed, the first three attempts at the hour record failed. One was due to a mechanical fault and the other two due to magneto trouble. It was ironic that they had managed approximately 55 minutes on one run and about 58 on another before trouble occurred. When the magneto failed, Nigel left by plane for England, having previously arranged for a Bosch magneto to be flown from Germany so that he could pick it up and fly back to France with it. Within a couple of days they were motoring again and Denly was able to complete his successful effort.

The switch to AJS had taken place during the previous winter, after AJS had made a handsome offer to Nigel to run their machines with the promise of back-up facilities from their drawing office and workshop. He saw Mr. Mansell at Nortons and told him exactly what had transpired, whereupon it was put to him that for the sake of himself and those who worked with him, it would appear to be an offer that he could not refuse. In consequence, he and Norton Motors parted company on the best of terms and remained so in subsequent years. Indeed, he remained associated with Mr. Mansell in a business sense, from which they both derived a lot of happiness.

It is only fair to say that Nigel now devoted much more time to racing development work, which meant he spent a lot of time in Wolverhampton. He used to call in and

Denly (AJS) took the 500cc 'Hour' back from Lacey at 104.51 mph in 1929. Lacey regained it within a month at 105.25. But, with more thought from Spring, Bert and his AJS took it back in 1930 at 108.60. Here, the two are seen after winning 500cc Solo 200 Mile Race at 97.26 mph in 1930.

And at Arpajon – they took sidecar records –

– as well as the 500cc Solo Flying Kilometre at 118 mph.

have lunch at Nortons and more by way of amusement he can recall that one of the Stephens brothers seemed to think it was a little odd that he should be going to Nortons when he was employed by AJS. When he pointed out that there was nothing underhand about this, they appreciated the point and all proceeded as it should. The AJS drawing office was absolutely first class and he had a machine shop at his disposal with something like 16 to 18 mechanics. Over the winter they produced engines which were successful in breaking no less than 117 records in the first year with which he was associated with AJS.

Not unexpectedly, he has no clear recollection of the individual record-breaking attempts. So many records were broken during such a short period that very little stands out in his mind.

It was during September 1929 that he and Denly went to Arpajon, taking the 350 flying start at 107 mph and the 500 cc kilo at just over 118 mph, feeling a bit guilty that they hadn't quite managed to reach 120 mph. For this purpose they used one of their Brooklands track machines, which was in the 114 mph class. They concentrated very much on the reduction of wind resistance, taping up poor Denly until he could scarcely breathe. It marked the early beginning of this type of approach to record breaking.

Asked whether he kept the big 750 cc single because race after race had proved the big twins were so unreliable over long distances, Nigel confirmed this. The big single had an engine that was very easy to build, had fewer reciprocating parts and he felt it was a good engine to have to cater for certain classes in the long distance events.

When the depression of the late twenties/early thirties came about, manufacturers had to pull out of racing and record breaking. It was about this time that Spring and the AJS company parted too. In point of fact the parting of the ways occurred for at least two valid reasons. In the first instance, whilst Nigel loved racing and enjoyed it immensely, it was not his sole source of income because he had other business interests. Furthermore, the motorcycle manufacturers regarded racing and record breaking as a form of advertising but no amount of advertising is going to sell a product if the potential customer just hasn't the money to spend. So the writing was on the wall for all to see and it turned out for the best because just at the point when he realised what was going on in the minds of the AJS board, he had similar thoughts, for he knew the time he was devoting to racing could be spent more profitably elsewhere.

That was how each went their separate ways. Two different minds, but with a single thought. Whilst the decision had to be regretted, it had become obvious that to carry on as before would have been wrong.

I enjoyed my day with Nigel immensely and, apart from being grateful to him for helping me forge one more link in the chain, I must express my gratitude both to him and Mrs. Spring for their kindness and hospitality. At the time I went to see him, he was convalescing from a major operation and I don't know whether, in similar circumstances, I would have felt like seeing or talking to anyone. Even so, he applied himself enthusiastically in answering my many questions and I am grateful because, in a sense, he is a major link in the chain.

Had I not been able to talk to him, I would have had to relate his part of the story from references only. But doing it that way, one can't get the inside story – little things like the Stephens brothers not at first being able to grasp that, apart from working with Nortons, he had, during the time he was with them, established friendships which in no way cut across his loyalty to his new business commitments.

GEORGE TOTTEY

During my time at the track, my old friend Charlie Brackenbury used to refer to Eric Fernihough as 'Tottey'. I asked him, one day 'Why d'you call him Tottey?' and he replied 'Well, he's brainy, isn't he? He's another 'Tottey''.

In Charles' rating there were only two categories, his mates who, as Nigel Spring would put it, were 'men of light thought', and the others, all of whom were 'Tottey'.

George Tottey was racing at Brooklands before I went there to take up residence so I never met him until after the war, when we met for the first time, I believe, in the Isle of Man. While I would agree with Charles that George is certainly 'brainy' I would have said that, without any doubt at all, he falls into both categories for no one who has been with George at a party or a re-union could possibly think otherwise.

He is also a 'character', very much loved by his friends and respected by all who know him. He was obviously very much part of the Brooklands scene of his time because, when I was there years later, his name often came up in many different contexts.

He was good rider and an even better engineer and I have heard it said that, as a qualified consultant, he is or certainly was at one time, the only man qualified to inspect and report on a road or rail vehicle, or a ship. From the racing viewpoint I would think that the engineering aspect held his greatest interest and that, while he enjoyed racing, that was really just a means of proving or disproving his theories. He had good results, of course, and these alone must prove that many, if not all, of his theories weren't far wide of the mark.

Although he was not well at the time, it was a great experience to sit and talk with George at his home in Cheshire, hearing how he got into the sport and listening to his views on Brooklands and on machinery in general.

His interest in motorcycles came about when he used to stay with his uncles on farms in Lincolnshire. They were all motorcyclists because there was no other means of fairly rapid transport and all used to ride Bradbury machines with controls on the tank – the very early models of 1911 or 1912. He first rode a motorcycle around 1913 or 1914, when he was 12 or 13 years of age. Of course this was quite unofficial but he did not actually have a machine of his own until 1919, when he acquired a second-hand 90 bore Zenith twin, which was a very good and famous machine in those days. It was a very powerful machine on which to start. When learning to ride one had to push off down a hill and either get on or suffer the consequences.

The 90 bore model had a 'Gradua' gear and a very over-square engine. From that, design progressed to long stroke engines, but now modern thinking has reverted back to John Prestwich's original idea of an over-square engine. George did quite a lot in the JAP works during the winter, preparing engines for New Imperials. He had the pleasure of staying at the home of John Prestwich, with his sons, and it was a great experience to listen to him talking at night. He always remembered so much of what JP had said when he rubbed in the mathematical formula plan. He said, 'Don't forget, plenty of area, not too long a stroke, lots of revs and you've got the pressure and the number of times its applied. The product of that is the power'.

Towards the end of the first war, George was studying at Manchester University on a B.Sc. Honours course, which would have preceded employment in the dye industry,

G. E. TOTTEY
344cc NEW
IMPERIAL
1924

George Tottey (344cc New Imperial). Isle of Man, 1924.

but when the opportunity came, the prospects seemed nothing like as good, so he changed to engineering. After leaving University in 1920, he went to Zenith Motors at East Molesey and took a job in the Assembly Department.

He went there on his motor bike, and when he saw a notice that said 'No Vacancies' he immediately walked in, asked for a job, and got one. He did a little work on Freddie Barnes' motorcycle and had his first ride at Brooklands in August 1920, on a 1000 cc side valve V twin Zenith, in a race which was run for Zeniths only. He also rode as passenger on odd occasions in Freddie Barnes' sidecar. He can recall one rather exciting experience when they were crossing the Fork, about to overtake Osborne De Lissa on a Motosacoche, when his sidecar wheel came off and careered across the track, so that they just missed it.

The first race in which he actually competed was with the 1000 cc V twin Zenith. Then he returned to his home in the Wirral, Cheshire and built Tottey's Garage, which opened in February 1922. He had a New Imperial which he raced on a small, three lap, banked track at New Brighton and also he managed to break all the records on the 3 1/2 lap shale track at a place called Fallowfield, near Manchester. Neither of these tracks were licensed by the ACU and he got a very severe reprimand from them for having ridden on unlicensed tracks. He rode in the 1922 Lightweight TT, in which he entered himself. As far as he could remember, the entry fee was £20 in those days so he cannot understand why people grumble at the very small entry fee nowadays. The only tarmac on the course in those days was between Governor's Bridge and Quarter Bridge. The rest was an old stone road from Ramsey to Creg-Ny-Baa, virtually a cart track with three ruts. In 1922, the 250 and 350 races were run simultaneously and whilst going along the middle rut up the mountain, a 350 overtook him and jumped back into the centre lane. A stone that was thrown up punctured his petrol tank so that he ran out of petrol, but those were the kind of conditions under which one rode in those days. Subsequently, he was entered officially by New Imperials in 1923 and 1924.

In 1924, he tried to straighten out Ballaugh bridge, not very successfully, and spent a few months in Ramsey Hospital. In the meantime he was at Brooklands almost continuously from the beginning of 1923 until about 1929. He won quite a number of races and one he remembers very well was the 1923 350 cc 200 mile race, in which Bert Le Vack was competing. Just towards the end, he happened to be leading and Le Vack was second, when the ball end of a rocker pushed through into the top of the push rod which meant the inlet valve was scarcely open at all. He had to drop down to about 60 mph and Le Vack just passed him before the finish. Nevertheless, the bike managed to average just over 70 mph for 200 miles, including two petrol stops.

One other incident he can remember very well occurred in the first Hutchinson 100, which was supposed to be a hundred mile race but actually necessitated the completion of 37 laps, which represents 102 miles and a bit. On the last lap, when he was leading, the petrol pipe broke when he was on the far side of the track and he had to push in a long distance, to finish about sixth. He complained that the race was supposed to be 100 miles, not 102 and a bit, and after that he was quite sure that the timekeeper used to watch the bikes emerging from under the Members' Bridge going down towards the Railway Straight, to see who was leading at that point. He would be the winner of the race, even if he broke down between there and the end of the 37th lap.

Although George rode for New Imperials, he was independent and not directly involved, as he was then running his own business. But he was connected and officially working for the Company as an outside Engineering Representative.

His business specialised in both cars and motorcycles. Fortunately, his racing successes had encouraged very good motorcycle business. In those days there were a lot of engineering requirements in the area and he built up quite a good business in general engineering too. His business did practically everything that could be done such as their own electrical work, painting, machining, welding and so on. At the time there were a lot of commercial concerns like laundries, gasworks, one or two locomotive works, waterworks and so on and he had frequently to help them out when their own machinery broke down, so that his machine shop was quite capable of dealing with most emergencies. He certainly had quite a big motorcycle trade, especially with New Imperials and other popular makes at that time.

George could not ride his machine to Brooklands and in any case, he had more than one, and often as many as three, machines of different capacity. He started off with a small shed there and later had a larger one, which formerly was used by the late Cyril Pullin. He had an old Darracq which he used as a transporter, but it was not very reliable and later he managed to buy an 11 litre 4 cylinder Fiat. It was a 1914 vehicle which the owner had purchased in London, driven to North Wales, frightened himself to death and rarely used again. George bought it for a song, took off the body and put on an ordinary flat wooden base, so that he could use it for transport to and from Brooklands. Each time he went there, it involved a journey of 220 miles there and 220 miles back. He can remember that in one season alone it involved a total of 19,000 miles, just going to Brooklands and back, so even in those days motorcyclists had to do a bit of travelling.

Running expenses were not too bad, because the Fiat had a top gear of 2.2 to 1 and the tyres were of 950 x 150 section. It used to do about 14 miles to the gallon but as petrol was only about 1s. a gallon it was not too dear. It was a very fine vehicle. He used it occasionally to go up the Test Hill for half crown bets, using third gear. He once took a well known rider round the track in it. There was only an open front seat which necessitated hanging on very firmly. His passenger did only one lap and never got in it again.

Arrangements with manufacturers and sponsors varied. With some manufacturers he had just a straightforward bonus arrangement for certain races and for world records. He had a part retainer from New Imperials towards expenses and one or two people paid him a retainer for the whole season. So the arrangements were not in any way fixed on one scheme alone. They varied according to individual circumstances and what he was able to arrange.

One of the agencies George held was for Omega motorcycles and one day, whilst he was talking to Mr. Green, who was then the Managing Director of the Omega Motor Cycle Company in Coventry, he said that he thought his three-wheelers could be improved by certain alterations and improvement to materials. Green said 'well, try one of the 500s'. So George took a 500 home, got a 500 cc racing JAP engine and tried it on the road. Every time he changed up into top gear, (there were only two gears) the cross shaft used to twist, so he made a cross shaft out of an old Ford motor car propeller shaft, which was of excellent steel and would stand up to the hammering. The two-speed type of transmission was similar to that used in the Morgan, although the front end had a different type of suspension. But it was not really satisfactory. One reason for this was that the clutch was incorporated in a heavy bronze wheel, which was welded on to the crankshaft, and when pressure was applied to withdraw the clutch, this put a side thrust on the crankcase and frequently the side of the crankcase would pull out completely.

He thought this design could be improved so in the winter of 1926 he built a quite different type of machine in which he used the normal bevel box half way along the chassis with a sprocket driving a Sturmey Archer gearbox, fixed where the original bevel box used to be. This drove the rear wheel with a single chain. The rear wheel could be changed in one and a half minutes as it had a knock out spindle, which was very handy when they were going for records and the tyre had to be changed. The arrangement for driving the propeller shaft was a steel disc bolted on to the end of the mainshaft with three holes in it and a corresponding disc on the end of the propeller shaft with three pegs, so one could slide the engine in and out quite easily. It was possible to change an engine for one of a different capacity in less than half an hour, which also was very handy when going for records.

Having done fairly well with the 500, George installed a 730 cc V twin JAP engine, having 74 x 85 bore and stroke dimensions. This proved to be the most reliable engine he ever had and never once did it break down through the whole of the period that he used it. Actually it was really a miscellaneous collection of parts, being one of the 85 mm stroke 1000 cc V twin crankcases with shortened connecting rods, 84 mm cylinder blanks that had been bored out to 74 mm only and fitted with 350 cc pistons, which were 74 mm diameter. An 84 mm cylinder head, not bored out to quite the full sphere formed the top end. The valves were very large and the gas feed was fairly low, but the engine was certainly reliable.

Although George raced a 350 and sidecar at Brooklands, quite successfully, he was not very fond of sidecars because when going round cutting the grass, the front forks used to bend rather ominously towards the sidecar. He recalled the day when Ted Prestwich was travelling as his sidecar passenger when, observing the movement of the forks, he came to the conclusion that it was rather a dangerous occupation. George managed to get a couple of records with the 350 cc sidecar outfit in 1923 but otherwise he raced solos until his three-wheeler era.

Questioned about who impressed most as a rider/tuner, the only person with whom George had any real contact was Bert Le Vack. He was very friendly with him and he certainly had some help from him. George believes that in all probability he was the best tuner and rider he ever knew, although possibly Victor Horsman was an even better engineer and designer and certainly a good rider. Also, one might think of the late Dougal Marchant, who was really a carburation expert and, of course, quite a good engineer. But in the top flight of motorcycle racers at Brooklands there were at least five or six between whom it was very difficult to differentiate in view of their respective abilities and riding.

When asked for his views about 'Woolly' Worters and Freddie Dixon, George agreed that Worters was certainly a very good rider and a good tuner, and that he had overlooked him when he mentioned the other good engineers and riders. With regard to Freddie Dixon, he was in a world of his own. He was the most amazing man, stocky as a post and extremely powerful. Whatever the machine wished to do, Freddie could control it and fight it very successfully. He recalled one very amusing incident when Freddie was going for the 5 kilo and 5 mile 1000 cc sidecar records and on the way round the sidecar wheel spindle broke. He continued on two wheels with the sidecar in the air and pulled up at the timing box, where he said to Ebby, 'Can I go on?' Ebby said, 'No, if you do, you'll be in the solo class'. So Freddie turned to George and said, 'Have you got a wheel spindle, Totty?' George replied that he had, but only out of a 350. Freddie said it didn't matter, so George dashed down to the Paddock, brought back the wheel spindle and put it into the hole in Freddie's sidecar chassis, although it was far too small and wobbling about. With a wheel fitted, Freddie took off with his passenger, flat out and with the sidecar wheel raised in the air, he lapped at 103.30 mph without the sidecar wheel touching the ground. Nevertheless he qualified as a three-wheeler, although he was only riding on two wheels. That was the type of man that he was.

The arrangements made between riders when record breaking seemed worthy of comment, especially as the late Eric Fernihough and George Tottey were probably among the busiest contenders with their 500 and 750 cc three-wheelers. They were great friends but equally great rivals. Nevertheless, Eric would perhaps come to George one day and say that he was thinking of going for the 1 Hour, 50 mile, 50 kilo or whatever it may be, record and ask whether he would work the schedule out for him. George would do this, allowing 10 seconds longer for the standing lap than the average required for the record to be broken by the minimum possible amount. He would then go down to the Fork, stand there with the usual lap boards and chalk and as the late A.V. Ebblewhite called down to him the going time, he could indicate to Eric how many seconds plus or minus he was on the schedule. Eric, of course, would reciprocate when he was going for records. So to that extent he was virtually manager

George (498cc New Imperial JAP), after winning the 3 Lap Experts Handicap at Brooklands in March 1925. Speed 81.51 mph.

Together again at a recent reunion. Gordon Cobbold, George Tottey, A.C. Squillario and E.C.E. ('Ted') Baragwanath.

for his rival while his own record was being broken.

George considers that two-strokes were not so predominant in those days because research on gas flow and the inertia of gas was lacking so that there was no knowledge of charging through the reaction pressure of induction and so on. Also crankcase compression was not very high and therefore the charge into the cylinder was not as great as it might have been. In addition, there was to some extent trouble with cooling because in the early days alloys which conduct heat far better had not been developed. As soon as one got fairly efficient charging with a cast iron cylinder, overheating occurred, causing distortion or seizure. So to some extent the development of the two-stroke without the present inertia knowledge was restricted by the heat developed. Nowadays, of course, one had tube exhausts which are really effective, and the modern alloys are much better at heat conducting. Pistons are more reliable, and furthermore one now has forced lubrication which is quite an advantage in most cases, when racing, over petroil.

It has been suggested that it is the life of a big end that determines the life of the engine in racing. George was asked whether he considered this applied when he was racing, or whether other parts of the engine tended to fail before the big end. In his experience, big ends were in those days sometimes the cause of trouble, but not the major cause. Major causes of failure were broken valves or valve springs, the burning of pistons and connecting rods breaking. He only ever had one big end go in the whole of his racing career and he was fortunate enough to break only one valve. He experienced one piston burnt out and he believed he had one connecting rod break.

Those were the extent of his breakdowns.

The most alarming cycle part failure occurred, fortunately, as he was wheeling his 500 cc machine up a small ramp into the shed, when the crankcase just touched the concrete. He thought that was peculiar because it didn't normally do it, so he had a look round the machine and found that the front down tube had just about parted from the head. One more bump and it would have broken completely. That was lucky. The only other awkward experience occurred when going down the Railway Straight when the front axle of his three-wheeler, which was tubular, and carried on quarter elliptic springs, broke in two. He managed to stop without too much damage. He went back to Coventry and in the Omega works there was a marvellous old blacksmith, who forged two stub axle ends suitable for 1.5 in. diameter special Reynolds tubing. He worked all night and the axle was rebuilt. He returned to the track the next day and the axle survived for the rest of the racing life of the vehicle.

Asked to recall any particularly humourous incidents at Brooklands, George recounted a day when the track was going to close. Although racing itself had finished there were still quite a number of people working there on experimental jobs, and on this particular Saturday the motorcycle boys had organised a farewell dinner in the dining room in the Paddock. The authorities had taken the precaution of removing all the pictures in the event of riotous behaviour, but this proved to be the last occasion on which a dinner was held there, for it developed into a snowballing match with Christmas pudding and custard. This was the last time they allowed the motorcyclists to have a meeting in that room, as it took some time to redecorate the walls. Other things happened such as tipping the big water tank over, which George thinks was done by George Patchett, which made them decide that motorcyclists were not suitable people from whom to take a booking on future occasions.

George had very vivid memories of three Brooklands personalities, none of whom were riders. He recalled that on one occasion Col. Lloyd happened to be in the Paddock when the gates onto the track were closed. However, Freddie Dixon went down the back road and over a small bridge by the aero sheds to do a couple of laps. Col. Lloyd was jumping up and down in the Paddock and when Freddie returned he was called in front of him. Col. Lloyd said 'Do you know who I am?' So Freddie said, 'No'. He said, 'I'm Col. Lloyd', whereupon Freddie said, 'Oh, I'm Freddie Dixon, how do you do?' and shook hands with him.

Ebby was also a character and he hated to have his handicapping system beaten. If a rider won a race rather too quickly, he decided that that would be the last occasion on which he would win a race that year on that particular machine. He was extremely helpful and a great man when a rider was going for records, taking great care to keep his assistant fully informed.

George Reynolds himself was Secretary of the BMCRC for many years and was a well respected and well-liked man. In fact Brooklands had two very fine time-keepers.

One other incident George could recall was when Tommy Allchin was riding the 4 hp flat twin Harley-Davidson in a handicap race start and Ebby was not available. In those days a clutch start was permitted. As was the custom, the limit man went off, then it was the turn of the two men on the next handicap, when the starter stepped back smartly two paces and dropped the flag. On this particular instant, Col. Lloyd stepped back one pace too few and when the flag dropped, Tommy Allchin took off and bowled him over. That was the end of clutch starts at Brooklands.

Col. Lloyd, of course, used to operate the electrical timing apparatus which was used on short distance records. It was not too reliable because the pens which inked the track on the recorder occasionally wobbled about a bit and scribbled. At one of the international meetings for the approval of records, these rolls had to be produced, and when one of the foreign representatives asked why there were so many marks, he was told that that was the wheel of the motorcycle. He said, 'How many wheels has it got, about 20?'

Asked whether he considered Brooklands would serve any useful purpose were it still available today, George suggested that had Brooklands not been constructed with great foresight by the late Mr. Locke King, the British motor industry would never have got to the height it eventually attained. There is no doubt that it was the only place where prolonged high speed testing, even to destruction, could be carried out and he considered it was this that put the British motorcycle and car industry ahead of everyone. Of course the track was not just a saucer with two straights as so many people seemed to think. One needed to have a fairly intimate knowledge of the contour of the track in order to avoid the bumps where sometimes the bays had dropped or there was broken concrete.

If one took the trouble to learn the course properly, as one has to do with any other course, Brooklands was a wonderful place. He doubted whether it would serve any good purpose today. Before the track was sold in 1939, the limit of possible speeds had almost been reached, due to the maximum angle of the bankings and their radius. He had witnessed on one or two occasions in the late '30s, cars going very close to disappearing over the top and even before that, one or two cars and at least one motorcycle went over the top, with fatal results. Now cars are getting up to the 200 mph mark, he could not agree that Brooklands would be very much use as a testing area, especially for racing cars at present day speeds. This fact had been appreciated when the late Malcolm Campbell produced a semi-road circuit, but not even that would be very suitable for racing and certainly would not provide a spectacle comparable with normal Grand Prix racing, on circuits such as we have now at Brands Hatch and Oulton Park. It is his belief that Oulton Park is the finest track we have because it is almost a natural track in beautiful surroundings.

When asked whether the reason why he pulled out from Brooklands, at the same time as many other well-known names, was on account of the monetary situation, George was emphatic it was not so in his case. He was never particularly interested in the total amount of money and on more than one occasion he actually made a loss during a full season. He was always extremely keen on the racing and to him it was worth a great deal to be able to enjoy the racing alone at Brooklands, and, of course, at other speed tracks, but it was a change of circumstances and business commitments which made him have to withdraw from active racing. If these conditions had not arisen, he would have raced right on until the track was closed.

The comments of a 'brainy' man? Yes, but very practical and down to earth. I found it interesting to hear George's views on whether or not Brooklands would have any value today and it certainly can be argued that if it was inadequate for a lap speed of a hundred and forty miles an hour plus, how much more inadequate would it be with speeds in the region of today's.

I don't feel qualified to hold any strong views on this but could it, I wonder, be argued that even if speeds have escalated, suspension and tyre techniques have moved forward to meet them. Certainly, when Brooklands opened in 1907 there wasn't a car built that, from the point of view of adhesion, couldn't lap it flat out. That had changed by 1939 and even earlier and, of course, when John Cobb turned in a lap at 143 mph he described it as 'leaning out of a window without actually falling out'. There were, by then, many cars that couldn't be driven flat out all the way round.

Maybe, even with all the improvement of modern suspension, no way could be found to avoid the lightweight racers of today being shaken to bits by the pounding. If not then, even at today's speeds, might the old track not become just a road racing problem, taking into account its inadequate bankings?

One other small thing that might mystify a reader not knowing the track well. George refers to the 'bays' of the bankings sinking. This was a factor because the surface was laid of concrete cast in bays some twenty feet square and, now and again, one of these would subside due to weather conditions or even as a result of the growth of tree roots.

J.S. WORTERS

When I first started thinking about writing this book and how to slant my approach, I sat down and made a list of the riders to whom I would like to talk. The first name that came to mind, I think, was that of J. S. 'Woolly' Worters.

It came out of the hat first because of all of them, I had known Woolly best and I felt pretty sure that he would help me if he could, even knowing that he was in happy retirement down in Devon and that he had then severed his connection with Brooklands completely.

I remember Woolly when he was ending his period of riding – all of it highly professional and successful – and was about to turn to running and managing his own team consisting of Chris Staniland, Maurice McCudden and 'Muffin' Hewitt. Over his whole span of racing and managing, the record shows that, in terms of sheer results, he was by far the most successful of any who competed on two-wheelers at Brooklands.

He was agent for Wakefield's at the time I first met him. Wakefields had a shed in the Paddock and, while he had his own business at Chertsey, three or four miles away, he was the chap to 'phone if one wanted a gallon of Castrol 'R'. I still recall 'phoning him on that first occasion, not understanding at all why he didn't seem too keen to make a round trip of seven miles to dispense a single gallon to a youngster who might or might not have the money with which to pay for it. I recall being surprised when he asked me if I knew how much a gallon of 'R' would cost and being shocked when he told me. But, by a hair's breadth, I had the money and, to his credit, he made the trip. But it wasn't a meeting I enjoyed and, from then on, I was rather in awe of him.

That would have been in the very early thirties, I think, and by the mid-thirties he was preparing and tuning my Manx Norton engines so that they were very much better and faster engines than they had been when they arrived new, from Bracebridge Street. During that period I got to know him quite well and later, when he built the single seater Multi Union for Chris Staniland, I felt I knew Woolly very well. But even then, I was still slightly in awe of him.

He has a 'presence' and, with one look he can cut you down to a size so small that you feel you're in danger of being trodden on by anyone passing. But, despite this, he is in fact a very nice man indeed and would do anything to help anyone for whom he had regard, provided he felt that that person was genuine and wasn't going to waste his or anyone else's time. With the record of his motorcycle racing at Brooklands set out and, bearing in mind that he built for Chris the second fastest car ever to go round Brooklands – a mile an hour or so slower than Cobb's giant Railton, and a 3 litre car at that – nothing more need be said about his engineering capabilities.

So when I asked him if I could make the trip to Devon to talk to him about his achievements I ought not to have been surprised at his polite refusal – but I was. We then talked on the 'phone a bit about other things (it must have been some twenty years since we'd talked) and that seemed to be that.

A few days later I got a letter saying that although he felt there wouldn't be much interest in such a book, he would, if I cared to send him a questionnaire, answer it as best he could. I sent off the questionnaire and, a week later came another letter saying that, on starting to answer it, points had occurred to him which made him think he would rather put his thoughts and recollections on tape, and would that do as well.

I wrote back, saying that that would be even better, waited a bit and, some time later, received the tape which, when transcribed, turned out to be the finest bit of original material I've ever seen on the subject of bike racing at the track in that period. It need hardly be said that I am immensely grateful to him because I feel that no one, other than myself, can have as good an idea of how much work and thought such a project involves.

'Woolly' made just one proviso regarding the publishing of his tape – that it should go into the book verbatim or not at all, to which I readily agreed because I had envisaged it being included exactly as in the taped conversations I had had with him. In this instance I am glad because I really don't think there can ever have been a better example of 'straight from the horse's mouth 'Brooklands' reminiscence. I hope, very much, that readers will feel the same and that they will enjoy it as much as I have.

Before setting out on the first of my journeys to talk to these great men, I prepared a 'questionnaire' which I took with me on each occasion because, at the time, I expected their recollections to be few after so long a time lapse. I needn't have bothered, as it turned out because time seemed to have erased nothing. But when 'Woolly' initially asked for a questionnaire, I sent him the same one and, besides setting out the whole story on tape, he also replied to it. So, since part of it does raise other points, that, too is included at the end of his narrative.

THE J.S. WORTERS TAPE

I started riding motorcycles about 1910 upon an old Motosacoche belonging to an uncle of mine. It was a glorified pushbike with an engine hung up under the top tube with side shields on it. The first bike I owned myself was a 1912 ex T.T. Scott with water cooled cylinder head and air cooled cylinder barrels. It overheated and I knew nothing at all about two strokes. I estimated once that I pushed it as far as I rode it.

The next bike was a three and a half hp Zenith Gradua which I started riding without any success in hill climbs at South Harting and elsewhere. Then I changed for a Martin JAP. Harry Martin was a man with a wax moustache who turned out bikes somewhere in South London. It had in it an overhead valve, 500 I think JAP engine, it was very fast, single gear, belt drive. One night when riding back to my lodgings at Dartford, where I was serving my apprenticeship with Halls the engineering works, an exhaust valve fell in about midnight on the middle of Dartmouth Heath and as I couldn't turn the engine to get the belt off, I had to push it about three miles with it on, which was a bit hard work.

After the 1914-18 War spent mostly working on aircraft at Sopwiths, which is now Hawker Siddeleys at Kingston-on Thames and Martinsydes, the latter being inside Brooklands Byfleet banking, where I had met O'Donovan during the war, I bought a side valve 500 cc Norton with Sturmey Archer 3 speed hub gear which went like a bomb. Then I spent about a year flying in the Air Force. Coming out, I went first to Gillett Stevens at Bookham, which was afterwards the headquarters of Burney and Blackburne, and worked on car parts – Vauxhall and various other firms. Then Martinsyde, the flying people with whom I had been, were in business at Woking, making motorcycles, twin cylinder efforts, and after that, when they folded up, I joined a small sheet metal firm making side car bodies in Addlestone. It called itself Toronda, concocted from the names of the then owners. With some money I raised, we took some premises in Ship Yard, Weybridge and started to make complete sidecars, one of which had the hood concealed when down. George Brough showed it on a bike at Olympia. Also we made tanks and bits and pieces for Brooklands racers, who sometimes paid and sometimes not. I was still riding in hill climbs and now I had a small Velocette. In Weybridge also lived Dougal Marchant who, with a partner named Jones, invented and made a carburettor named Flexi. I bought one and Dougal became a sort of God Almighty to me. He fitted the carburettor to the Velocette, tuned it and from then on I listened to every word he said with baited breath. He eventually showed me the innards of a 250 cc Blackburne he had started to race, the crankshaft etc. polished like chromium plating. This fired my enthusiasm and I believed everything Dougal said as Gospel truth. He completely convinced me that high compressions were no good and in consequence I thought a 7 to 1 compression ratio was absurd and concentrated on better means of filling the cylinder with shaped valves and ports and with these ideas I continued right up to 1930, gradually getting better at it, when Hatch of Burney and Blackburnes convinced me otherwise. Paddy Johnson, who had surreptitiously taken the head off one of Marchant's bikes while he was away, told me that the piston almost came out of the plug hole. However, I was so full of enthusiasm after all this that we at Toronda built the one and only bike of that name around a second-hand 250 cc outside flywheel Blackburne which I bought off Dougal and I joined the BMCRC. Previous to this I had raced my Velocette in I think an Essex Motor Club meeting handicap, where I was limit man. The motorcycling report said, "Worters, after an excellent start, got slower and slower". I finished last by some minutes.

About this time our business folded up and I went to Brooklands and worked for C.G. (Cyril) Pullin. Also about now Marchant joined Chater Lea, the one with the flat camshaft, so Blackburnes in 1925 gave me more and more help but they didn't give me a retainer. About this time, in 1921, the 500 mile motorcycle race was held and I well remember seeing the start and the 100 or so riders do their push start and the sight of

Toronda – a small sheet metal firm making sidecar bodies.

them all running and jumping. It was I believe Dixon's first appearance at the track. According to the report, he fell off several times and once having a puncture, he sat in the middle of the Railway Straight and mended and pumped it up.

Pullin's works were in the Paddock but he was mostly on Douglas motorcycles but also on cars which were tuned for Woolf (Babe) Barnato and also for George Duller to drive, the famous jockey. One of these cars was a Wolseley Moth, a bulbous sort of streamliner with an almost rigid suspension. Working inside it one day, George Duller looked over the side and said, 'Come out of the way, Woolly, and let me look'. I then wore my hair very long and untidy. The name stuck around the Pullin camp and eventually spread, Chris Staniland being the one to alter it to Willy. Rex Judd and Fred Dixon made periodic visits to the track and were of course based on Cyril's place, thereby livening things up more than somewhat, having excellent ideas on extra-curricula entertainment, and these two became and remained, with Chris Staniland and Ron Hopkins, my closest friends. Whenever Rex and Fred came up from Bristol they came to our bungalow at Weybridge and my wife had to order about two dozen oysters apiece for us – imagine the cost in these days! During this time Bert Denly had joined O'Donovan over at the aerodrome and used to go home to Byfleet every night on a Norton, coming into the track in the morning and very often stopping at Cyril's place for a chat before going on to O'Donovan, who was a great stickler for people keeping time. One morning I remember Cyril kept him talking in the shed in the Paddock while the rest of us, there were about four of us, got Bert's Norton upstairs, up the steps into the bar and he nearly went frantic when he couldn't find it, thinking of O'Donovan tearing his hair out the other side of the aerodrome, until eventually we had to carry it all the way down again for him.

Then Cyril sold the Brooklands business to Col. and Mrs. Stewart. Mrs. Stewart was originally Gwenda Glubb if you can remember the name. Whilst Cyril had been agree-able to my riding my own bike in meetings, the Stewarts didn't want me to at all, and wanted me to tune for them all the machines and for me not to ride, so after a few weeks I quit and decided to start racing on my own, on the strength of a few minor successes in club meetings and hill climbs. Incidentally, reverting to Cyril and me riding, one BMCRC meeting, we were both entered in sidecar outfits, with me on a 350 with the engine loaned by Blackburne giving Cyril on 500 cc a start. I don't know why that was. When he saw the programme, Cyril said, 'O.K., but you get the sack if you pass me.' This I did on the last lap and Cyril, letting go with one hand, took a piece of paper out of his pocket and waved it at me as I went by, luckily in fun only. When I started I had the Toronda, a sidecar, a lot of tools and ambition and the loan of a good 350 Blackburne from Harry Hatch, the chief man at Blackburnes and Bookham now. I rented a shed at the track up the hill and under the tunnel and then straight on, instead of going round to the right and out of the gate, which was promptly burgled of all movable bits and pieces, subsequently recovered due to my own reading of all the small adverts. in the local motorcycling papers and finding an advert that corresponded with them, thereby the thief was caught and given 18 months' imprison-ment. The police had given up about 5 or 6 weeks before that. As obviously I wasn't likely to make a living for myself, wife and baby son out of BMCRC meetings, records it had to be. The timekeeper's fee was, I believe, about 1 guinea and the oil firm, Castrol, then would pay about £5 per record. The lords of the 250 and 350 cc. classes then, Marchant and Le Vack, being apparently uninterested in the standing start mile and kilo, and in any event now spending most of their time at the recently opened track at Montlhéry I decided to have a go at the 250 standing start mile and kilo, which I got at first attempt on 19th June 1925, I think, with my old 3 cylinder holding down bolt Blackburne in the Toronda frame. Thus encouraged, I put in the 350 engine Hatch had lent me and again had Col. Lloyd and his electric timing working but only got one of the four records. At first the Colonel said, 'Well done, you've got all four' and then, 'By Jove, no, you missed the kilo', then, 'No, By Jove you missed the kilo on the reverse'. I went hurriedly down the steps of his box in case he took away the last one. Thinking big, I announced that I would go for the 5 and 10 miles and kilos, only to be told jointly Marchant and Le Vack, just back on a trip from France, that if I did, one of them would break it the next day, and if I wanted to go for 250 cc or 350 cc records and be left holding them for the required time, I had better start with about 100 miles and kilos and work on from there. Despite your earlier comments, Charles, there was very, very little co-operation between rival camps. I'll say more about that later on. One standing mile and kilo I wanted especially was the 350 solo, then held by George Dance of Sunbeam fame and set up a long time previously. Incidentally, when I mentioned taking a 350 out after the 250 records, it was a 350 and sidecar then. This record was held by George Dance, TT rider extraordinary. He set it up a long time previously but working out his maximum speed by his time from the kilo box to the mile box and then against my speed, I reckoned I had 10 miles an hour in hand so I thought this easy but his reputation and skill at this game were no imagination and I couldn't get within seconds of his time. Remember all bikes had hand change in those days. And after weeks of practice, for quite a long time really, I managed to get inside his time, hand timed. So I rang up Col. Lindsey Lloyd, who did all the electric timing from the little box opposite the paddock gate, and next day had a go. If you remember, the electric timing strips were large flatttened, heavy rubber tubes, with metal strips fastened inside the top and bottom of them. Air was pumped in to separate these strips and the edge of the bottom rubber tube was screwed down to a wooden strip let into the concrete right away across the track with a screw supposed to be about every 18 inches. On the day in question, the track gang had only screwed the mile strip down about every 8 feet or more. In consequence, as I went over it the first time, the strip lifted and as I had then a very bad habit of riding with my toes down, I collected the strip with my left foot and broke the entire footrest off, plus the second toe of my left foot. I coasted to a stop half the way round to Byfleet and fell off on the grass in some pain. After ten minutes or so, during which Col. Lloyd went red with rage, as I afterwards heard, and having no staff to come and look for me, I managed to get up, start the bike and ride to the Paddock, to be taken to Weybridge hospital by Rex Judd. Incidentally, I had bettered George Dance's time but only one way and standing start records require a run both ways, as you know. I never did have another go at it, I don't know why.

In 1924 and 25, Marchant and Le Vack were both very occupied at Montlhéry They lived over there most of the season and they were presumed by their respective firms, JAPs and Blackburnes to be competing there in deadly earnest for world records and were certainly sending back a few results but on periodic visits to the track they both said conditions over there were terrible, there was no money to be made. However, they still kept on going back. At one of our occasional convivial evenings during show week, the truth came out. They lived in the same lodgings, they kept their bikes in the

1925 200 Mile Solo Race. J.S (Woolly) Worters, 250cc Cotton, refuelling.

1925 200 Mile Race. 'Woolly', 250cc winner at 69.24 mph.

same shed at Montlhéry, the Superintendent of which was a M. Lamblin. One of them would get a record and the other another record, each breaking the other one's record after the minimum period. On other days, M. Lamblin would call and ask them to give a demonstration for the large public who came there at that time at weekends and they would stage a race. Every record or race entailed a visit to Hutchinson Tyres which they were both using, in Paris, where the very amiable M. Mellano would write out cheques at once. Once Dougal said they had got hard up for records to break so they invented some intermediate ones, 150 kilos and miles, 250 kilos and miles and so on, for which Hutchinsons were quite pleased to pay. I don't think anyone tumbled to their scheme to keep Montlhéry private until Nigel and Denly went over. Incidentally Dougal always called Nigel Spring, Nigel (with a hard g). It annoyed him but he loved doing it. I added it up and I find that in 1924 I rode in 5 hill climbs in all for four firsts, two seconds, and four thirds. I also rode in 17 Brooklands meetings for eleven firsts, thirteen seconds and three thirds. I did 310 laps of the track in all, where I had five big ends go and broke three con rods – quite a season. By now Hatch at Blackburnes was sufficiently impressed to lend me a better 250 and 350 cc engine. Also a Cotton frame, known then as the flying bedstead. I entered the 250 in the 200 mile in the Cotton frame. The favourite by about 10 mph for this was Bert Le Vack who was so sure of winning that he geared up his new Imperial to the exact revs where the vibration broke both his valve springs in the end. He played cat and mouse with me for about 100 miles, sometimes in front, sometimes at the side grinning at me, and sometimes just behind. When we came in at half distance to refill, with him one lap in the lead, I got

Though the engines were always JAP the frames were Rex Acme –

– or Excelsior, according to Vivian Prestwich's arrangements. Among numerous other wins and record successes, 'Woolly' won the 200 mile 250cc Solo Race in 1925, 1926 (with a lead of 17 minutes over the second man), and in 1927.

away first and after one lap was amazed to see him still in the pits with Vivian Prestwick looking at the engine. I was in the lead but next time round he had gone and depression set in again until I found him pushing the New Imp down the straight. Next lap round to Byfleet and so on, so I throttled back and coasted home several hundred pounds better off and with two feet on the ladder. However, it wasn't all success. I lasted one lap in the 200 miles sidecar race and blew a piston head.

The 1925 season ended with some more records and wins and show time at Olympia arrived. This was our mecca. We walked in pairs, or threes, from oil stand to oil stand to plug stand to tyre stand, asking how much they would pay next season for our services. Ditto with everybody you can think of. You name it and we just got something. I signed up with Little Andy, Anderson of Castrol, and stayed with them till I left Brooklands. He was a real friend to me and helped me at JAP's and helped me in every way. I was also signed on by JAPs with the magnificent sum of £50 for the seasons, Le Vack having joined new Hudson, I think. I took a better shed in the square opposite Dunlops, took on a youth named Hewitt, who lived at Addlestone, whom I called Boy and he called me Boss, until we parted in 1932, and whom I taught to ride and who ended up a better rider than I was. I spent the winter shooting with Bert Denly and friends at Clandon as ever. We shot hundreds of rabbits, not much else. Le Vack had used overhead camshaft JAPs. Only about six were ever made and all for him and on leaving JAPs all the bits and pieces were suitably dismantled and stored as was customary as far as I can remember whenever a rider left one factory for another. Anyhow, I rather horrified Vivian for a start by saying that I would have nothing to do with the overhead camshaft but would race the standard push rod types, 250 and 350 only. I inherited Le Vack's frames, all of which, three or four, were built of very light tube.

Vivian was still very much opposed to low compression ratios but I looked at some of Le Vack's old pistons and the centre of the crown stuck up so high that I didn't reckon the plug could get a good look at the gas on the other side at all, so I started working on getting the cylinder full and I got the results eventually.

We all had some of our special parts made outside the factory for the reason that if they gave us an advantage over our competitors, they were worth keeping secret and paying for out of our own pockets. I had all my valves, valve guides and other parts made by a very clever young engineer at Walton named Stafford Macey. Dougal Marchant and Jack Emerson, who lived in Weybridge and Walton respectively, also had parts made there but Stafford Macey never deliberately exhibited anyone's bits and pieces to anyone else. I'm sure of that.

About 1923 - 25, JAPs and Blackburnes suffered greatly on these racing engines with big end trouble. Le Vack once told me he couldn't get one to last 200 miles without a lot of luck but suddenly Marchant had no more trouble with his Blackburnes. One day over at Maceys, I with my to this day incurable interest in anything mechanical and particularly 'how was it made' looked at a small bronze circle with rectangular holes in it, standing on the bench, and said to Staff, 'What's that?' He covered it up and said, 'You're not supposed to have seen that', but I had and suddenly after a bit of thought guessed correctly, as he eventually admitted, to its being a cage for a big end bearing for Marchant. I said, 'Make me one' but he said, 'No, I can't, but if you go home and make me a drawing of it, I'll put the clearances right and if anyone ever asks, you can always say it was your own idea'. He made it and subsequently several more, expensively, but that trouble was over. For me also. It was so simple and in retrospect so obvious a solution to big ends burning out but the sequel was that Jack never got a penny piece from anyone for it.

1926 was a good season for me. I got a quantity of records and you probably have got a record of what they are in all those *'Motor Cycling's* you have bought. Chris Staniland started riding my bikes and I started tuning his Bugatti. I won the 200 mile 250 cc race again and I rode my 350 in the 500 cc class in the afternoon, getting second to Jack Emerson, who was riding a 500 Zenith Jap I think. I led for several laps while Jack was in the pits with trouble of some sort, but as at the time I was sitting on the side of the Railway Straight trying to thing out how to tighten the engine shock absorber ring nut without a spanner, I knew nothing of this distinction until, having got some sort of result with my hands, I rode slowly to the pits to find them frantic. The spanner and a hammer completed the repair and I finished my 400 miles in the day second in the end with a nice handful of cash.

During this year Chris and I and Maurice McCudden, brother of the First World War flying VC, started on long distance records, some successful and some not. Mac was full of guts and full of good humour and kept us cheerful when depressed, which was customary, especially the night before a BMCRC meeting, with stories, blue and otherwise. He worked at the RAE at Farnborough. Once again, no luck in the 200 mile sidecar race but a lot of trouble, ending in the conrod broken, I believe. I spent the winter again shooting with Bert and other friends. I went towards the end of the year down to Bristol on our Austin Chummy car for the Douglas Club dinner which was supposed to be a great thing down there. It was a dinner and booze up with Rex and Fred. They asked me down there. At the Douglas Club, we got through the dinner all right but then they started some dancing – they had women in this one – but Fred

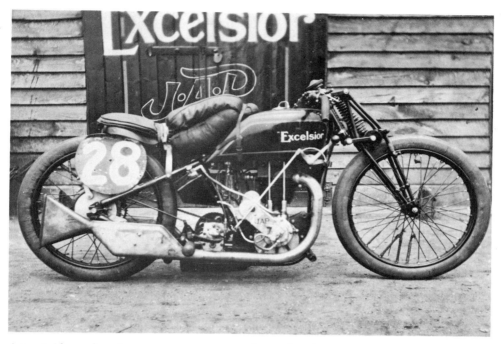

A great rider and, perhaps an even greater experimental engineer. Note the gearbox position in this 'Worters' Excelsior –

– and in this one!

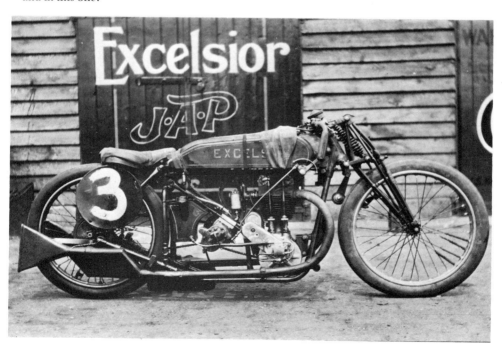

Brooklands most successful race winning and record breaking team. From left to right – **J.S. Worters** (Manager), Chris Staniland, W.J.C. Hewitt and M.V. McCudden.

With the **1925, 1926 and 1927 250cc 200 Mile Races** won by Worters, Staniland, under his management, continued to win the same races in **1928, 1929 and 1930**.

decided he had had enough of it so he went and pulled the main electric light switch and there was a riot in the dark. I woke in the Kingswood Hotel the next morning, woken by Rex coming through the first floor window carrying a bottle of champagne to revive Fred and myself. I also tasted the best hare soup I have ever tasted in my life, which was then, and may be now for all I know, a speciality of certain restaurants in Bristol. If you are ever down there, try hare soup.

Once again I reminisce. By the middle of the year, I had managed to break Marchant's 250 cc record for 5 and 10 mile and kilos. This stood for several years at just over 85. Vivian once told me he was sure it had been done on a 350 as no-one else could get within 8 or 10 miles per hour of it. The standard fuels for motor cycles in those days were either Discol PMS2 or Discol RD1. Both alcohol based and made and marketed by the Hammersmith Distilleries. I don't remember what PMS2 stood for but RD1 was Ricardo Discol after the famous Harry Ricardo, who once raced a Triumph at the track in his spare time for engine research etc. But at JAPs we had tried methyl alcohol with great success but only on short races and records. This fuel, unfortunately, varied in quality, and I remember Staniland's annoyance once when I sent him out in a 250 cc five lap race one championship meeting, telling him it was an easy race for him from the next fastest man, which was Fernihough. Chris only won by half a length, due to bad fuel. It occurred to me that pure ethyl alcohol would be the thing to find the 2 to 3 mph extra I wanted but how to get it without dealing with Customs and Excise etc. I didn't know. Eventually, Monty Bird, the famous Jazz of Discol's Paddock representative, wangled me two gallons of 98% absolute alcohol from the Hammersmith Distillery at about £1 a gallon I think and with Brewster and Johnson, if you remember them, and several other regular track inhabitants up to see the fun, and Ebby time-keeping, they all trying to see what I had put in the tank, but we kept them far enough away not to be able to smell it. They wanted to know what I had been using over the last week which had apparently given the 250 a kick in the pants in practice. I set off and got all four records at 88 mph plus. I phoned Vivian who was very excited and I got a real welcome at JAPs next day. I then cleaned up the 50 kilo and mile and a week after the 100 also, but the latter on RD1, failing to scrounge a lot more ethyl alcohol. The odd half pint or so we had left after the 50 Kilo and mile, we put into our morning coffee, with great effect, rather good. Vivian now wanted me to go over to Arpajon to ride in the speed trials down the famous route. Arpajon is just somewhere near Montlhéry. Wright, Brewster and Teddy Prestwich were going over by boat but due to matters which delayed me a day, I got them to take my bike over and I decided to fly over. I chartered a DH9 open cockpit three-seater, an old ex-wartime machine, the three seats in tandem, with a Captain Travers, I think the man's name was, who was to fly me to Le Bourget for the sum of £40 double trip. Having a spare seat, I asked George Patchett, another famous Brooklands rider to come along for free. George said he had never flown before, but I having piloted during the last year of the war said, 'Oh, there's nothing to it'. We left Weybridge at 6 a.m. arrived at Croydon and found thick fog, which didn't lift until 8.30 or so. Once off I cheerfully tapped George on the shoulder. He sat in the middle seat, and I pointed down at Croydon cemetary just to cheer him up. Arriving after an easy flight at the Channel we found we were above 10/10th cloud and the pilot wandered about looking for a hole in the clouds and decided to turn back and I managed to spot a hole just as he was going. He turned and we went down through the hole. There was the

Channel, very bumpy, and the air was very bumpy and to my horror I was very airsick indeed, George being perfectly OK and thoroughly enjoying it. We landed at Beauvais as the pilot was completely lost. Madame, the wife of the aerodrome keeper, gave me a glass of cognac, and we took off again. We arrived at Le Bourget to find Major Carreira of JAPs and Teddy Prestwich and a driver in an enormous open Peugeot, which he drove through Paris as if the streets were completely empty, frightening me to death. On the way to Arpajon, we heard the toot, toot of a French train, which we saw, running on a converging track. Our driver took no notice whatever, went across the level crossing in front of the train with about sixty yards to spare. Eventually, we arrived at Arpajon to find the rest of the gang, who didn't look too happy, sitting on the side of the road. Some of them had ridden and got nothing, but by now I had more or less recovered. After getting the bike warmed up and changing the plug, I set off down the very slightly sloping half mile before the start to run down this road. The road runs perfectly straight. It is not very wide. It goes through a few woods and every time it emerged from the woods, the wind seemed to push you to one side. At the far end I stopped in trying to turn and was restarted by two obliging Gendarmes. The reverse run was much the same and after some long time, Teddy got the result, which was a mile and kilo at just under 90 mph. I changed a gear and tried again, but couldn't make it any better. I was now anxious to get home. No-one arrived at our end of the road to take me, so Ted set off on my bike, leaving me alone with one bottle of French beer and half a French loaf. After a long wait our car arrived, having, I afterwards learnt, been deliberately delayed so that the plane could take the London press photos back. Due to the delay we left Le Bourget later than planned. The weather turned very rough and I noticed that the pilot was zig-zaggging across the Channel from ship to ship, just in case. It was definitely dusk when we started across Kent and increasingly obvious we should not make Croydon before dark and as I had been airsick all the way across, I had ceased to care. The pilot passed over many, to my eye, very suitable fields and eventually landed us safely with an act of God in the middle of a sewage farm at Penshurst, in Kent. He missed a wide and deep ditch by about three feet or so. George Patchett decided to stay there with the pilot for the night but I insisted that I had paid to get back to Croydon so they got me a taxi to get me back and after coping with a puncture when I got back to Croydon in the little Talbot we had then, I arrived back in Weybridge about 2.30 a.m. where my friend Ron Hopkins, who took on Chater Lea after Marchant went to FN, who had looked after my family with his wife all day, was still waiting. He had to drive home to Camberley afterwards.

Several people had achieved good speeds that day though. Machant did 102 on a Chater Lee, Mrs. Stewart 101 on Terrot JAP, Brewster 86 on a 600 Zenith and sidecar. Temple did 122, one of his runs being the fastest a motorcycle had ever then been timed at. My chief memory, however, was Ernest Eldridge on his enormous Fiat, with pistons almost as large as dinner plates, driving down the road hitting alternate kerb-stones or verges. The road was comparatively narrow and even at my modest speed I kept seeing first one kerb and then the other appear below my right or left arm. I used to ride very flat in those days. Marchant had riding dress for records down to a fine art. He rode in some sort of tights with insulating tape round his thighs to keep everything from flapping about.

1927 went better than ever. I drew over £1,440 in retainers before I ever put a leg over the saddle. We got a lot more records and I won the 250 cc 200 mile race for the third year running. Chris drove my 350 in the 350 race and if I've got the year correct, it rained the entire way and despite the fact that he must have passed me at least three or four times, we never saw each other from start to finish. In the afternoon it cleared up and I had arranged with Pat Driscoll to ride one of his Nortons in the 500 cc race. He was now running a stable and he had entered three Nortons. I had been too busy to do more than one lap on the one that I was going to ride, which I subsequently discovered had been tried and discarded by the other two riders as definitely difficult to steer. In the race with a full fuel tank plus a top tank, making it something like a camel above the bar, the steering had no trail at all as we measured it afterwards and after wrestling with the bike all the way down the straight on the first lap I came off at about 70, going round the Blyfleet Banking, noting with glee as the bike and I passed and repassed each other along the floor, that one handlbar had gone through the side of the tank and let the fuel out. I walked back to the Members' Hill where my wife and small 5 year old son were sitting. Robin was inconsolable for the rest of the afternoon, not because I had fallen off, but because I wasn't riding for him to watch. My only damage was bruises but I did my leathers no good at all. Pat was most apologetic about the bike afterwards but he said, 'The other two riders thought that as an expert, you could manage it all right. They had tried it and they didn't like it.'

At the end of 1927, I personally held every 250 cc World and British record from the standing kilo to the six hours and, I think, with Chris, Mac and Hewitt, the longer ones as well. But I was 33 years old then and I suddenly realised I had gone on long enough. I was on top of the 250 class, I couldn't get any higher and I found that I was inclined to watch the front tyre in case it burst or I got very tired early on long distance records and it was having a very bad effect on my wife's nerves. Twice during this year, coming to the track to meet me, she met the ambulance coming out. Once it was Jim Hall and I forget who the other was, but either could have been me, I think she felt. It's time to leave off when you are at the top and not go on too long – that goes for everything. Trying to compete with younger riders who are on the up and up, physically, and more attractive to the trade and public – witness poor old O'Donovan, who went on in my opinion much too long. So at Olympia, having managed to almost essential pre-show crop of records and results I told Vivian I had decided to be a manager and with Staniland, McCudden and Hewitt already doing a lot of the riding and able to step into my shoes, he thought it a good idea and actually increased my retaining fee. Chris and Mac both rode for fun and anything I cared to pass on after big races or records. Hewitt worked for me and was paid weekly as well as bonus on results and did all the test riding, however many bikes there were in races. He had ridden them all for the riders. Eric Walker of Excelsiors was also very happy with the idea. Now while we did very well financially in 1928, I soon found out the snag of being a manager. When you are riding and tuning your own bikes, all your worries, or most of them, end once the flag is down, but as manager they only really start. You are worried the moment your rider is out of sight until he reappears and practically die if he is a few seconds late on any lap. If eventually he does not appear, you imagine the worst at once – he has crashed, the engine has blown up, a tyre has burst etc. And had miniature two way radio sets been invented then, a lot of grey hairs would have been saved. The riders in our stable at least classed everything as occupational hazards, I think, and never quite understood what the old man was bellyaching about.

Once again we won the 250 cc 200 mile. I got told off by Vivian afterwards for having the timekeepers down twice to get the 250 cc, 5 and 10 miles which seeing that the lot only took four laps, it was customary to do in one go. We got the 5 and 10 on one day and 10 mile and 10 kilo a week later, thereby getting two lots of bonus. I believe my excuse was engine trouble but I doubt if Vivian believed it.

By now, in additional to my own shed, I had the Castrol shed next door and dispensed free Castrol R galore to all and sundry. A lot of the amateurs were scrounging such a lot that I think they must have been using it medicinally as well. One of the racers, meeting racers not the regular ones, F.J. Young of OK fame, ran a motorcycle business somewhere up in London. He was a real Cockney and always brought his wife and family down with him, some of them quite small children. He brought them down to the meetings and on one occasion, a boy of about eight or nine turned up and said, 'Two gallons for F.J. Young, please'. Knowing that Young was only in one 5 lap race that day, I said, 'No, you can't have it', whereupon the boy lent out of the shed door and yelled to his father across the paddock, 'Hey, Dad, he says you can't f-ing well have it', which was rather a shock as in those days, small children didn't swear. We also supplied the car people and Castrol paid a retainer. Also Castrol paid me a retainer for looking after the shed. Also across the Paddock, near where you had a shed, Charles, we did a similar service for Amal with jets and carburettor spares. By now we seemed to have added the 175 cc class to our stable and I rode this myself for some short records but in the 1927 championship there were I think four 175 JAPs and one 175 Blackburne entered. The Blackburne was ridden by a complete newcomer to the track named Dallison. I found out later that day that Marchant, very jealous of the records the JAPs had had on the 175, had taken Dallison's engine and modified it suitably on the condition that he had it back after the race to unmodify it. Anyway it took me down several pegs because I was beaten by quite a distance by him. We had two dozen records with it later on, some as long as seven hours, and all the shorts. But what happened to Dallison, I don't know. I don't think I ever saw him again or heard of him.

At this stage, Charles, I must appeal to you for information from all your books. I have mislaid my 1928 diary and I can't remember exactly when I gave up riding, so perhaps you will correct any wrong dates. I do know that in November 1928 I had peritonitis. I was lucky to come out of Weybridge Hospital alive – all due to Sam Beare the surgeon. This finally finished my riding if I hadn't finished before. In 1929 we got thirty to forty records and races and the money still came in, but with more people to share it now of course. I entered Staniland and Hewitt in the 200 mile solo race again with instructions to Hewitt that Chris was Number One rider and, despite the fact that towards the finish Chris's engine was getting very tired, and Hewitt's was still full of beans, the boy kept his place and they finished first and second, a few yards apart. We also got the three to twelve hour records with the 250 cc in July.

At the end of the 1929 season Vivian said they were not quite sure how much they could pay next year, etc. etc. They only paid £250 for the entire stable this year and as Marchant had served his connection with Burney and Blackburne and the latter were in the market for a rider or a stable of some sort, I went over to Bookham at Hatch's invitation and had a long talk with him. He was very keen to get my stable but dubious about the Brooklands crowd, about whom and their goings on he had heard a lot, he said, and nothing very good. I convinced him that he was utterly mistaken and eventually signed up. They also had Bernard Hieatt under some sort of a contract and they added him to my riders. He was a very nice, quiet, willing lad, full of guts, who had an old Gypsy Moth, which he flew from his home near Reading to the track when he was racing. Now Freddie Dixon used to come down from Middlesborough on an old saloon Chevrolet and about now his brother was riding solo down to Brooklands, solo until a wasp came in. Fred's brother tried for quite a while to drive at 60 mph and swat the wasp at the same time and eventually turned the Chev over without damage to himself but a lot to the Chev body. Fred managed to buy another body and get it to the track where the old body was taken off and the new one fitted. Now, what to do with the old one, which lay not far from my shed, between me and Dunlops. 'Burn it', said Fred, so after pouring petrol on it, it was set alight. Just then Jim Hall turned up – I expect you remember Jim Hall – he could have a chapter to himself very nearly. He turned up and several other of the Brooklands blithe spirits, who started to dance round the flames, occasionally rolling a scrap tyre from Dunlops across the square on to keep things going. Fred shouted to Jim Hall, 'I think we'd better put it out, put it out'. And he handed Jim a Pyrene which he had previously filled with petrol. Jim squirted it on the fire and of course the flames ran back up the stream of petrol to the extinguisher and he kept pumping faster and faster and the flames kept coming up and up. As he danced round, he eventually threw the Pyrene on the fire and started mopping his face with a suspensary bandage, a jock-strap, which he took out of his pocket, but by now we were all exhausted with laughter and I turned round to find Hatch. standing beside me not altogether convinced of the sanity of the Brooklands inhabitants after all. After a marvellous winter shooting on a marvellous new shoot Bert and I had taken over at Tillingbourne, near Friday Street, we started 1930 with new Blackburne engines. Of course the same old frames again with transfers on the tank to suit Hatch's requirements. These engines had inclined push rods which was a 1930 innovation. The other ones used to come off at an angle. An over-enthusiastic Temple Press reporter, in an article on my arrival at Bookham, had attributed these inclined push rods to me. Hatch was furious and despite my denials of having been responsible, was never quite so co-operative afterwards.

The first meeting of the season was, I believe, sponsored by *The Motor Cycle,* the paper. The crowds were colossal. I think there was some sort of half-price admission if you had a copy of *'The Motor Cycle'* or something. I went home to lunch to collect my wife to come up there and I found when I arrived back at the box at the gate complete traffic jam and I was told that like the others I would have to wait my turn. However after a lot of arguing that unless I got in quickly, the entries would be severely restricted, because no-one could get any Castrol oil and they couldn't get my bikes out because they were all locked up, they let me through. We really gave Blackburnes a good show that day and we won five races, but the memorable part of the meeting was the crowds, many of whom parked round the Members' Hill and ran across the track up and down the banking, irrespective of whether races were in progress or not. We were quite popular at Blackburnes for a bit after that.

The season went well until the 200 mile sidecar race. Our jinx – we never won it. We got seconds and things like that but this time had Chris and Hewitt out on 350s and sidecars, and Bernard Hieatt on a 500 cc sidecar and at half distance, the 100 miles, the 350s were lying one and two and the 500 first. Jack Linton the bookie called out to me, "How much, to manage your pit for the rest of the races?" Less than ten laps later, it came on to rain hard and both the 350s went out, one with a broken piston and the

But, by 1930, having started with Blackburne engines and switched to JAP the team were again using Blackburnes. Faired forks and even exhaust pipes were now being fitted.

other with a broken con rod and then the rain came on really hard. Bernard Hieatt was leading Vic Horsman by about two laps I think. With four laps to go he came into the pits without his goggles on and a badly leaking tank. Vic Horsman was one and a half to two laps behind. Hieatt was so excited that I had a job to make him put on a clean pair of goggles and wait while we filled up his tank with enough fuel to keep him going for the odd few laps. He had about four laps to do I think. Off he went into the pouring rain, after I had done my best to explain to him that if he went round at about three-quarter throttle, Vic couldn't possibly catch him. He reappeared after a lap, again with no goggles on, apparently flat out, although I had done my best to explain that Vic couldn't catch him. Next lap round I watched him with horror come off the Byfleet and making no attempt to straighten up whatsoever, ride at full speed into one of the large wooden posts which held up the corrugated iron fence on the river bridge. I shouted 'Ambulance' and drove up from the Fork on the side of the track. Bernard lay dead in the middle of the bridge but his passenger was still in the sidecar, which had looped. The passenger had nothing worse than bruises. What with the inquest, meeting Bernard's parents, our own inquest on the bike and going over and telling Hatch at Blackburns and then the funeral to which Hatch came with me, at Reading, the job of manager seemed even less desirable. It was weeks before I really could get down to work again. In addition, when Hatch and I arrived back from the funeral and had just reached the bar in the Paddock needing a drink, two Talbots in the 'Double Twelve

Hour' race came down the straight, and round a chicane and out onto the Members' Banking. They collided just opposite the Paddock bridge, killing several of the crews, some of the spectators and generally putting a very bad end to a day, a bad day.

In 1928 Grand Prix races were also included in the BMCRC meetings. The circuit would start at the Paddock, down the Finishing Straight, through an artificial chicane, turn right under the Members' Bridge, down to the fork and down the straight again. Stanland had had many successes in these. One sidecar race there, I remember, George Tucker's passenger fell out at the chicane, but this was not noticed by George until the next lap when the sidecar wheel lifted in the same place. George turned round to swear at his passenger and found there was no-one there.

Wal Handley and Jimmy Simpson on OK and AJS also came down for these races sometimes and on one occasion coming round the fork together, Wal Handley came off and tore a thumb nail half off. I was deputed to take him to Weybridge Hospital. We set off in the car, taking also a large brandy for Wal. Sister Damant, well-known to Brooklands riders, instructed me how to hold his arm and wrist while she took off the nail, but I never saw the operation as I next found myself on the floor, having passed out cold at the sight of the mess Walter had made of his thumb. The tail-piece of this story – I had to drink the brandy.

At the end of 1930, all the oil barons, manufacturers of bikes, tyres, chains, plugs and other accessories got together and announced to an amazed motor and motor cycle racing world that they would no longer pay retainers and bonuses but would lend us bikes and engines for us to continue for our own pleasure and any prize money we could find. So the golden years had finished. All my engines went back to Bookham and I sold some of the frames, notably the 250 cc with the JAP engine, which Chris had in 1929 lapped at 96.9. About this time, or rather before this, I had become the first to try and streamline bikes to some extent. I can't really remember any streamlined before. First I started by fairing the front fork blades. Then having a small aluminium cowl over the top of the front forks. In 1929 I had a complete enclosure of the machine with two side panels, and an air intake in the front made at the sheet metal works in Weybridge – Les Anstead's place. He had taken over the works where we originally had Toronda. Chris wasn't very keen on this bike as he said that in any sort of a breeze you got too much of a side draught but he did prove that it put on about two miles an hour. He had two or three futile attempts at doing 100 mph over the half mile. So when eventually I left the track in 1932 and went down to Bristol, the streamline parts were stored with Anstead in Weybridge. Eventually I think Les Archer achieved the coveted 100 mph on a New Imperial. He was the first one to do it.

1931 was spent by Hewitt and me tuning Nortons for Jock Forbes, Charles Mortimer and other racers. Also we did a lot of dirt track engines, JAP dirt track engines, for several up and coming stars in that line. I also borrowed one of this type of JAP 500 and a semi-machined cylinder head which I modified to such an extent that in the last BMCRC meeting before we went to Bristol, Hewitt lapped at 115 mph on it, riding the inside line on the Byfleet and grinding quite a bit more off the corner of the Excelsior frame, which always bottomed round there at over 100 mph anyway.

Cyril Pullin now offered me the Competition Manager's job at Douglas's, but would give me no contract. However, I accepted, provided I could take Hewitt also. We sold our bungalow in Baker Street, Weybridge, and bought a house at Hanham near Kingswood, Bristol, where Douglas had their works. I also had C.J. Williams alloted to me as a rider and also a draughtsman, and I set out to redesign the 500 cc Douglas head, valves and pistons, which new parts the works made with amazing speed and accuracy and we had quite an increase in horsepower on the brake with the prototype engine. We made a raid on Brooklands where Williams ran in a Grand Prix, losing narrowly due to brake failure. Williams and Hewitt also went over to the TT where Williams tried hard, without much success, to teach Hewitt to be a road racer. According to C.J., Hewitt spent more time riding on the grass verges than on the road. Shortly after this, and less than twelve months since we arrived in Bristol, Douglas Motors folded up and the directors and staff having paid themselves in £1 notes presumably, paid me with a rubber cheque. So after hanging about a further six months in the hope of the firm starting up again, I sold the house at a loss, bought a caravan and had a holiday fishing for trout and salmon in Wales, eventually coming back to Chertsey, where my wife's people lived, and I started a garage. What a fool I was. If I had done what Rex Judd and some of the others did, and kept in the motorcycle industry, cashing in on the small publicity my riding had got me, I should have done a lot better. Hewitt went into the dirt track business as manager/mechanic.

In 1938 Chris, who after the Bugatti had bought a Monoposto Alfa, on which I had done some tuning with some success, said, "Could you turn this into a modern racing car for £200?" It sound a silly figure nowadays but it was quite a lot then and eventually we had a go and for £250 produced the Multi-Union, the name arising from the many firms who Chris had persuaded to donate or finance the making of bits and pieces, the chief one being Lockheeds with the Emotts, father and son, the driving forces. They produced new and larger brakes etc. There was also W.C. Devereux, who was the head of High Duty Alloys and made us special supercharger castings and pistons and Chris got things like valves machined by Faireys. I was kept busy on the drawing board.

Eventually Chris went to the USA for Faireys, leaving me with a lot of things to sort out, also a draughtsman from Lagondas who he introduced me to, who was to design us a four speed gearbox, which I had to get made and assemble myself. Also another draughtsman, whose name I have forgotten, but I believe connected with the track somewhere, who was to redesign the front suspension and rear. Chris came back, and the latter draughtsman had covered sheets and sheets galore with ideas but nothing workable so I had to have a go at the back end and Robin Jackson's people the front end. Eventually a new car emerged which had a modern, streamlined body reminiscent of a Mercedes a la Ulenhaut, made at our works. The car appeared on the track. I well remember standing at the Fork with John Cobb and Tim Rose Richards, clocking Chris, saying to myself 141.9, whereupon John said, 'Impossible'. His best lap – he held the flying lap record in those days – being 143 or so. But on that and one other occasion, Chris was just one-tenth of a second outside the record. Many things weren't right with the engine but it never had a fair crack of the whip, on race days. Chris would say, 'I'll have a go at the lap record, next meeting', and then he'd go and enter the car for two Outer Circuit races, two Grand Prix ditto and so on before the attempt, by which time the car was out of breath or a valve had stretched or something. That was Chris, always impatient, but a marvellous driver, or rider, in everything he conducted.

Then the war broke out. We stored the car and Chris was killed, test flying. The silly

The Multi Union. Owned and driven by Staniland, produced and rebuilt by 'Woolly' from a 1934 Monoposto Alfa Romeo – Plus £250! First Brooklands practice lap after the rebuild was 141.9 mph!

part of it was that he wasn't killed doing anything risky. They had a machine there that was to be delivered to Martlesham Heath next day and there was nothing to do and Chris said, 'I'll just take this for a fly round', and that was all there was to it. He was found with the machine lying apparently quite flat on the ground. He had jettisoned the hood so someone said it was due to fumes but no-one ever really knew why he was killed.

I never raced cars. I tested the Wolseley Moth for Barnato and the Multi-Union for Chris but never faster than just over the 100. I don't think I had enough lead in my boots. I did several hours as passenger to Alastair Miller on records in a Wolseley and I ran a big end in Barnato's Wolseley on a Friday night before a meeting and still got it into the line in time. I also went as a passenger with Dougal Marchant, driving a contraption called a KRC, which steered like the proverbial brewer's dray and had a twin Blackburne water-cooled engine, in a light car club meeting this was, 200 miles I think. But after wrestling with it for about twenty laps, Dougal shouted in my ear, 'I've had enough of this – next time round on the Byfleet'. I didn't know what he meant by this but when we reached the aero sheds and hidden from the Paddock, he proceeded to change gear from top to reverse without taking his foot off the accelerator, with easily guessed results.

At the time I was entered for some Brighton speed trials on a Bleriot Whippet, a four wheel belt driven cycle car with a twin Blackburne air-cooled engine which did about 65. Dougal and Hatch persuaded me to cancel the Whippet entry and substitute the

KRC. This, incidentally, stood for the initials of the makers, Kingston, Richards & Crutchlow. The latter car with a new gearbox, of course, and with the big twin water-cooled Blackburne engine, so I said, 'Yes, I would', and went out to practice over Brooklands half mile, timed from the Paddock stand by Dougal and Hatch. After a couple of laps to warm up, and to get used to the awful steering, I came round the home banking at full speed but halfway down the straight with a loud bang, one of the cylinders came straight through the bonnet, luckily missing me. I never got to Brighton after all.

While I worked for Cyril, an old friend of his, an ex-Brooklands racing driver named, I believe, Toop, was there one **BARC** meeting and stood at the shed door of Pullins watching cars arriving in the Paddock. He suddenly said, 'Look, there's my old car'. It was a Peugeot and I can't remember who it was owned by. 'I wonder if he'll let me drive in one race today'. He rushed off and returned to say, yes, it had all been fixed up, he was going to drive. So I said at once, 'Take me as a passenger', and he agreed. When racing started, Cyril had some urgent job to be done on a customer's car and when I finally got away it was just in time to see the Peugeot go through the Paddock gate with no passenger. I watched from the Paddock stand the start and then went back to Cyril to hear the ambulance bell almost at once. Toop had gone over the Byfleet Banking and was killed at once. It was a classic example of they never come back once they have left the sport, the drivers. It made me think a lot, of my lucky escape, and possibly contributed a lot to my dislike of car racing.

In the early 1920s the car racers were practically all amateurs and well to-do, with mechanics to do the work, and drivers turning out in immaculate white, or coloured, overalls and helmets and definitely with few exceptions like Barnato, Duller, Parry Thomas, Campbell and Purdy, looked at motorcycle racers as an inferior breed, common and scruffy, which latter I am afraid, we mostly were. I found Parry Thomas ever ready to talk technically about his and my problems and his only complaint was that while he was practicing and we were practicing, we all wanted the same line of the Fork. Malcolm Campbell was known as the old friend, his customary greeting to those he knew being, 'Hello, my old friend'. He also had a small son who got in the way whenever possible – Donald Campbell. George Duller was very quietly spoken, very sardonic and very amusing company, especially in the bar. He flatly refused, and as far as I know never did, give anyone racing tips, saying that he had seen too many good friendships lost that way. Barnato was very quiet but his eyes saw everything. I didn't know intimately any of the other Bentley boys.

In later years, when Chris Staniland, Fred Dixon, Charles Brackenbury and company were about, we felt more equal. Charles Brackenbury and Chris both grew up at Louth in Lincolnshire and Chris once told me that they had a good way of catching rabbits. Chris had a 3 litre Bentley in those days, also a greyhound and the plot was to go out at night with a spotlight, one of them sitting on the running board, holding on to the spare wheel with one hand and the greyhound with the other. The driver then put on his spotlight and headlamps and drove until a rabbit appeared in the beams. Then when they got somewhere near, the passenger launched the greyhound off the running board and having a flying start it quickly caught the rabbit. The only snag was the wear and tear on the greyhound's feet so they made some chamois leather boots which improved things quite a bit.

My introduction to fast cars was at a **BARC** meeting about 1923. I went as a

spectator to practically every meeting and always managed to get into the Paddock somehow. At one meeting the BARC were running a 3 litre championship, running two cars in a heat. With much trepidation, I asked the great H.O.D. Segrave if I could go as his passenger. His car was the famous Indianapolis Sunbeam, a 2 seater thing with a round petrol tank behind the seat and after looking me up and down, dressed in my best grey flannel trousers and sports jacket, he said, 'Yes'. Eventually, we went up to the Fork, with Cook on a Vauxhall as his opponent. The Sunbeam had a strap down by your left leg and a handhold on the body behind the driver's back for the passenger to hold on to and stay in his seat if possible. I soon discovered that the Sunbeam gave a very rough ride. By the time we even got to the Railway Straight, the only thing I was thinking about was staying in the car and certainly not looking about admiring the view or Segrave's driving. He sat quite imperturbably as if driving down a very flat, smooth road. We won our heat by a street and I got out of the Sunbeam in the Paddock and I found my best and only pair of grey flannels soaked up to both knees in castor oil. I pointed this out to Segrave, that there seemed to be an oil leak, but all he said was not that he was sorry about the trousers but that it was lucky it was discovered before the next race. Our lap speed was 112 and I was told afterwards by a number of people that I couldn't have chosen a rougher ride than the Indianapolis Sunbeam.

There really were very few whole time residents of the track even if you include the staff and the Hawker and Vickers pilots, who were always good company and with all of whom I flew as a passenger at some time or other. When I worked for Pullins and JAPs the inhabitants, starting down from the top in more senses than one because his office was at the top of the clubhouse, was Mr. Rance, the Superintendent, a very quiet, friendly and I imagine, efficient person. He had a secretary named Kitty. Then the bartender or tenderess, Mrs. Durrant, known to hundreds of people as 'Auntie'. Ask her to have a drink and she always said, 'Yes, I'll have a gin, thank you', pouring water unseen into her glass and putting the money in her pocket. There was also a barman at one time there named Bitts who did not drink water and sometimes the last of us to leave the Paddock, seeing a light in the bar, would go up and find him fast asleep snoring and say, 'Come on, Mr. Bitts, time to go home', whereupon he would wake up, wipe his face and nose on the glass cloth and be taken to Weybridge station to go home by train. Then we come to the famous Mrs. Hodges. I'm not sure whether it was Mrs. Hodges or Miss Hodges, who managed the catering with a staff of two or three girls. Mrs. Hodges was very awkward when so inclined. A classic example of this was one afternoon when Dixon and Judd were at the track. Fred said, 'Come on, I'll buy you all some tea and toast'. So about six of us went up to the dining room and Fred ordered tea and buttered toast for all of us. This duly arrived plus plates of bread and butter, jam, cakes and so on. We ate the buttered toast and Fred asked for the bill, which was made out at 2s. 6d. each for the standard tea plus extra for the buttered toast. When Fred protested to the waitress, Mrs. Hodges arrived and was adamant that tea meant bread and butter, jam and cakes, and that it didn't matter what Fred thought. The price included all the other things on the table, as well as the toast. So Fred paid and said to Rex, 'Get hold of the two corners of the cloth', and proceeded to empty all the bread and butter and the cakes and sugar from the basins on to it and carried it downstairs past the astonished Mrs. Hodges, saying, 'Our landlady will like this lot'.

He and Rex always stayed at the same place, somewhere down in Thames Street, Weybridge.

Then there was Jack Cann on the Paddock gate out on to the track, very quiet and polite but quite difficult to get past when it came to it. He knew who could, and who couldn't, go through. Taffy at the box at the entrance was partly crippled. He had been in the railway start timing box when Zbrowski I think spun off the track with a Merc and hit the box. Taffy's chief grievance was not so much about being hurt himself but it had also broken his 12 bore gun and the replacement Zbrowski had got him was not as good.

Caswell, another man, foreman of the repair gang, which broke up and remade vast areas of concrete in the winter. I once spent an hour with them, operating a pneumatic drill – very hard work. The concrete was not thick enough when the track was made and history has it that S.F. Edge making his 24 hour run on a Napier soon after the track was opened – (they had hurricane lamps all round to illuminate the edge) – did it too soon, that the concrete hadn't properly set and this run permanently damaged the surface, which as anyone who rode or drove on it knew was very rough. I once fixed a 7.5 mm Pathé cine camera on the back of one of my 350s operated by a Bowden control and rode round at about 75 to 80 with Hewitt tracking on another bike to be photographed at twenty feet or so. I took a long time to make the film as the bumps broke the little steel governor springs in the camera and I had to make several new sets before the film of a complete lap was made but it was quite good when it was done.

We often had some of the TT cracks down at the track, Jimmy Simpson, Wal Handley, Ernie Nott, Tyrell Smith, but they all disliked the track and said how much smoother the Island was. Then there were the fuel depots at the track and their reps. Discol with Monty Bird, who was always known as Jazz, a willing helper on record attempts, turning up once for one of our long distance records very shaky in the morning, he had had a very thick night the night before. So I said, 'Oh, for the Lord's sake, go down to the Paddock and get yourself a drink', which he did, so he cheered up a lot. But at the end of the day, when I went up to the bar, Auntie Durrant said, 'Oh, Mr. Bird had a double brandy and dry ginger', which was rather over the odds.

Next there was Crouch of BP and Reg Tanner of Pratts or Esso, a very clever operator of a stop-watch, who took considerable profit on a Saturday sometimes, no doubt.

Then there was Algy Garrett, an always cheerful man who dispensed good advice and KLG plugs which, when I started riding were virtually the only ones which would stand the pressure.

In the square where we had our shed, the Castrol sheds, were also Dunlops to which Big and Little Mac and Fiddle, whose name I believe was Hicks, arrived every day from London in their black and yellow van, during the season, and would fit tyres for use whenever asked with great speed and a lot of cockney humour. So much of our livelihood depended on them and I now wonder if we appreciated it as we should have done. Over the opposite end of our row, was the Brooklands Engineering Company, owned when I first arrived by a giant of a man named Major Hertzel, I think it was, who made Celerity valves, a speciality of which was a hole drilled up the stem some way from the head end, presumably for lightness, but having other odd effects. In one long distance race, I remember seeing Norman Norris, who was afterwards killed at MacGilligan sands in Ireland driving a Lea Francis, riding an Ivy. He came into the pits, complaining that his engine had lost power but not noticing at all that his magneto platform had broken off, ditto the magneto chain, and the magneto was hanging upside down. As the engine was still firing evenly and continued to do so, he went off on it, presumably the ignited fuel in the valve stem turned the engine into a diesel. After Hertzel left, Sammy Lee continued the business until the War, making very good Martlet pistons, designed by Brewster and Johnston, and also good valves out of the then new KE 965 steel, which mostly cured our valve breaking trouble.

Then there was our shed and the Castrol shed, where Hewitt and I spent most of our waking hours during many seasons.

Then there was Cyril Pullin's shed, that was the first one on the right as you came under the tunnel into the track, which was later the headquarters of Mr. and Mrs. Stewart.

No-one with any sense or knowledge of track etiquette ever walked into another rider's shed, uninvited. We had a stout beam across ours, which discouraged visitors, but there was an unwritten law about that. I think every other shed was rented at some time or other but other than those I have mentioned, only occupied before or at meetings. Vic Horsman had a gloomy sort of place underneath the club house but the gloom didn't affect the results he got for Triumphs with his faithful mechanic, Curley Quinn.

No story of Brooklands would be complete without a word about timing. Everyone owned a stopwatch and quite a few of us, two. O'Donovan would stand on the Byfleet Bridge with Bert Denly to write down times and with his two split second watches have a lap speed of everyone practicing on the day before meetings. We could time laps from our shed window, the usual start being the Railway Straight box, but so could everybody else time then, so we changed to the Half Mile box, that's up the other end of the straight which we could just see, but that also became known and seen as we could tell from the bookies' boards on a Saturday morning, so we sent our riders out of the Paddock gate, not up the Fork as it was customary to start but down the straight to the members banking and opened up starting from the half mile box flat out until a mark we had just after the fork, then throttle back and open up round the Byfleet, flat out from the Fork mark to the Half Mile box again. It sounds a big complicated but if you think it out it's all right. The result was two half laps. This worked quite well as the bookies and the spies couldn't decide whether we were really trying for a lap or not.

Then there was the electric timing, operated from the box by the Paddock gate, by Col. Lindsey Lloyd. The machine itself had a paper strip marked off in minutes, seconds, tenths etc. The current from the timing strips came via telegraph wires across from the railway box and the half mile box and the kilo and the mile. They sent in a signal as the wheel crossed the strip or rather you got two signals for a car or a bike, front and back wheels. This operated a pen with an ink reservoir on it. The ink reservoir made a mark on the strip as the wheel passed over and by measuring the distance between the marks, the Colonel could determine the time over the various distances. Unfortunately, if the reservoir were newly filled, the pen usually made a mark wider than necessary. It could make one or even two-tenths of a second difference to the time, depending which end of the mark you took. So as far as we were concerned and soon found out, the Colonel's times were always open to argument. At the end of 1925, just before the show, Dougal Marchant was determined to have the Chater Lea to be the first 350 to exceed 100 mph over the flying kilo or flying half mile and when the day and Col. Lloyd arrived there were at least six, and possibly more, people with stopwatches on the paddock stand to see the attempt and, I must admit, to assist Dougal to argue with the Colonel if there was any dispute about the time. Some wit said afterwards that when Dougal flashed across the first timing strip, it sounded like a boy dragging a stick along a chestnut paling fence, there was so great a difference between the first and last click. This was of course somewhat of a libel. The majority of us agreed, that he was one or two tenths out. Dougal came in and was cross when Col. Lloyd told him he had missed it. He took the Chater Lea over to the shed he was using and reappeared in a few minutes having altered something, told the Colonel he would have another try, and once again tore down the straight. This time we were fairly evenly divided between, 'He's got it' and 'He hasn't got it' but eventually we decided probably he had got it. When Dougal arrived in the Paddock, he went over the Colonel and the Colonel said, 'No I'm afraid you missed it again, Marchant'. Dougal said, 'Well, that's all wrong, Colonel. These chaps are all very good with the stopwatch, and they say I've got it.' Then the Colonel said he would go up and check his tape again and after a lot more arguing and measuring, he decided that 100 mph had been exceeded. Ebby once tried to operate the device when Col. Lloyd was away, but he could get no good results but by report he had paper chains all round his neck and everything else.

On one occasion when Vic Horsman was out for some sidecar records, standing start, I think, he had been instructed by the Colonel to set off for the Railway Straight and wait for the signal to start. Unfortunately the Vickers test pilot then, Tiny Schofield, who was an enormous gentle giant of a man, who was afterwards killed at

Brooklands or just near it, and was a friend of all motorcyclists, was out testing an ultra lightweight biplane with a 6 hp Douglas engine. The propellor was chain driven. He was shooting up the Paddock, flying under the bridges, but in so doing he cut the telephone wires linking the Paddock to the track and linking the irate Colonel with Vic. The situation which took some time to disentangle, necessitated a profuse apology to the Colonel from Tiny. The Paddock stand was a favourite place from which to time all and sundry. I remember once being there with Cyril and Rex, who were timing one of Cyril's proteges, an enthusiastic amateur, I think he was. His name was Glover and he was on a 750 Douglas. He completed his lap and came down the Straight from the Fork. As he approached, Cyril having missed his time, waved to him with a circular motion of his arm indicating that he wanted Glover to go round again, whereupon Glover, misreading the signal, changed down, opened the throttle full and shot up the Test Hill, rising about fifteen feet into the air over the top and vanishing from view. We all quickly jumped into a car and on reaching the top of the one in four Test Hill found a very shaken Glover, undamaged luckily, but sitting on the ground looking at a somewhat bent Douglas. One of the bookies, Jack Linton, was very good with the watch, arriving early on motorcycle and car race days and when he put up his prices, the other bookies, Long Tom and George Cooper, were quick to copy them. Generally speaking, all the Brooklands bookies were scared of being badly caught and prices were ridiculous – 4 to 1 the field in a race with 20 entries and so on. But as, unlike horse racing, there was no book of form by which to judge the riders' or drivers' respective chances, they were almost entirely dependant on who was putting on the money, and how much money they were putting on and it required considerable cunning to get even a £5 bet on one's fancy. There were, of course, other bookies, mostly over the hill but betting with them, although generally more profitable, involved a quick trip over the bridge and back, before they got wind of the prices in the Paddock. Very often, they would all stand there with no prices up on their board at all and wait for the first man, whether it was Tanner of Pratts or one of us, to go there with money. Directly we arrived there and wanted to bet on somebody, he was automatically the favourite until someone else turned up with more money.

No account of Brooklands activities would be complete without a word on sidecars. These came in three classes, from the passenger's point of view, bad, very bad and bloody awful. When our sidecar firm, Toronda, was still working, we designed and made a completely streamlined shell in aluminium, handbeaten with a chassis which was composed of a two inch tube down the centre with cross struts across each end, one end of which went onto the bike and the other went onto a wheel. All the chassis was inside the body. The seat was of the hammock type. We built one for Cyril, but Rex complained bitterly that over the bumps the centre tube hit him in the backside all the time.

Dixon had a sidecar shaped like a slipper with no back to it and a strap fixed inside the bottom for the passenger to hold on to. One evening he had a disagreement with Cyril and Rex about how fast he had been over the flying mile and I happened to come round at that time and he said, 'You come in the sidecar, Woolly, and take a watch and we'll get it right'. So we set off up to the fork, with me vainly trying to find the strap, which broke when I did. He swung round at the fork and he set off round the members banking with me holding myself in with pressure from my feet and knees, thinking every minute I should fall out. However, the time came out more to his liking.

Vic's sidecar I don't remember much but it had a bad reputation and I remember his mechanic, Curly, who had done something to displease Vic, promising to go in it for a 50 mile record attempt, I think, as a punishment, if only Vic would stop nagging. Vic also nearly became a casualty in a most extraordinary sidecar escapade. In a 200 mile race, with a 350 Excelsior and sidecar, we had terrible attacks of misfiring and eventually stopped on the Railway Straight. We made several attempts at a push start and got to the Byfleet Banking without any result. Then a track marshal named Hart, I think it was, arrived and encouraged us, now completely exhausted, to have one more go. This we did but just as we were going to give up, my passenger slipped and fell, and the engine fired at the same time. I had let go of the handlebar and I also fell but the outfit went off by itself, straight up the banking and under the Byfleet Bridge, just missing Vic, going by at speed. It straightened itself up and disappeared from our sight round the banking. The marshal said, 'Well, I'm damned' and went off in pursuit and we followed as fast as we could. We eventually found the outfit with its nose in the ditch just past the aero sheds. We hauled it out and it started first push and did four more laps before breaking a con rod. Meanwhile, several other competitors had seen the outfit in the ditch, stopped at the Fork and reported an accident, so on our next lap round we met the ambulance, vainly looking for us.

One more race Vic may remember, a three lap sidecar handicap where he had a 600 sidecar and he had to give me a start of course on a 350 sidecar. Once again, we had misfiring trouble. Half mile go and half mile stop and so on like that, or no stop but half mile slow and in the last lap Vic passed us about half a mile from the finish, grinned at me and throttled back so as not to let Ebby see too much of how fast he could go. He was throttled back just in front of us. As we got sight of the Fork, our engine decided to work again and we were quickly catching Vic up. Feeling sure he would have a look round before the finish, I suddenly decided that if he looked at all, he would look over his left shoulder, as we were still on a little bit of the banking, so I pulled out to his right exactly as he looked over his left, passed him and crossed the line about a length in front of him, much to his, as ever, good-natured annoyance afterwards.

I had no serious accidents. In 1924 I burst a front tyre in a 50 mile race and tried to ride back to the Paddock with the result that the tyre came off the rim and I came off the bike which fell on top of me and burnt my arm as I was underneath the exhaust pipe. I spent the rest of the afternoon in Weybridge Hospital with Dr. Eric Gardiner extracting pieces of woollen jersey from the cuts in my arm. I couldn't afford leathers then. Dr. Gardiner originally invented the crash helmet.

I also broke a toe in contact with the timing strip as I have described before. I fell off Pat Driscoll's Norton, also described already, but I had two contretemps with wasps, once on a long distance 350 record. It being a hot day, I was riding without gloves and a wasp flew up my sleeve and stung me on the arm. As the Railway Straight was about the only place I could let go with one hand, I rode down still at about 80 mph slapping my arm trying to kill the wasp. It stung me again round the Byfleet and I had to wait for the straight on the next lap and I had to repeat the performance of slapping it but it was on my shoulder. This happened once more but just when I decided to pack up the record attempt, the wasp died and I continued, to get the three hours I think. The other episode was not so amusing to me, but provided a good deal of amusement among the unsympathetic characters of my friends in the Paddock. Going out to warm up a bike before doing some fast laps, I was not fully dressed in leathers and crash hat and coming back to the shed felt a sharp pain in a very private part of my anatomy. I came into the shed and handed the bike over to Hewitt and a wasp flew out of the top of my leather trousers. My worst fears were realised and to try and get something done for the enormous swelling, I rushed down to my great friend, Dr. Sam Beare, at Weybridge. He sat in his chair laughing till the tears ran down his face and eventually gave me an injection, only somewhere near luckily. Back at the track, my alleged friends almost queued up, begging to have a look. That year, the cartoonist, Grimes, who did the cartoons in the BMCRC dinner programmes, depicted me riding a standard road model Excelsior with lamp, carrier, mudguards etc. trying to swat at a wasp with the caption underneath, 'The man who was stung on his production model'.

Going back to sidecars again, when the regulations permitting ballast instead of live passengers came into force, I was out for records with the 350 with a home built sidecar body shaped very much like a coffin. I put a sack of sand in and started but after a dozen or so laps, the front anchorage of the sidecar body to the chassis broke, due to the sack shifting slightly backwards, I believe. The body tipped up, the bag split and the sand all streamed out of the back. This ended the attempt and also inspired Grimes to include another cartoon in a dinner programme, one of me with the sidecar tipped up and the sand running out, and the caption underneath, 'Dastardly attempt by Worters to lighten his sidecar during records'.

In one of my early 200 mile sidecar races, on reaching the pits to refuel, my passenger leaped out of the sidecar, and 'That's enough of that', and disappeared in the crowd. Luckily one of my pit crew took over at once. The original passenger was very apologetic afterwards but I knew just how he had felt.

Freddie Dixon was down there in 1930 or 31 with a twin JAP and sidecar, going for short records but he hadn't a passenger. During the day a youth arrived from Tottenham, with some JAP part for Fred, so he seized the chance and asked him to go in the chair. He told him there was nothing to it and so on. So they started. Going into the Byfleet banking flat out around the 100 mph mark I suppose, the sidecar wheel came off and the sidecar wheel raced ahead and careered over the Byfleet banking. Fred continued at speed, keeping the sidecar off the track. It had very little clearance anyway and stopped at the fork, unharmed. The passenger got out a bit shakily and seeing no wheel said, 'Look, no wheel', so Fred said, 'Ha, ha, ha, funny isn't it, how they sometimes come off' and the passenger went back off to Tottenham, apparently quite convinced that this was all part of the business and not in any way worried

The BMCRC dinners at the end of each season were all male affairs. One special feature – they were never twice held at the same London restaurant. The reason, we did so much damage, they wouldn't have us. I remember one year when so many got in the lift – I can't remember what restaurant – to come down, that the side bulged out and jammed it so we had to come down the stairs. Another year O'Donovan and Denly chose a wine to drink which seemed to turn them a delicate shade of green about the face. I forget what happened to Don but we carried little Bert down a lot of stairs, pausing at each landing for a change of carriers and a rest. I think Dougal drove him home.

I can also recall one year seeing Dougal overturn a table laden with glasses etc., wrench off one leg and proceed to beat up all the other tables and chairs in range. A little Italian waiter looked at him, shook his head, and said sorrowfully to me, "I see no fun in this at all". One year at the track some of us decided that we would also have our own special dinner for the real track people. There were a lot of 'me too's' at the BMCRC dinners. Rex and Fred and I decided that the menu should start with one dozen oysters per man, those people who didn't like oysters having to pass them on to those who did. I think we had about 30 or so. We had this dinner up in the dining room of the Clubhouse at the track, drivers and their mechanics, and Mrs. Hodges did us very well with turkey etc. to follow. As customary, the dinner ended in a riot. People were throwing those very hard rolls from end to end of the room and I remember seeing Bill Lacey's father hit on the top of the head with a roll going off at high speed. Ebby decided when he came to the dinner that to start any function like that there should be a big bang and he knew where there was a maroon, so he took it outside but unfortunately decided to put the maroon inside an old cast iron drainpipe. The drainpipe burst of course and Ebby's assistant, I don't know who he was, had to go down to the hospital for sundry minor repairs to legs and arms but arrived back in time for the fun.

Whilst on the subject of dinners, when Dixon was at JAPs with the big twin, he invited a very quiet and inoffensive man from the JAP office – I can't remember his name, I'll call him Smith – to come to a BMCRC dinner. This little man was nearly a teetotaller to start with and passed out before the end. When Fred asked him where he lived, all he could say was something about 'Pull the wheel to the left, pull the wheel to the left'. However, he eventually got sufficiently coherent to give Fred his address in Tottenham. Fred drove him to his door and then left him and walked down the garden path and said to a forbidding female who answered the door, 'Does Mr. Smith live here?' She said, 'Yes, do you want him?' Fred said, 'No, I've got him'.

Now some answers to some of the questionaire, Charles.

Did you meet with parental opposition or support in starting to race?.

No, I was too old when I started for my parents to worry.

Was it long before you began to feel established as a race motor cyclist? The first 200 mile race I won helped a bit but I didn't really feel established until about 1926, or 27.

Preparation and tuning. In the early stages, and later, when you rode Works, standards were generally high, but can you recall any retirements that could have been avoided by better preparation?

Things like broken chains due to use spring links instead of riveting the chains. Fuel pipes, the rubber tubing wasn't so good as the polythene now. Bolts working loose, due to lack of lock nuts and split pins. Tanks splitting and things like that. Incidentally, talking of chains breaking, several track riders had a trade mark – a terrific scar up their backside where a chain had broken and slashed them about half a dozen times before falling off. Reuben Harveson was one and Rex Judd was another. I was hit once but luckily it didn't cut my leathers and fell off at once.

Travel and Transport to and from Brooklands?

I lived in Weybridge.

How tough was the competition? There was money in it then and there is now. Today, it is a long haul in order to get established and tough when you get there. Would you think both eras comparable in that respect?

Very, There is so much more money in it these days that it must be harder and I imagine sponsorship essential. It was unknown in my days.

When you were at the top, how much help were you able to give each other in emergencies. One imagines you were all good friends, but you had divided loyalties here in your committments to manufacturers. Can you recall any instances?

Comparatively little. Some riders would go to almost any lengths to hinder the up and coming. Dixon and Judd would help anyone at any time. They once came to my shed on the night before a 350 Championship and on being told that I couldn't steer my 350, something had gone wrong with the frame, took the bike out of the shed, walked ten yards in front while I held it up straight, bent down forwards and viewed the frame from between their legs, Freddie seized the bike by one handlebar, jumped on the engine sprocket a few times and said, 'That's OK now'. It was, and for ever afterwards steered perfectly, but he, Rex, Ron Hopkins and a few others were rare exceptions in my experience.

At the peak, were you full or part time?

Full time.

Can you recall, or maybe you would prefer not to go into too much detail of the sort of arrangements you had with manufacturers, entrants and sponsors. Flat rate for the season? Bonus on successes? Probably no start money?

My old account book for 1929 when I was running a stable read: Wakefield £200, Dunlop £75, Amac £45, KLG £100, Wellworthy £45, Japs £250, Excelsior £175, Castrol shed £50, bonus £491. 1928 I got about £1,450 and so on – it went back to about 1925 when I only got £700.

I was always the entrant and had no sponsor. Bonus for races – BP paid about £5, Castrol about £5 per race or £5 per record and so on.

Particular races that stick in your mind for the same reasons or because the results were particularly rewarding or disappointing. Or for any other reason?

Plenty I enjoyed, some I didn't. The best race I ever had was in a 5 lap Championship, I think. Marchant was the favourite on a Chater Lea, Wal Handley was on a Blackburne and myself. Dougal didn't get away very well and went out after two laps. I led the entire way. I don't think we were ever more than two lengths apart but Wal having no objection whatever to riding round the bottom of the Members Banking, due to TT experience I suppose, despite the terrible bumps. For a start I kept to the 50 foot line. This lost a lot of ground, most of which I made up every lap on the straights. On the Byfleet on the last lap, I came round the bottom with Wal just inside, trying to get inside me, and I got about a length on him up the straight by the Byfleet Bridge and we suddenly caught up with Cobbold on a Sunbeam. Although I pulled out to miss him, Wal trying to get inside me, eased up for a second and we arrived at the Fork with me about half a length ahead. We rode side by side back to the Fork after the race, handed our bikes to the mechanics and fell on each other necks, laughing and nearly crying, I think. Neither of us knew or cared who had really won but I still remember every second of it. I won at 92 I believe. Lacey was third

Bad races? – A 200 mile 250 cc race in pouring rain. I had read the weather forecast and cunningly fitted mudguards to my and Staniland's bikes in anticipation. Chris was going to ride my 350. Chris must have passed me several times but we never saw each other the entire way. We both won our classes and I hated every yard of it.

I believe that neither you nor any of the other Brooklands riders involved in this story ever rode big twins at Brooklands. Generally speaking, they tended to be temperamental and, as a breed, less efficient over long distances than the big singles. Their records of even finishing in the long races were apalling and when they did finish, their speeds were often poor. To some extent, one can understand the problems of keeping two cylinders firing for a couple of hours or so. But do you think their record need have been as bad as it was. In long races particularly, so many different people seem to have ridden big twins just once or twice. Apart from Baragwanath, few people seem to have stuck to big twins in long races in the way that, say Horsman stuck to his Triumphs. Why do you think this was? Was one experience of riding a big twin in a long race enough?

I hated them for their weight, bad performance and general discomfort and like a lot of riders I was quite a bit scared of them I think.

Nowadays, it seems to me that riders tend to change from one make to another more frequently than they used to in your day and this seems to me not always a good thing. I remember that, for instance, when Bira was racing cars so successfully in the 1930's he usually had what was considered to be the latest and best cars at the start of each season but never parted with the car he had raced during the previous season until the new one was proved better and as reliable in races. Did you ever adopt such a policy or think it a good one?

We stuck to the engine we had tuned and got to know, as long as possible, in case the next ones were worse or harder to get going. All the bikes are so good now that the rider counts more than the engine and it doesn't really matter what you ride. They are tuned at the factory in any case, aren't they?

Riders. Do you think anyone stood out, in most respects, head and shoulders above the others. Le Vack for instance. And , if so, what were the qualities he had that made this the case. What about Dixon, Staniland, Marchant, Fernihough and Baragwanath, Hicks. Any others?

I should say definitely Le Vack in spite of his irritating drawl. He always said 'Ye e e s'. He rode all sizes except a 175. He was a very clean rider, his one concern was winning, but I never heard that he was a bad loser. I and others were probably a worry to him as contenders for his position but he never showed it as far as I can remember. I didn't know him really well but I had enormous respect for him and his mechanic, Sid Moran, as a tuner and an engineer.

Chris Staniland. Chris's idea of motorcycle or car racing was to arrive a few minutes before the first race, beautifully attired in spotless white overalls and helmet. He had a mechanic push the bike out to the line say to me, 'Will this one win, Woolly?' and then ride as perfect a race as humanly possible, with the throttle hard against the stop, come in, make any pertinent remarks on the bike, and then go off to talk to the other riders or friends, repeating the performance as necessary throughout the afternoon. A marvellous rider and friend. His flying and car driving were all of the same type and the Lord knows why he had to get killed in an unexplained accident.

Marchant – see my previous comments. Very good tuner but he worried too much about the man on the rung below.

Dixon – rough and very tough. Not a tidy rider, he had footboards fitted to some of the Douglas machines so that he could walk about a bit while racing, he said. I helped him a lot the year he came to JAPS and he won the 350 TT on an HRD, and still somewhere I have a telegram sent from the Isle of Man, "Many thanks for all your help". Also very good with the twin JAP and sidecar in 1930 I believe.

Fernihough – a great character, who knew that putting an engine together with dirty hands lost 2 mph or so. Frank Longman borrowed an engine from me once to use in the TT by arrangement with Vivian and I heard afterwards that Ferni spent the whole night taking it to pieces to see what made it tick. Frank said that Ferni used clean newspaper to wipe parts on but wouldn't allow more than one piece of paper per part as it was wasteful. I don't think they found much out in the engine and I doubt if they know what to look for.

Barry – one of the great Brooklands characters, with his three inch high wing collar. Always very tough and very popular.

Bert Denly, who after years of good riding at Brooklands and Montlhéry went with George Eyston over to Salt Lake with Thunderbolt and drove 'Speed of the Wind' for hours at over 150 and 160. He apparently did nearly all the night driving in the long records. George couldn't see too well, I believe, also a very fine shooting companion and an excellent and safe shot. Rex Judd – the spirit of good cheer at all times and a good TT as well as a track man.

Vic Horsman – quiet and reserved. Everyone liked him.

Wal Handley – moody, sudden-tempered, charming all by turns, but a good TT man, didn't like the track much. Could also drive a car. One evening, finishing our last drinks at the Hand and Spear, Dixon said "Let's go to the Palladium" and he, Vic, myself got into Wal's Alvis fabric saloon. As the box office manager happened to be Billy Simpson, who was also Bert Le Vack's sidecar passenger on race days, we got front stalls for the asking and spent most of the evening in Billy's office, drinking and talking. When we started for home, we started two stopwatches and went like the wind, sometimes on the left hand side of traffic islands, sometimes on the right, and after Dixon had accidentally switched off the headlamps approaching Walton bridge at 70 mph, we arrived at the Ship Hotel in Weybridge in 20 minutes 21 seconds, quite safely to my surprise.

Billy Simpson was there for some years after this and when in 1932 I was at Douglas, we came to Brooklands and I decided that the crew wanted a bit of entertainment. There were seven of us in all, I think, myself, my wife, Williams and a girl, Hewitt and two very good mechanics, Frank Baker and Jack Clapham. We stayed at the Hand and Spear but one evening I thought they needed some entertainment so we all got into my Hudson saloon and off to the Palladium to find hundreds of yards of queues. To the astonishment of my troops and I think myself, Billy Simpson never forgot Brooklands and within minutes we had seats in the front of the circle, and saw the Crazy Gang, ending up at the Ace of Spades on the way home for bacon and eggs. Going back to your questionnaire, there were many more riders – think of a name and I'll probably think of something.

For a start, you have left out Jack Emerson. I see you mentioned him in your little piece you have already written and his trouble in getting and keeping the hour record. He was so determined to be thorough that he several times went out for a practice hour run just beforehand just to make sure the engine would do an hour and then blew up during the actual timed run.

Another piece I missed out when I was talking about Major Hertzel, who made Celerity valves for the Brooklands Engineering Company. Once Rex Judd was sent down there by Cyril Pullin to complain about something and Hertzel picked Rex up with one hand on each shoulder and shook him. Now, going back and answering some of your questions.

Going back to the show for a minute, we usually ended the evening with a dinner for about four or five of us at the Clarendon at Hammersmith, or a little place in Soho – the name I forget – where on one to me memorable evening the other three were Ebby, Marchant and Le Vack and I felt much honoured and bigger in the head I expect next day. The conversation inevitably turned to our respective speeds and handicaps, every one of the three of us agreeing that Ebby was wrong in our particular case. Eventually Ebby said, 'Allright, each of you write on a piece of paper what you think your respective handicap should be. Fold them up, give them to me and I will arrange a special race for you'. But he never did. Going back to these frames of Le Vack's – they were built of very light tube. The petrol tanks were all short race tanks. In this connection the frames were Excelsior, Rex Acme etc. according to Vivian's arrangement, the only difference being the tank transfer; the bikes went on just the same. The bikes steered well for those days but the quality of the tube in a frame, which I believe then was called an 'A' quality, was very prone to crystallisation and I had two break under the head, one at 95 mph in a BMCRC Championship and the crankcase grounded and ended with the bottom ground off it but the bike was no problem at all until down to about 30 mph when it was a job to control. I borrowed a leather belt from the coat of a travelling marshal, strapped up the back and rode it back to the Paddock. JAPs gave me marvellous service and tool room machining, making special con rods, flywheels, camshafts etc. very quickly and well to my drawings usually but they were, I felt, prone to hand out my ideas to other riders. This I have dealt with later on, during some of your queries that you set me. I think you will find a big reference that will cover this.

Reverting, for a moment, from riders to manufacturers. You were, yourself, always associated with Excelsior. Was there, at any time in your career, a point where you might have been associated with another make. Could you tell us what it was?

Anything with JAP or Blackburne engines, also Douglas.

Most of the big names at Brooklands in the 1920's rode both solo and sidecar machinery. One imagines that for financial reasons alone, this was necessary. But did you have a preference for solo or sidecar. Would you think that the hazards of one were greater than the other? and would you consider either a greater test of the rider?

Financial reasons. Solo was the best I think. It was certainly the greatest test as far as my experience was concerned, but a big twin and sidecar must have been very hard work. The largest sidecar outfit I ever rode on the track was one of Pat Driscoll's Norton outfits in a 5 lap handicap. This outfit definitely had its own ideas about the best line round the Byfleet which was not the line I would have chosen.

At the time you were riding, tyres were still quite a headache, weren't they? How much of a worry were they? Did you ever have any alarming moments caused by tyre failures. Long distance record attempts with the bigger bikes must, presumably have involved tyre changes at a time when there weren't such things as knock out spindles and this must have involved some careful lining up of rear wheels and a lot of thought as to how it should be carried out quickly and accurately.

In my early days I tried several makes, none of which did me any harm, but got onto Dunlops quite soon as they gave a marvellous service and best of all expert fitting and advice. Some of the big twins at that time suffered with throwing the back treads off. George Patchett notably didn't enjoy some of the whackings he got on his backside.

Nowadays, of course, two-strokes form the hardcord of race machinery but at the time you were racing at Brooklands and even a number of years later when I was competing there, they were considered a 'spent force' and unworthy of further development. As one who has a 'built in' and, therefore, old fashioned preference for the four stroke, it sometimes seems to me that the engine designers of the 1920's and 1930's must have overlooked something. Would you agree?

Engine designers missed such a lot, myself included. I once thought of writing a book called, 'It was all just over the page'. No-one took the two-stroke seriously or thought of making 250cc or 350 cc twins, or fitting twin carburettors, until the Triumphs came along with them. And cars likewise. I got Staniland's Bugatti going simply by trying to imagine that I had got four motorcycle cylinders there and making them all do some work, and I got even nearer to this with the Multi-Union special manifold I had made. Dixon made the Riley go by putting on one Amal carburettor per cylinder instead of as most racing cars seem to be, you have an engine, give it one carburettor and hope it would make do with that. I'd give a lot to see the insides of a racing 250 or any other size, come to that, today.

Again, nowadays, despite the fact that racing engines generally are much more sophisticated and complicated than those of the 1920's and 1930's it is the life of the big end that determines engine life. Would you think that this was the case during the time you were racing? What, would you feel, were the other components, in your day, that needed most frequent replacement, apart, obviously, from tyres. Clutches, for instance?

See my story on big ends. Incidentally, I wonder what those in Charles Junior's engines are like these days.

Returning, now, to Brooklands itself. You must have a lot of recollections of the place itself. Everyone grumbled about its bumpiness and, in retrospect, seem rather to have taken its existence for granted because so many of the people who grumbled about its shortcomings were the same people who were so outraged when, suddenly, it was no more. Would you agree with this and do you think it could have been, in any way, useful today.

I doubt it.

What was your feeling about the track itself. At the time, of course, it was virtually the only thing we had and although many people criticised it, it always seemed to me that we were not only luck to have the use of it for testing as well as racing and record breaking, but, also, that we owed a debt of gratitude to the Locke King family for its very existence. It certainly had deficiencies but, in retrospect, it does seem to have served its purpose fully, not only to everyone who competed there and to the spectators, but also as a testing ground and a means of development.

It was a marvellous experience. I worked there in the first world war on aircraft. I flew from it and to it. I raced on it and I worked on it. I made most of my best friends there. It was very kind to me and I think it was the best period of my life.

Another bit that may or may not be interesting – hill climbs. In the days when I was doing quite a lot of it, we went to Kop Princes Risborough, which was one of the most famous hill climbs. Lots of track riders who went there took their machines to this very famous hill and sheer speed naturally enjoyed a big advantage. I once took the Toronda with a 350 Blackburne. I had never ridden up Kop before. It had three or four fast swerves and could, I was told, be taken flat out on a 350. The crash hat regulation was being enforced and not having brought one with me that day, I borrowed one which turned out to be two sizes too large. I was first off in the class and having changed into top gear set the throttle lever flat out against the stop. I charged

Brooklands Re-union 1978. Worters and Lacey. 'Now if I'd wanted those records, Woolly'.
'Nonsense, Bill'.

up the hill and charged up the first swerve which was not only more of a bend, at the speed I was travelling than I expected, but also very bumpy. The over-sized crash helmet came down over my eyes and I couldn't let go with one hand and push it up or shut the throttle. I negotiated all the bends somehow and ran onto the grass verge and after a struggle, managed to shut the throttle, completed the tour round the back lanes to get back to the start and I was told, 'Sorry, but the timing wasn't working. You must have another run". I did later on, but considerably slower this time and lost that class to Stan Greening on an Enfield JAP. I did however win the 350 and sidecar and I think the 500 and sidecar class but oh for a twist grip throttle Charles.

Another character I didn't mention, I don't know whether he did figure in anything was Jim Hall. He wasn't notable so much for his race and record achievements so much as for his brilliant ideas. Daft ones at that. He decided that people could earn good money by getting records on 175s, 250s etc. machines and that he would take up the sport. But he couldn't obviously cash in any of those, so he built a 50 cc machine on which to go for long distance records. In his day, 50cc travelled very slowly indeed and were not reckoned much. I suppose nowadays they do about 100 mph. The report was going round that Ebby and George Reynolds, having started him off, had gone down to the Paddock for a drink or a cup of tea before returning to clock the next lap. His shed door carried adverts, for most unusual sponsors. One I remember was a famous cough syrup. He was a clergyman's son and he lived in some little cottage down in Sussex and he was perpetually hard up. Some of his stories about raising money would beat anything you would read nowadays in the financial papers. Well, Charles, I think that's about all, I can't think of anything else that's interesting. You've got about an hour and a half tape here, I should think, and you might be able to pick something out of it that's worth listening to. All the best with it.

The
BMCRC Gold Star

From time to time one hears it said that so and so won a 'Brooklands Gold Star' and it's sometimes clear that the donor of the information isn't at all sure what winning a 'Brooklands Gold Star' really means, because it can, in fact, mean two completely different things.

The Brooklands Gold Star was an award given to the winner of a particular car race, an annual event at one of the meetings run at Brooklands by the Brooklands Automobile Racing Club and, while a handicap, it was an award that was coveted both for its prestige and because it was accompanied by a cash payment.

A Brooklands Gold Star was something awarded by the British Motor Cycle Racing Club, to all Members who succeeded at one time or another in turning a lap of the track on a motorbike at an average speed of a hundred miles an hour or more.

It was a star, albeit a very small star, but it wasn't gold and no money came with it. It was brass, about the size of the old fashioned halfpenny and it attached to the ordinary BMCRC Members Badge. It had the figure '100' in gilt against a dark blue enamel background and, on the reverse side, the member's name engraved.

In the 1930's, when I was competing, nearly all competitors were amateurs or, at least semi-amateur and I think one could then have counted the number of full time professionals on the fingers of one hand. So, at that time, a Gold Star was something rather nice to have.

But apart, possibly, from being the first to win a Gold Star in a particular class, I doubt whether such an award during the period covered in this book meant anything at all to the recipient, who would probably much rather have won the race and with it some cash. He wouldn't have worried at all whether his lap speed, in order to do it, had been nine or ninety miles an hour because, at that time it was wins and the cash that went with wins that mattered.

From the following list of British Motor Cycle Racing Club 'Gold Star' awards it can be seen that from the first, in 1922, to the last, in 1939, they were divided as follows:–

1000 cc	Twenty-five	750 cc	Twenty-one	500 cc	One hundred
350 cc	Twenty-nine	250 cc	One	Sidecar	Three

3 Wheel Cycle Cars – Four and, in addition, two 'Double Star' Awards were made for

lap averages of over 120 mph to Eric Fernihough and Noel Pope, both Brough Superior mounted.

Riding a five hundred round Brooklands to average between 100 and 105 mph presented no problems to someone who was doing it professionally as it were, every day. But it did present problems, even to riders of quite great road experience when tried for the first time. In the thirties, there were certainly as many who tried for a 'Star' with a machine able to do it, and failed, as there were riders who achieved it. To take the bottom line on a five hundred was a knack that wasn't easily mastered and the inclination was, if one failed in that, to try it half way up the banking. That, however, presented a quite different problem because, although the back end of the bike was no longer sliding in a broadside, one was then finding bumps with which it took much more experience to cope. Admittedly a rider who was using the track regularly could leave the grass verge at the bottom, if necessary, go up to the fifty foot line or even higher if necessary, round the Byfleet Banking, and still get back to the bottom. I confess I can't imagine circumstances which would render such a manoeuvre necessary but it was possible. Such a manoeuvre would, however, have needed most of the length of the Byfleet Banking in which to do it and unless there was an exceptionally good or urgent reason, one would stand a very good chance of being collected from behind by something overtaking.

By 1938 and 1939, the use of better forks and a sprung back end made the whole process a lot easier but, before that, with a rigid back end and girder forks, it wasn't much fun at all trying it for the first time. The magic triple figure itself seemed to be a barrier at times. Sometimes aspirants would circulate fairly happily at 99 mph as though thinking that the additional single mile an hour might take them through the barrier to eternity. I remember trying to help and advise one young lady, who was really a very trim and competent rider. In the end, when she had lapped at 97, I held out a board telling her she'd done 98.5 and when she'd got up to 99, a board saying '100 dead – keep going' whereupon she instantly turned in a lap of 101, followed by laps of 103 and then 104 which was all that bike was capable of.

I wasn't sure, even then, whether she'd be able to repeat the performance in her race the next day but she did, and got a very creditable 'Star'. A few meetings later, I found myself going off the same handicap mark with her in a race, with my second string Norton that had a maximum of 103, so I knew it was going to be a question of the standing lap and who could scramble into the Byfleet Banking first. If she got ahead, I would be behind the race for sure.

To make sure, I hired two of the most burly 'pushers off' that Brooklands had ever seen and, as a double indemnity, as the flag was raised for us, I leant across to her and said 'follow me'. If I hadn't done so there would certainly have been headlines next day 'Girl rider beats men at Brooklands'.

With a three fifty or a two fifty it was just a question of having an engine that gave enough power but sidecar 'Stars' were obviously hard to get although I didn't realise it at one time, from the riding point of view that is. The 'Three Wheeler' stars were harder still – and dangerous too. With a 'thousand' or 'seven fifty' and a top speed of between 105 and 110 mph, it was a question of using as much banking as you were entitled to, bearing in mind anything that might have been coming up faster astern. And when it came to a 'Double Star' – well, one must just have had to start learning all over again.

LIST OF GOLD STAR HOLDERS

Class 'E' 1000 c.c.

1922 H.Le Vack	1926 R.Charman	1937 S.H.Goddard
1923 C.F.Temple	1926 G.W.Patchett	1938 R.C.Appleby
1923 F.W.Dixon	1930 E.C.Thomas	1938 J.F.Kentish
1924 T.R.Allchin	1931 G.Davies	1938 G.E.Gott
1925 J.L.Emerson	1933 N.B.Pope	1938 E.Fullam
1925 J.S.Wright	1933 B.L.Pickford	1939 E.J.Frend
1925 H.J.Knight	1934 C.K.Mortimer	1939 M.N.Mavrogordato
1925 O.M.Baldwin	1935 E.C.Fernihough	
1926 E.W.Guyler	1935 H.Trevor Battye	

Class 'D' 750 c.c.

1925 H.M.Walters	1929 R.R.Barber	1936 C.B.Bickell
1925 V.E.Horsman	1929 M.E.Davenport	1936 N.B.Pope
1926 C.S.Staniland	1929 H.W.Collier	1936 G.Newman
1926 W.L.Handley	1930 L.P.Driscoll	1936 C.D.Allen
1927 A.Denly	1930 C.T.Atkins	1937 J.M.West
1928 H.Le Vack	1930 C.W.G.Lacey	1938 D.C.Minett
1929 C.J.Williams	1930 A.R.Quinn	1939 F.W.S.Clarke

Class 'C' 500 c.c.

1925 H.Le Vack	1932 H.J.Bacon	J.Lamb
1927 A.Denly	S.Wood	1936 O.S.Doulton
C.W.G.Lacey	W.H.Rigg	G.W.Webster
T.F.Bullus	J.O.Britton	I.B.Wicksteed
R.N.Judd	H.Levings	E.J.Lemon
G.C.Cobbold	H.G.Tyrell-Smith	C.K.Mortimer
1928 W.A.Colgan	W.Kilmister	N.B.Pope
C.J.Williams	J.H.Fell	R.H.Newman
R.Gibson	1933 J.M.Muirs	C.D.Allen
E.M.Thomas	E.Ovens	J.B.Waite
G.E.Nott	Erik Nelson	G.R.Stanley
R.R.Barber	L.M.Gregory	D.C.Minett
	J.M.West	E.J.Tubb
1929 C.W.Johnston	1933 H.Stevenson	A.C.Perryman
A.L.Loweth	P.A.Refoy	D.A.Loveday
P.M.Walters	A.C.Dobson	J.B.Moss
B.L.Hieatt	J.W.Forbes	1937 G.M.Gatley
1930 C.S.Staniland	1934 Miss.F.Blenkiron	M.D.Whitworth
M.V.McCudden	R.Harris	A.C.Bartlett
G.S.Grose	D.W.Ronan	G.Newman
A.R.Quinn	Miss B.Shilling	T.F.Pullin
J.Levene	F.W.S.Clarke	W.L.Handley
V.E.Horsman	1935 B.G.P.de Mattos	R.C.Appleby
J.D.Duncan	A.Paul	H.Rayfield
1931 H.Clifton	H.C.Lamacraft	M.O.Klein
W.H.Phillips	R.Somerville Sykes	1938 J.Naylor
C.B.Bickell	R.J.Borradaile	M.R.Tufnell
N.A.Anderson	J.C.Gaythorne	L.Pike
L.R.Courtney	W.J.Shortt	J.Lock
J.H.Pringle	J.H.Greenwood	V.N.Hood
C.T.Atkins	E.C.Nicholls	E.F.Cope
F.K.Anderson	P.R.MacIver	1939 A.Leveson Gower
W.C.Marshall	G.Brockerton	L.A.Howe
		M.W.K.Tisdall
		G.E.Gott

Class 'B' 350 cc
1928 F.G.Hicks
1929 A.Denly
     C.W.G.Lacey
1930 C.S.Staniland
     W.J.C.Hewitt
1931 L.J.Archer
1932 R.R.Barber
     A.G.Mitchell
1933 E.C.Fernihough
     C.B.Bickell

1934 J.H.White
     H.C.Lamacraft
     H.E.Newman
     J.M.Muir
     J.H.Bacon
     H.Clifton
1935 N.Christmas
     L.R.Courtney
1938 J.W.Forbes
     D.C.Minett

     D.Vincent
     J.Sandison
     W.R.Lampkin
1939 F.W.S.Clarke
     J.Lockett
     F.W.Fry
     T.F.Pullin
     Miss T.Wallach
     V.H.Willoughby

Class 'A' 250 cc
1933 M.B.Saunders

1000 cc with Sidecar
1927 F.W.Dixon

1931 E.C.Baragwanath

1938 N.B.Pope

1100 cc Cyclecar
1930 H.C.Lones
1936 H.Laird

1930 R.R.Jackson

1934 T.A.Rhodes